"This book shares helpful and abundant examples from both caretakers and their partners that give a real feel for the dynamics of these relationships. It shows ways to understand the high-conflict partner while also setting limits on their negative behaviors. And, it helps caretakers see how healing their own trauma, not buying into gaslighting, developing compassionate detachment, and not invalidating their partner can ultimately make changes in the relationship."

—**Margalis Fjelstad, PhD**, author of *Stop Caretaking the Borderline or Narcissist*

"So happy to discover that the authors of the *Stop Walking on Eggshells* series have turned their focus to include narcissistic personality disorder (NPD) since the two disorders make up so many high-conflict couples. The authors did an excellent job of defining the two disorders, discussing the similarities and the differences, helping readers discover the unmet needs that drew them to their partner, and offering them important skills to help them improve their relationship."

—**Beverly Engel, LMFT**, author of *The Emotionally Abusive Relationship*

"Empowering and enlightening, this book is a beacon of hope for those navigating toxic relationships with partners suffering from narcissistic or borderline personality disorders. It unravels the intricate web of psychological and emotional manipulation with clarity and compassion, providing solace and understanding to those who have felt silenced and invalidated. It is a vital resource for reclaiming one's sense of self and finding the strength to break free from destructive patterns. A must-read for anyone seeking to heal and thrive."

—**Lisa A. Romano**, best-selling author, life coach, expert in the field of codependency and narcissistic abuse, and founder of The Conscious Healing Academy

T0191046

stop walking on eggshells *for* partners

What to Do When Your Partner Has Borderline or Narcissistic Personality Disorder

RANDI KREGER
BILL EDDY, LCSW, JD

New Harbinger Publications, Inc.

Publisher's Note

NEW HARBINGER PUBLICATIONS is a registered trademark of New Harbinger Publications, Inc.

New Harbinger Publications is an employee-owned company.

Copyright © 2024 by Randi Kreger and Bill Eddy
New Harbinger Publications, Inc.
5720 Shattuck Avenue
Oakland, CA 94609
www.newharbinger.com

"Wise Up" by Aimee Mann ©1996 Aimee Mann (ASCAP). Used by Permission. All rights reserved.

Cover design by Amy Daniel

Acquired by Catharine Meyers

Edited by Gretel Hakanson

Library of Congress Cataloging-in-Publication Data on file

Printed in the United States of America

26   25   24

10   9   8   7   6   5   4   3   2   1   First Printing

Contents

Part III: Kids, Custody, and Making Decisions

It's not

What you thought

When you first began it

You got

What you want

Now you can hardly stand it though,

By now you know

It's not going to stop

It's not going to stop

It's not going to stop

'Til you wise up

—Aimee Mann, *Wise Up*

PART I

Understanding BPD, NPD, and Yourself

CHAPTER 1

An Introduction to Borderline and Narcissistic Personality Disorders

Part One, Differences

When someone shows you who they are, believe them.

—Maya Angelou

Is your relationship not at all like it was in the beginning? For example, do you feel that anything you say or do will be twisted and used against you? Have you lost hope that your needs will be met? Perhaps you feel controlled, manipulated, and lied to. Are you accused of doing things you never did? And does your partner alternate between intense, violent, and irrational rages and normal, or even loving, responses? Most of all, does the following description sound like a page from your life?

You're confused and heartbroken about a romantic relationship that's driving you crazy and making you feel helpless, hopeless, and depressed. Perhaps you think you're alone and that no one else could possibly understand or believe you. You're having a hard time believing it yourself, because you never imagined that such a perfect fairy tale could become an endless nightmare.

Things with your partner were fantastic at the beginning. Your partner was so into you, thoughtful and attentive, great in bed, and constantly giving you compliments. They "got" you like no one else. You couldn't believe that someone this great thought you were so special—they practically put you on a pedestal. They were your soulmate, your princess, your knight in shining armor. You saw a few red flags; perhaps your partner needed constant attention, adoration, and praise. But nobody's perfect. They wanted to move faster than you, but you adored them so much, so you surrendered to the flow. You made some kind of commitment; perhaps you moved in together, got married, or decided to have a child.

Maybe your partner flipped right away, or perhaps it took a few years. Or it might have come after a major life change. All you know is that things quickly started to take a turn in the opposite direction. No matter what you do, you can't make them happy or convince them that you love them and aren't interested in anyone else. They have morphed into a heartless critic who must be right all the time, blames you for everything, and is never accountable or at fault. And what happened to all the plans and promises you made together?

Your partner repeatedly criticizes you, and says, for example, "You're selfish," or "You're self-centered." Is that true? They continually deny your experiences, saying things like, "You shouldn't be upset about this," "You're a bad parent," or "Nobody would want to be in a relationship with you—you'd just ruin someone else's life." They fly into terrifying rages that make you feel unsafe. When they're not yelling at you or putting you down, you're stuck in the same endless circular argument in which they spout their complaints from an alternative reality while you logically explain, justify, and defend yourself and your position. You know your partner needs therapy, but they won't go because "nothing is wrong with me—it's everyone else's fault."

You never know what to expect, and you're walking on eggshells all the time. But you can't deny that your partner's control tactics make you feel bullied—tactics such as giving you the silent treatment, belittling you, making threats, dominating you, putting you in no-win situations, and trying to isolate you from friends and family. They withhold affection or sex or demand it when you don't feel like it. They keep you awake until the wee hours fighting.

The continual walking on eggshells is playing havoc with your body and mind. You feel like a shell of yourself. You don't know what's true anymore or even what you want. You used to like yourself, but now your head is spinning, wondering if anything about you is good and worthwhile. You're confused, you're depressed, and you feel hopeless. The continual gaslighting and the emotional and verbal assaults on your self-worth make you second-guess yourself and wonder if you're too sensitive. After you've *been away from your partner, you may feel physically ill when you're about to come home.*

Some people probably would have called it quits by now, but you believe it's your job to heal this relationship. You need to fix your partner and get your soulmate "back" by getting them to see reason, convincing them to see a therapist, and trying to get them to understand how much they're hurting you. But they can't see anything from your perspective. How long can you just trudge through day to day? Will they ever change, and why don't they appreciate all you've done for them?

If all of this sounds suspiciously familiar, there is a very good chance the person you fell in love with has the behavior patterns of a high-conflict person with either borderline personality disorder (BPD) or narcissistic personality disorder (NPD), or both. You are not alone, you're not going crazy, and millions of people share your experiences because they're going through the same thing. So let's look at personality disorders in more detail, particularly the different subsets of borderline personality disorder and narcissistic personality disorder.

General Information About Personality Disorders

BPD and NPD are caused by both nature and nurture. With some people, genetics play a larger role, and with others, a dysfunctional childhood environment is the major risk factor. Either way, you can neither change their genetics nor go back and change their childhood environment. The effect on you is the same.

While there is treatment for BPD, it won't work unless the person wants to change and is ready to do very difficult work on themselves. Without the motivation and willingness to acknowledge their problems, treatment is useless. Sadly, there is limited treatment for NPD. There is a handful of clinicians who treat NPD, but narcissists usually don't go to therapy unless you threaten them with something they don't want, such as leaving the relationship. Don't make any threats like this unless you are prepared to find a lawyer, change your living arrangements, and go through with a divorce (see chapter 12). When they do go to therapy, narcissists may use it as a way to convince the therapist that they're a hero and you're abusing *them*. Once they have that confirmation, there is no way back.

So what exactly is a "personality disorder"? A person can be said to have a personality disorder when their personality patterns cause them and the people around them to have considerable problems dealing with life. The patterns must be significant, long-standing, pervasive, and inflexible. Essentially, personality disorders are an enduring pattern of dysfunctional interpersonal behavior. Now, let's look at BPD and NPD individually.

Borderline Personality Disorder

My boyfriend is convinced I am going to leave him because he thinks so little of himself. If I tell him I'll call him at 6:00 p.m. and it's 6:05 p.m. and I still haven't called, he thinks I've dumped him. He's extremely jealous of my male coworkers no matter how often I tell him I'm not interested. He also has incredible mood swings, shifting from elated to down in the dumps within a few hours. When I tell him I'm going away with my family for a weekend, he screams and shouts that I'm selfish and don't really care about him.

—Eva

People with borderline personality disorder may find it very difficult to regulate their own emotions. While you can do something to bring yourself up when you're feeling down, they need other people to keep them on an even keel— and that's hard to do because their emotions are often going from one extreme to another. Driving their emotional life are feelings of emptiness; an unstable sense of self; a constant, acute fear of abandonment; and shame and feelings of worthlessness. They have super-rages that can frighten or cause trauma to the people who love them the most.

When their emotions overwhelm them, they impulsively take "pain management" actions they think will make them feel better, like shoplifting, binge eating, acting recklessly, and spending too much. The intense emotional pain can even lead them to harm themselves or have suicidal thoughts. What people with BPD want most from a partner is someone who will heal all their core wounds from childhood and perpetually make them feel loved and wanted. They don't want to be your highest priority. They want to be your only priority. When your needs clash with theirs, they will argue with you until you finally give in. If their manipulation works, they will try it again and again. So it's essential that you stand your ground.

Types of BPD

BPD is an unusual personality disorder because people who have it can appear completely different from one another—even diametrically opposed. Over the decades, researchers have tried to tease out these differences and develop names for each type. But different researchers have come up with their own findings, and currently there is no consensus on subcategories of BPD. However, in my own twenty-five years of research,* I have come up with terms for what seem to be the two basic types: the "conventional" type and the "unconventional" type. There is also a large gray area in the middle.

The Conventional Type

I call this subgroup the "conventional" type because people in this group meet the stereotype of the "typical" person with BPD described in books, on the internet, and so on. The major criterion of this group is that they self-identify as having BPD, and they seek treatment for it. Aspects of the disorder (like self-harm, suicidal thinking, suicide attempts, and co-occurring disorders, such as bipolar and eating disorders) bring these individuals into inpatient and outpatient mental health settings. They often have trouble keeping a job. Their enormous pain, low self-worth, and self-loathing are directed inward and lead to the self-harm and suicidal feelings that some researchers and therapists believe, incorrectly, typify all people with BPD.

If you have BPD and meet these criteria—including you self-identify as having BPD—you are of the "conventional" type, and I did not write this book for you. This book focuses on the "unconventional" high-conflict type.

The Unconventional Type

People with BPD in the "unconventional" group do not identify as having BPD or any other mental health condition. They take the pain, emptiness, low self-worth, and self-loathing typical of the conventional individual and project it outward, taking characteristics about themselves that they don't like and attributing them to others. To cope with their unwanted feelings, they find a target of blame—mostly you (their partner or spouse). They will insist that all relationship problems are due to your many faults—things like you won't "improve"

---

* Throughout this book, references to "I" and "my" mean Randi Kreger. Bill Eddy, as coauthor, contributed some sections and was consulted with on mental health clarifications and overall review, but Randi completed the vast majority of the writing and personal commentary based on her extensive work in this field.

yourself, "make" them happy, or capitulate to all their demands. To control their environment and feel better about themselves, they rage, blame, criticize, and make false accusations. They may even become physically violent.

Unconventional borderline individuals act normally much of the time—at least to people outside the family. They hold jobs, sometimes impressive ones, and are more independent than the conventional types who usually need psychiatric help. They don't project vulnerability. They mostly fiercely refuse to accept help unless someone threatens to end the relationship. If they do go to counseling, it may be because their partner gives them an ultimatum. Forced therapy, however, seldom works. They are stuck in denial as much as someone with alcohol use disorder who insists they don't have a problem despite it negatively affecting their life in serious ways.

Causes of BPD

Research studies suggest that between 37 and 69 percent of people with BPD have genetic factors predisposing them to the disorder (Kendler et al. 2008; Torgersen et al. 2000). People don't inherit BPD itself, but rather they inherit traits that define this complex disorder. Two parents—neither of whom may have BPD—can give their child these traits, which include:

- aggressiveness

- excitability

- quickness to anger

- impulsivity

- cognitive (thinking, reasoning) impairments

When you combine these inherited traits with certain environment triggers, the person is at risk for developing BPD (Kreger 2008). These environmental triggers include family and peer influences, such as:

- emotional, physical, or sexual abuse

- neglect by one or both parents

- an unsafe and chaotic home situation

- a poor fit between the temperaments of parent and child

- a sudden loss of a parent or a parent's attention

- environments that are invalidating, meaning the child is constantly being told that their perceptions aren't true

There is a myth that all people with BPD have been abused. But many people with BPD had parents who gave them plenty of love and care, but they developed BPD anyway. Many of them have perfectly healthy siblings. This is confirmed by coauthor Bill Eddy's work for thirty years with high-conflict divorce cases, including many people with BPD traits. Often others in the family appear to lack these traits even when raised by the same parents.

A person with BPD must be willing to acknowledge some of their problems and work in therapy before their relationships improve. They don't need to believe they have BPD, but they need to acknowledge that some things about them need to change. That only happens when the pain of things being as they are is worse than the pain of changing. The client does most of the work in therapy; the mental health professional facilitates this.

Narcissistic Personality Disorder

My wife always talks about how she does more work than anyone
else at her job. She thinks her boss and other coworkers are stupid
and she knows better than them. When there's a problem, it is always
someone else's fault. Because of these behaviors, she's lost job after job.
We moved recently, and she had some hoops to jump through to join
a union. She is furious about the extra steps she has to do that other
people don't. She had a screaming match with a union rep about it.

—John

People with narcissistic personality disorder also rely on others for a vital function: to regulate their sense of self-esteem. Just like people with BPD, they rely on other people to fill the gap, to make them feel important, special, and superior. Although they may appear highly confident, most experience shame and have lurking doubt about their self-worth underneath their confident façade. People with NPD develop a "false self" that feels entitled and self-important.

People with NPD are often arrogant, have no empathy, and may take advantage of others to get what they want. They believe they should only spend time with other "special" or high-status people. They are never accountable for their actions and can fly into a rage when they don't get what they want. In my experience, what a person with NPD wants from a partner is someone who will give up all their needs to satisfy theirs (sound familiar?); devote themselves to giving them endless attention and admiration (this is called "narcissistic supply"); handle the mundane tasks of life, like childcare and housework that they don't deign to do; and back them up when they feel like a victim.

Types of NPD

There are two types of narcissism: the confident, charming, textbook "grandiose" type I've been talking about and the "covert," or "vulnerable," type. You can easily find signs of grandiose narcissism in politicians, celebrities, and CEOs. But my readers tend to have spouses of the vulnerable, or covert, type.

Vulnerable (or covert) narcissists can appear modest, humble, and empathetic. They can fake empathy. If they are emotionally or verbally abusive to their partners, it's often more subtle, insidious, and passive-aggressive. They have many of the same traits as the grandiose narcissist, but they may attempt to hide those traits when they are around nonfamily members. Their demeaning actions are more subtle, and you may not notice that anything is wrong at first. But over time, they drain you of energy without you realizing it. As time goes on, you lose the ability to tell what is normal and what is not. Signs that your partner is a vulnerable narcissist include:

- They may be introverted and shy.

- They act as though they are the center of the universe. They are always thinking about themselves, not others—even in extreme situations.

- They are especially sensitive to criticism, even when criticism was not intended. For example, one woman bought a Toyota even though her spouse denigrated Toyotas because he had a bad experience with them. When he saw the car, he acted highly insulted and refused to talk to her for two days.

- They have a victim mentality. For example, after a woman had been fired for cause five times, it didn't occur to her to look at her own behavior as a reason for the job losses.

Keep in mind that a person can have BPD with co-occurring NPD or NPD traits, and someone with NPD can also have co-occurring BPD or BPD traits. These disorders don't mix to create something else, like flour, sugar, and eggs together make a cake. Rather, when someone has both BPD and NPD, it is more like a cake with several layers. The frosting between the layers of cake represents the mix of BPD and NPD. Sometimes the NPD traits appear, and other times the BPD traits appear.

Differences Between BPD and NPD

Now let's look at the differences between BPD and NPD so you can see which one describes your partner. It is essential that you understand which personality disorder(s) your partner may have because once you have a working theory that your partner has BPD or NPD, or both, you can better predict their behavior, understand what's behind it, and develop the right skills.

Borderline Personality Disorder Traits

Following are the major characteristics of people with BPD only. If your partner demonstrates the following characteristics, it is likely that they have BPD. This doesn't mean you can rule out NPD though because nearly 40 percent of people with BPD also have NPD (Grant et al. 2008). To make it even more complicated, people with BPD may exhibit traits of NPD without actually having NPD.

Fear of Abandonment

It wasn't until we were six months into our relationship that I realized something was really off with my girlfriend. She got jealous about someone, and it threw her into a crying fit—she curled up in the fetal position on my bed and sobbed for hours. I left on a trip to see my family, and the next thing I knew, she showed up on my parents' doorstep 250 miles away!

—Carla

People with BPD constantly question whether you want to be with them, because in their mind, there must be something wrong with you to love someone so worthless. Hence, they're always afraid you're going to leave them. Fear of abandonment, a hallmark symptom of BPD, shows itself in a multitude of ways:

- Exaggerated reactions when you are late, spend time with someone else, or give up your needs to satisfy theirs

- Threats to leave you (they reject you before you can reject them)

- Demands that you be immediately accessible to them, such as expecting you to respond to their numerous texts within minutes

- Statements such as, "You love them more than me," or "You've never loved me," or "You'll do this if you love me"

- Constant jealousy, not only of other potential romantic interests but also of your family, friends, and even pets

- Stringing out the divorce process so they still have contact with you, even if it's negative

- Stalking you online or in real life after a breakup

People with this disorder seesaw from fears of abandonment to fears of engulfment, which is feeling submerged in the relationship. Sometimes they push you away, and other times they pull you in. For example, after a wonderful night of lovemaking, they wake up the next morning and tear into you because you left your clothes all over the floor.

Trying to use logic to convince your borderline partner that you are not abandoning them is usually fruitless because the fear exists in the limbic system (the "emotional brain") and not the prefrontal cortex (the "thinking brain"). For people with BPD or NPD, their feelings equal facts. They easily ignore facts when the facts differ from their feelings.

Impulsive "Pain Management" Behaviors

To know what it's like to have BPD, imagine a world in which you are positively sure that you are a complete and utter failure, and everyone thinks you're an idiot, aren't worth listening to, and can't be trusted. When you get a chance to show them differently, it turns out wrong no matter what you do. So, you wrap yourself in self-loathing.

—Ruth

The combination of your partner's exquisite sensitivity, black-and-white thinking, and feelings of shame and worthlessness means that they are almost constantly in emotional pain—even if you don't see it. When something happens to trigger them (and it could just be a thought), they look for comfort immediately. They may impulsively try to manage their pain by doing things like shoplifting, binge eating, acting recklessly, and spending too much. Some people with BPD self-harm or have suicidal thoughts. But as I said earlier, people with BPD depend on others to manage their emotions. Making you the target of blame is a pain-management measure.

People with BPD think negative thoughts about themselves, their world, and their future much more often than the average person. This rumination increases the severity of their symptoms and leads to an "emotional cascade" that leads to more impulsive pain management behaviors (Selby and Joiner 2009).

Difficulty with Empathy

My borderline wife has difficulty recognizing the needs and feelings of others. She is oblivious to the way I hurt when she says mean things to me or acts like she doesn't care. I have always had empathy for her, especially knowing her background, but I don't feel it coming back in the other direction. Doesn't she realize that I need to be comforted too?

—Stephan

When people with BPD are in a highly emotional state, they're either not aware of how their behavior is affecting you, or they are indifferent to it. Again, feelings equal facts. Remember they're almost always in emotional overload, encumbered by negative painful feelings. Their problem is not so much a lack of empathy as much as an inability to set aside their own intense emotions and focus in on yours. Some self-aware people with BPD highly regret it when they've hurt someone. They feel shame and guilt and apologize. But unfortunately, many others don't. If they were to acknowledge their mistake, their low self-worth and shame would make them feel even worse.

Severe Mood Swings

How my wife's mind works is a mystery. For example, we were having a great time in the car. It was day one of our three-day getaway. One minute we were chatting about our daughter, and then suddenly she asked me to never talk to my brother's wife again. She thinks my sister-in-law doesn't like her. I hesitated and tried to think of an answer that wouldn't cause her to blow her top. My hesitation was all she needed. She pulled over, yelled that I didn't love her, and began punching and kicking me.

—Jamie

People with BPD tend to have extreme mood swings. One minute everything is fine, and then there is a sudden and intense mood change. Borderline emotions have the following qualities:

Extremely intense. What might make you feel depressed and in need of some chocolate ice cream may strike someone with BPD as a personal tragedy. If most people's emotional range is from one to ten, people with BPD go from minus-twenty to plus-twenty.

Mostly negative. Their mostly negative emotions come from their feelings of shame and worthlessness, along with the expectation that bad things will happen to them, including rejection and being abandoned. When they feel like a mess, they think something is wrong with you because you chose them.

Last a long or short time. Once emotionally aroused, your BPD partner usually takes a longer time to come back to baseline. You might be feeling better a day after a significant argument, but your partner might need a week. Or the opposite can happen. Once they feel better, they are surprised that you are still hurting from an argument. Then again, sometimes they will act as if the fight never existed and want something you're in no mood to give.

Swing widely and often. People with BPD are hypersensitive and triggered by things you would consider small. Many of their mood swings won't make any sense to you. But they are very real to your partner.

Take away from their ability to concentrate or be logical. Rumination, or thinking "attentively, repetitively, or frequently about the self and one's world," can take over the life of people with BPD (Segerstrom et al. 2003, 909). Rumination is a drain of mental energy that can take up so much space in your partner's mind that they have less room for concentration, memory, and problem-solving (Whitbourne 2021).

Feelings of Emptiness and a Lack of Identity

For me, having feelings of emptiness is like having a piano on my chest and stomach, and I'm overcome with loneliness, boredom, and apathy. There's a big piece of me missing. I'm desperate for something that'll take up my time, make me forget about it, and make it go away. I try to fill it up with relationships, but then I end up driving people away. Someone once said that it's due to a

*lack of a solid sense of self, and I would agree. I don't know who
I am as a person, and I don't feel like I have any real identity.*

—Brad

Feelings of emptiness and a lack of identity are hard to explain to someone who's never felt them. Nothing on the outside of the person may look different. They may go to work, see friends, and so on, but for them, none of it fills in what is missing. It adds to their pain and the likelihood of pain-management behaviors. The emptiness is related to a lack of identity or sense of self.

Differences in Men and Women with BPD

Research shows that just as many men are diagnosed with BPD as women, despite the stereotype that it affects mostly women (Grant et al. 2008). The following attributes are more common in men with BPD than in women with the disorder:

- substance abuse

- impulsivity

- aggression (even after controlling for differing levels of the trait by gender)

- co-occurring narcissistic personality disorder

- co-occurring antisocial personality disorder

The following attributes are more common in women with BPD than in men with the disorder (Grant et al. 2008; Sansone and Sansone 2011):

- a history of being in therapy

- eating disorders

- anxiety disorders

- PTSD

- a major mood disorder, such as depression or bipolar disorder

---

Brief Stress-Related Paranoia

My wife and I broke up. I told her the day and time I was going to come over and pick up my things so she could arrange to be elsewhere. At the arranged time, I entered the house with my keys and went to the basement. The next thing I knew, my wife was screaming and calling the police because she thought a stranger was coming in to rape her. I am lucky I wasn't arrested.

—Danny

People with BPD find it difficult to trust others. This is magnified under stressful situations, such as being criticized, facing real or perceived abandonment, or under the influence of alcohol or other drugs (including prescription drugs). During these times, they can become especially jealous, suspicious, and worried about other people's motives. It's even more difficult for them to think rationally. They may believe that others are plotting against them or want to hurt them. These episodes can last for hours, days, or even longer.

Narcissistic Personality Disorder Traits

Following are the major characteristics of people with NPD only. If your partner demonstrates the following traits, they may have NPD. This doesn't mean you can rule out BPD though, because nearly 40 percent of people with NPD also have BPD (Grant et al. 2008). Additionally, to make it even more complicated, people with NPD may exhibit traits of BPD, but without actually having BPD.

The False Self

To cover up feelings of inadequacy, feelings of worthlessness, and shame, people with NPD construct a "false self." Developing a false self (versus an authentic self) is like putting on a Superman (or Superwoman) costume that covers up emotions and painful events that need to remain hidden. While their deeply buried authentic, or "real," self feels less-than, inferior, and small, their false self covers it up in a package that is successful, powerful, loved, smart, and attractive.

The key point is that to varying degrees, they forget they are wearing a costume. They believe they *are* a superhero. Constructing a false self and pushing all their feelings of "badness" onto targets of blame is a highly effective way to avoid confronting painful feelings or truths. But this Superman doesn't go around doing good deeds. In any situation, the person with NPD has one question: What's in this for me? Their beliefs and self-talk are different depending on whether they are a grandiose narcissist, or a vulnerable (aka covert) narcissist. I'll explain those variations shortly.

Narcissistic Supply

Let's look at the terms "narcissistic supply" and "narcissistic injury." As you know, people with NPD rely on others to supply self-esteem in the same way children rely on their parents to clothe them, feed them, and get them to school. They do this by finding people who will provide them with that self-esteem in the form of "narcissistic supply." Examples of narcissistic supply include admiration, praise, attention, being envied, having an impressive title, owning expensive things, special treatment, adulation, being feared, approval, affirmation, respect, applause, celebrity status, sexual conquest, notoriety, or any other means of being viewed as the "top dog."

In the beginning of the relationship when partners idolize each other, the narcissistic supply spills out like maple syrup over pancakes. This initial phase gives the narcissist hope that their new partner will maintain that level of supply throughout the length of the relationship. But as the relationship matures and the participants begin seeing each other more realistically and start eating takeout food on the couch while watching reruns of *The Big Bang Theory*, the nonnarcissistic partner expects the other to be able to handle constructive criticism. However, objections about anything, no matter how small, can disrupt the flow of narcissistic supply and become highly threatening to the psychic survival of the person with NPD. This distress is called "narcissistic injury."

To the person with NPD, their partner's primary function is to provide a constant flow of narcissistic supply. They expect you to agree with their fantasies of being the latest, the greatest, and the best at everything. People with NPD obtain narcissistic supply in as many places as they can: work, school, social groups, and online connections to old flames. Some people with NPD may have affairs or may have other potential partners in mind who can step in if something happens to you. If you don't give them as much supply as they need because you have your own life to lead or if you "betray" them by disagreeing with their assessment of themselves, your partner may call you selfish, castigate you, or complain that you're not giving enough in the relationship.

Narcissistic Injuries

Narcissistic injuries trigger feelings of pain and worthlessness, and the narcissist's way around this is to blame you for doing or saying something that triggered them. Because their self-esteem is so low, some people with NPD are unable to tolerate even the smallest slights. Even criticizing their favorite movie, song, or restaurant can feel like a slap in the face to them, because it implies there is something wrong with them for having a different opinion.

Narcissistic injuries can be overblown, like their partner showing too much interest in someone else; petty, such as not getting the best table at a restaurant; or giant, like being edged out as the CEO of a Fortune 500 company, losing an election, or having a spouse ask for a divorce. They find someone or something else to blame, even if it's only fate. They, of course, are innocent victims in need of sympathy (more supply).

Lack of Empathy

I can't empathize with anyone. I don't care about other people's feelings. I only care about myself. I developed NPD so early in life that I never had the chance to develop a conscience or the capacity to feel remorse or empathy for the way I treat others.
—Carlos has both NPD and BPD, and having BPD puts him more in touch with his emotions or actions than someone with only NPD.

When my brother called me and told me my father was in his last days, I canceled everything and flew across country to be with him. I couldn't believe it when my wife, whom I think has NPD, was only concerned that I wouldn't be able to accompany her to a work event! That and the fact that she had to take care of the kids by herself for a few days. She would call me looking for something for one of the kids and never asked me how my father was doing or how I felt. I was crushed.
—Roger

While people with BPD have trouble feeling empathy when emotionally aroused, those with NPD seem to lack it altogether. They understand it intellectually, but the feeling itself bewilders them. They may feel bored when you're talking about your bad day. They might get irritated when something great happens to you, because they're jealous of your good fortune. And when something terrible happens to you, it seems like all they care about is how your grief is going to affect them. This inability to empathize, or even sympathize, is often the reason why many narcissists' relationships eventually end.

Feelings of Superiority, Self-Importance, and Entitlement

Her sense of entitlement would show up in small and big things. For example, she would demand that I bring her coffee at random points in the day. But she doesn't even remember how I like my tea made. Once we went to a restaurant and were turned away because we didn't have a reservation. She was furious and insisted that we be seated. She acts like the rules are for other people, not her. She does this at work too. When she was found to be taking credit for someone else's work, she wasn't embarrassed. She just stopped speaking to the guy whose work she had co-opted.

—Chris

People with NPD may latch onto superficial notions of superiority, such as a designer clothing brand or a luxury car, to set them apart from others. They have an exaggerated sense of their accomplishments and will brag in an arrogant way to anyone who will listen. They pay special attention to their grooming, seem to have a high opinion of themselves, and are unwilling to listen to others, especially if those people are marginalized, underprivileged, or have feelings of inferiority, insecurity, or inadequacy.

People with NPD need to be well-fed by things like acceptance into an elite school, "likes" on social media postings, or recognition of their status (such as a promotion)—all are narcissistic supply. They feel, think, and act as if they are entitled to the best of everything and that the rules are made for other people, not them.

Interpersonal Exploitive Behavior

When I was pregnant, I learned my husband had a lot of debt. I offered to clear this for him so I wouldn't have the stress of debt collectors knocking at our door while I was pregnant. He agreed to pay me back. He didn't. Not only that, but he also refused to do any cleaning around the house or take care of our child. He wouldn't find a job, which he had promised to do, so I had to go back to work

even though I had a chronic illness. We had enough money, but he
spent any excess on cigarettes, alcohol, and junk food for himself.

—Sally

In the television series *Star Trek*, one of the alien races has the motto "Never allow family to stand in the way of opportunity." People with NPD go by the same rule, although they would never say so. People with NPD know that other people don't always do their bidding or meet their needs in the ways they would like them to. So they may be exceptionally good at spotting your vulnerable areas (such as the need to be giving, nice, and compassionate) and exploiting them by using power plays, such as intimidation, threats, and charm, to achieve their goals. They may also use passive-aggressive tactics, such as acting like a victim, acting helpless, and using emotional blackmail (trying to instill fear, obligation, and guilt in you). You are easy to manipulate because you are predictable: you always do the right thing.

The Need to Win at All Costs

I finally realized my husband doesn't have the same goals that
I do for a conversation. I want to find a win-win solution to
problems, minimize conflict, and increase intimacy. He just wants
to be right, and he will grab at any crumb to make himself so—
even if he has to make it up, totally misrepresent my position,
or only tell the part of a story that makes him look good.

—Debra

I get extremely jealous of other people and can't stand to see someone
better than me. I must put this person's self-esteem down to feel better
about myself. I sometimes self-sabotage and hurt others just so I can
get attention. I would rather be called a loser than to be called a
nobody! I get incredibly defensive whenever there is anything I perceive
as criticism. I make everything about me. And when someone tells
me I have hurt their feelings, I will try to turn it around to show that
they are the ones who actually hurt me. I will not apologize because
I'm perfect and special. Even if I say I'm sorry, it is not sincere, and
I will continue to do the same thing again and again and again.

—Carlos, who has BPD and NPD

The First Commandment: Don't Tell Your Partner You Think They Have a Disorder

It seems like it would be so easy: just tell your partner what you've learned about these disorders, and they will understand that their feelings, thoughts, and actions are distorted and try to change them because they love you. But sadly, that is just a fantasy.

When you call out a person with NPD on their manipulation and exploitation, they deny, attack, and reverse victim and offender: a process known as DARVO (Freyd 1997). You will hear, "I'm not the one with the personality disorder. You are!" along with some emotional or verbal abuse. For people with NPD, this counts as a major narcissistic injury (when their narcissistic supply of admiration and attention are taken away or they are confronted with someone treating them as inferior or not supremely special). People with BPD will immediately think you're going to abandon them and DARVO as well, but generally will not want to hurt you the same way someone with NPD would.

The exception to this is *if* they believe they have a problem and want to work on it, possibly by seeing a therapist, then you can mention what you have learned about BPD and NPD. If they're looking for answers to why they think, feel, and act so differently than most people, and you're sure, then you can risk this—but be prepared for DARVO if that's how they respond. Ideally, their therapist will go over the diagnosis. But if they don't have a therapist, or the therapist believes in concealing their diagnosis (in my opinion, a terrible idea when it comes to BPD), the best way to discuss this is to suggest a couple of different diagnoses and leave some URLs or printed materials where they will see them. Let them tell you if they see a match.

In the next chapter, I'll tackle the similarities between the two disorders. You'll also learn about what happens when someone has both BPD and NPD, which occurs in about 40 percent of people who have either BPD or NPD.

CHAPTER 2

An Introduction to Borderline and Narcissistic Personality Disorders
Part Two, Similarities

In this chapter, I cover the similarities between people with BPD and people with NPD. I have compiled this list of similarities based on my twenty-five years of working with family members, as well as my research, both formal and informal. At the end of the chapter, we'll take a closer look at high-conflict people—which can describe people with BPD, NPD, or both. There's a lot of information here, but I encourage you to stick with it because it will be useful later on, when you are building skills to improve your relationship and making tough decisions about kids, custody, and whether or not to remain in the partnership. You may find it useful to flip back to this chapter and review the similarities more than once.

Reality Is Based on Feelings

People with BPD/NPD are like children in that their entire reality is created by their feelings, which become their "truth." This is what I meant when I said "feelings equal facts" for them. Any observed evidence is disregarded or dismissed the same way someone who has a deeply entrenched view avoids reading articles that might contradict their beliefs. Confusing feelings with facts in this way is called "emotional reasoning," which usually originates from negative thoughts that are "involuntary, uncontrollable, and automatic" (Seltzer 2017).

Splitting, or Black-and-White Thinking

Some people consider splitting to be a BPD trait only, but it also applies to people with NPD. Splitting means that a person can't integrate the good and bad aspects of people, situations, and themselves. It's got to be one or the other. When someone is bad, they're evil, and when they're good, they're angelic. Splitting can last hours, days, weeks, or years before the person with BPD/NPD switches (and they don't always switch).

Splitting is called a "primitive" defense mechanism because it's common in young children; for example, when their feelings about their parents depend on whether they get a cookie before dinner or not. But people with BPD/NPD are stuck in this stage, and it makes them very difficult to deal with because when they feel one way, they can't remember ever feeling the opposite. People with NPD tend to "split people all-bad" who threaten their self-image or who have wronged them in some way, while people with BPD split when someone triggers one of their hot buttons, like abandonment.

Idealizing and Devaluing People

In the beginning of the relationship, your partner idealized you and thought you could do no wrong. You were going to heal their core wounds. But when you turned out to be just an ordinary person, not a magician with the power to heal them (BPD) or make them feel special 24/7 (NPD), they started devaluing you. No one can meet the incessant needs of someone with BPD/NPD and still have time to work, sleep, and eat, let alone have a life of their own. Things they used to like about you now become things that irritate them. Don't be confused by their sudden turnaround. Devaluation follows idealization like the seasons turn. It's essential to separate the disorder from the person. Love them, hate the disorder. But that doesn't let them off the hook. It's their job to modify their behavior if they want to keep you.

Having Feelings of Shame and Worthlessness

Why do I manipulate? It's to avoid feeling shame. Because of shame, I wear a mask. If it's on tightly, I feel prideful and safe. But if it starts to slip, I can't handle the shame, and I hide, lie to myself, or get angry at someone. Almost everything I do revolves around shame: what I do, what I don't do, and what I tell people about myself. People bring on shame by pointing out my flaws or mistakes, questioning my actions, ending the relationship, rebuffing me in public, talking about me, and even asking me questions that I don't want to answer—especially in front of others. Anything that might embarrass someone else causes me to cry rivers of shame.

Shame feels scary, like I am exposed to the world—and not just a naked kind of exposed. It's an eviscerated, everyone-can-see-your-innards kind of thing. If someone makes me feel ashamed, I go into a fight-or-flight response just because of the sheer terror of the situation. It's an unbelievably cruel and unnecessary thing to do to me, and if you cause me shame, you are an evil, hateful person, and I need to take you down.

—Nick, who has BPD and NPD

Guilt and shame are two different emotions. People feel guilt for something they've done, while shame centers on your very identity as a person. It's associated with self-disgust, self-contempt, self-loathing, and feelings of worthlessness. Toxic shame spins into other emotions, like anger, and makes a person feel small and worthless. People who get involved with someone who has these personality disorders often feel the same way when it comes to shame. They just deal with it differently. For example, they think of everyone's needs but their own because it makes them feel worthwhile.

What If My Partner Was Never Formally Diagnosed? Can I Say They Have BPD or NPD?

If your partner has never been formally diagnosed and is not likely to seek treatment, it may feel odd to "diagnose" them yourself. But you don't need to have a formal diagnosis, just a working hypothesis that your partner has BPD or NPD. In fact, don't get hung up on a diagnosis at all. What matters most is that the thoughts, emotions, and behaviors described here are highly familiar to you. If you can, do your best to determine if your loved one has BPD, NPD, both, or just one with traits of the other. Remember: Don't tell your partner what you have determined. Instead, focus on adapting your approach.

Unstable Relationships Due to Difficulty with Emotional Intimacy

> *My borderline wife wants intimacy but fears it at the same time. She has to be in control of it. When we are emotionally intimate, she says, "I am so scared that you are going to hurt me since I am so vulnerable now." I assure her that when she talks about her abusive background, it only makes me love her more. But she always finds some way to "prove" that I don't love her—for example, not answering the phone fast enough. She never completely trusts me, which hurts.*
>
> —Regan

People with NPD are also bad at intimacy. They can be good at emotional *intensity*, such as making a grand gesture on Valentine's Day. They can give you flowers and candy, but not a piece of themselves, which they keep buried because it is composed of shame and feelings of worthlessness. To build intimacy in a relationship, you need to be open and vulnerable and talk about what's deepest in your heart. But people with NPD use their disorder like a shield to keep others from getting too close. They must remain defended against outside threats, like their partner sharing their innermost self. Their conversations are transactional, and their goal in discussions is to win, look superior, and get the other person to do their bidding. None of this supports any kind of emotional intimacy.

Victim Mentality

> *My husband has either quit or been fired from six sales jobs in the last ten years. We have had to uproot our family six times. If you ask him, all his bosses were idiots or had it in for him. He takes no responsibility for this. He goes on and on about how his bosses are jealous of him, or have it out for him, and he is the poor victim. I know it's because he had a terrible childhood, but I'm sick of my children always being the new kids at school.*
>
> —Heather

Playing the victim makes people feel safe and comfortable, especially people with BPD, who hope that by playing the victim, their partner will care for them. People with NPD may *feel* like victims, but they also *play* the victim because it gives them a chance to gain attention.

People who struggle with a victim mentality are convinced that life is not only beyond their control but is deliberately out to get them. A victim mentality leads to blame, finger-pointing, and pity parties. Pessimism, fear, and anger also contribute to a victim mentality, as does extreme emotional sensitivity.

Stuck in Childhood

I always say I have three kids: my ten-year-old,
my twelve-year-old, and my husband.

—Dennis

Developmentally speaking, people with BPD/NPD seem to get "stuck" or impaired at early levels of development. People with BPD get stuck at age eighteen months to twenty-four months, and people with NPD get stuck at about age six. This is their "emotional age." Part of them functions in an adult way: they can hold a high-level job, for example. But their ability to navigate complex relationships, see themselves clearly, and handle their emotional escalations have not developed past childhood.

You can see childish behaviors in BPD/NPD traits, such as blaming others for everything, lying, name-calling, poor impulse control, protests at separation, problems with sharing, lack of awareness of others' emotions, needing to be the center of attention, and black-and-white thinking (splitting). It's helpful to look at developmental psychology to understand BPD/NPD patterns. For example, there are optimal times when learning patterns of human interaction are much easier, and later, it can be tremendously difficult to learn new ways of interacting (Fjelstad 2013).

Extreme Rages

The rage part is what scares me. It also creates great anxiety in my mind, as I am really worried about what I might do. I know that someone only needs to say the wrong thing (quite innocently on their part) and I will potentially turn into a wild animal. The anxiety and fear of losing my temper can build up to the point that I am literally shaking and cannot concentrate. The longer this goes on, the bigger the explosion of anger. I will try my very best to avoid any potential trigger situation, even to the point that I am almost paralyzed by indecision and fear of my own potential rage.

If it unfortunately does turn into a full-on fit of anger, well, that's when things get worrying. Property will be destroyed. My voice takes on a very deep and completely different tone. My lungs will project words so loudly that people nearby will stop to see what's going on. The recipient of the anger will have the most insulting and harsh personal insults literally spat out to them through bared teeth. Physical violence follows. And afterward, it is virtually impossible to rebuild any sort of relationship with the recipient.

—George, who has BPD and NPD

A rage attack can happen in an instant without warning, which causes family members to walk on eggshells. For some people, anger is a substitute emotion for feeling sadness, hurt, guilt, disappointment, or shame. When a person is angry, they feel energized and powerful instead of vulnerable. Showing those other emotions can seem "weak," and most people don't want to explore those underlying feelings.

People with BPD rage for many of the same reasons. Rage isn't just an emotional reaction; it's key to their defense mechanism. People with BPD are unhappy when:

- You aren't immediately available the moment they want to talk with you.

- You pay attention to someone they fear could displace them.

- Anyone gives them any kind of negative attention (such as criticism) or fails to give them positive attention (not saying "hi" when passing in the hallway, for example).

- You want closeness when they want distance, or you want distance when they want closeness.

- You go somewhere without them, especially for an extended length of time.

- They feel rejected.

- They feel misunderstood.

- They feel ignored or invisible.

- They are invalidated or are sent the message that their feelings are wrong, bad, invalid, or unimportant.

Lack of Accountability

Rule one: my partner is never at fault, to blame,
or wrong. Rule two: see rule one.

—Betsy

While you must pay with blood for each of your transgressions, your partner will never be accountable for any of their actions. Accepting accountability means admitting that they were wrong, and they are never wrong. Because of splitting, people with BPD/NPD think that one mistake makes *them* a mistake. So, this is an important survival tactic. Without it, they would lose face and feel the shame creeping out of the vault.

Pathological Lying

Most of the time I don't even know when I'm lying because I'm lying
to myself too. When I do know I am lying, I see it as a way to avoid
shame, and I feel entitled to avoid my shame. In that case, it feels
justifiable to lie, and it feels like I am rightfully trying to protect myself.
I thought nothing of this for a long time. Now I know a little better.

—Aaron, who has BPD and NPD

People with BPD/NPD lie, especially those with NPD. Randi Kreger, lead author of this book, has a website for family members of people with BPD/NPD and found that 20 percent of the searches had to do with lying. Lying includes keeping secrets, lies of omission (telling the incomplete truth), not speaking up when asked a direct question, making up facts that are not true, embellishing the truth in a misleading way, and insisting that the truth is false.

When you catch them red-handed, they will blame you for seeing through the lie, tell more lies, play the victim, make excuses, throw a fit about how unfair and selfish you are, or any combination of the above. Some people with BPD may lie more spontaneously, while some people with NPD do it in a more manipulative way. But they both do it to cover up their feelings of shame and worthlessness, and for the person with NPD, to avoid a narcissistic injury and keep their special and entitled false self intact.

Extreme Jealousy

My wife goes crazy when I watch a certain TV program because she's convinced I have a crush on the main actress. She told me she didn't want me to watch it because of that. So I watch it when she's not at home.

—Ken

People with BPD can be extremely jealous to the point of ridiculousness. One man was "forbidden" by his wife with BPD to answer the phone at work—his own business—because there might be a woman on the other end. The thought of you with another lover strikes at the heart of their fear of abandonment and rejection. Someone with NPD feels possessive about their sources of narcissistic supply and will be sensitive to anything that threatens it.

Infidelity

After I broke up with my narcissistic boyfriend, he was involved with another woman within a week. I think he was seeing her before we broke up. It makes me feel better when I imagine him doing the same thing to her as he did to me.

—Doreen

While they question you about any disloyalty, one of their survival strategies is to keep a potential partner in mind or waiting in the wings in the event you aren't meeting their overwhelming needs. One of the most active topics in online forums where partners hang out is cheating. The authors of one study say, "Relative to non-narcissists, narcissistic individuals tend to be less committed to their romantic partners and to play games with their romantic partners; they also tend to be less satisfied with their relationships and engage in infidelity more often" (Altınok and Kılıç 2020).

Since people with both disorders need others to give them what they cannot provide for themselves, cheating or having someone shiny and new waiting for them gives them the feeling of control.

You Can't Make Them Happy

My husband knows I'm a decent person who doesn't lie, cheat, or steal. He complains he isn't happy with me and starts fights knowing I will never admit to things I didn't do or agree with his interpretation of why I did something. He will just say I'm lying about why I (supposedly) did something, and it's always for deceitful or hateful reasons. He gets himself all upset for nothing, and he won't believe me.

Your partner has a few thousand complaints about you. They are sure that if you just change, they will be happy. I hear that from partners all the time. They believe that if they can just change in some way, their partner will be pleased with them and the complaints will stop.

All of this is untrue. You could turn yourself inside out and they would still be unhappy. Your partner is morose because of the disorder, and you happen to be the handiest target of blame. They feel upset and aren't self-aware enough to understand it's coming from them, so they convince themselves the problems emanate from you. Someone with NPD can put you down because they need to feel better than someone, so if you're of inferior status, their status is raised. People with BPD feel such intense pain that they may think if they can spread it around, perhaps they won't feel so bad. Remember, they're never accountable and they can't admit fault.

This is a good news–bad news kind of explanation. On the good side, I'll say it again: *their unhappiness is not your fault.* The bad news is that you can't change something about yourself to increase their happiness. You don't have that power, and you never did. What is happening is inside their mind. Becoming happy is an inside job, and true happiness lies in getting treatment for the disorder.

Using Survival Strategies to Maintain Control

In chapter 1, we explained that people with BPD need other people to manage their moods, while those with NPD use other people to manage their self-esteem. Not being able to depend on themselves represents a huge loss of control. Additionally, when other people provide them what they need, it doesn't last long. They need another "hit" very soon. Therefore, they try to exert control though a wide variety of "survival strategies" that may make them feel better—for a little bit.

All strategies have two things in common. First, they are meant to control their environment—especially the people in it—so they don't have to experience their many fears, such as being thought of as unimportant or inferior, or experience being ignored or humiliated. Having control also wards off feelings of shame and worthlessness. Second, the strategies are intended to make you feel small so that your partner has power and control over you. Some of these strategies are unconscious; others aren't. It really doesn't matter. What matters is their effect on you (see the box "Partners Share How the Toxic Environment Affects Them").

These techniques, or survival strategies, keep you confused, intimidated, off guard, and feeling stuck. The person with BPD/NPD makes it seem that they're in the driver's seat when it comes to defining reality. Naturally, they will tell you they are forced to do these things because it's your fault. It isn't. These are survival skills, and your partner is the last person whose critiques you should take seriously. For some, to make themselves feel good, they need others to feel bad about themselves.

Here is a list of twenty control-based survival strategies.

- Acting jealous and possessive, insisting you are interested in other romantic partners

- Unrealistic expectations, such as expecting you to do all the housework and childcare or expecting you to fulfill their every need this very minute

- Seeing everything as a personal attack, which prevents you from bringing up anything you want them to work on

- Using physical force, including kicking, pushing, shoving, hitting, or otherwise making physical contact toward you in an unwanted way, no matter your or their gender

- Trying to isolate you from family and friends

- Giving you the silent treatment

- Forcing sexual activity, which includes touching you in unwanted sexual ways when you're asleep, expecting you to have sex whenever they demand it, or persuading you to have sex to avoid a big argument

- Gaslighting, making you doubt your reality, like saying, "I didn't yell very loudly. You were the one who screamed at me"

- Using emotional blackmail, or using fear, obligation, and guilt to get their way

- Promising that things will change (but they never do)

- Making threats, like they will divorce you or not let you see the kids, including vague threats like, "You'll be sorry if you do that!"

- DARVOing: when confronted with misdeeds or the fact that they have a problem, they deny, attack, and reverse victim and offender

- Using sarcasm like a blade

- Throwing or destroying property, especially your prized possessions

- Misremembering

- Belittling you or calling you names

- Withholding affection or purposely not meeting your needs

- Devaluing and dismissing your viewpoint

- Putting down your interests and opinions

- Constantly monitoring you and trying to get you to believe you need their permission to spend time with someone, spend time alone, or have your own interests

Blaming and Criticizing

It was somehow my fault that the blanket was too warm.

—Kevin

While most people would try to cope with shame and worthlessness through therapy or in some other way, those with BPD/NPD have a different strategy. They deny they have these feelings and "project" them (plus any number of negative traits they secretly identify with) onto people close to them whom they "brainwash" (for lack of a better term) into feeling those feelings for them. Projection is taking an unwanted trait or feeling and attributing it to someone else. Sometimes the projection has a bit of truth in them, but your partner will twist it into a Greek tragedy. Projecting their shame onto you is one of the main survival mechanisms of most people with BPD/NPD.

The first step to feeling better is understanding that because of their internal programming, your partner is attributing their own painful traits and feelings to you. No matter what their specific criticisms are, it's never really been about you at all. Their words and actions are really about things like their fears, their feelings about themselves, and their need for control.

Needing to Exert Power and Control

Essentially, people with BPD/NPD need power and control to create the best survival strategies to play out. They do this with very little empathy (BPD) or no empathy (NPD) because their survival strategies are needed for, well, psychological survival. Only the fittest survive. Some of this is done unconsciously; some know what they are doing.

For example, people with BPD will test your love for them because of fear of abandonment. They push you past your limits or act even more unreasonable. The logic goes like this: if you really love them, you should be willing to put aside all your own desires and concentrate on fulfilling their needs. For example, if you and your partner agreed to meet at a certain time and place, they may show up an hour late. If you "fail" the test by becoming irritated or giving up and going home, they may feel their unworthiness has been confirmed. This makes the world more predictable and therefore safer. If you "pass" the test by tolerating their actions, they may escalate the behavior (perhaps by showing up many hours late next time), until you finally blow up in anger. Then you become the bad guy, and they become the victim. You may be wondering, *What kind of test is this? No matter what happens, we both fail!* You're right. It doesn't make any sense in your world. But it does in the borderline world (Mason and Kreger 2020). Other examples of exerting power and control for someone with BPD include (Greenburg 2021):

- Requests like "If you love me, you will announce our engagement on social media (even though we have only been dating for a month)"

- Crying and threatening to harm themselves if you don't do something they ask immediately

- Making you get out of the car during a fight or insisting you let them off on the highway

While people with BPD are trying to avoid abandonment (for example, isolating you from other people), power and control strategies for the person with NPD are done for several other reasons. They can only see their own ideas and preferences as meaningful, so want to control you to:

- get their way
- establish dominance in the relationship
- establish they are above you in the status hierarchy
- control access to resources

Here are a few ways they might do this:

- Asking you to move to another state where you have no friends, family, or job for support

- Offering to take over a "chore" (such as paying bills or investing money) and then not giving you the information you need

- Over time, taking over more and more of your life decisions

- Calling you selfish and ungrateful if you complain or want to do something for yourself

- Trying to make you feel too stupid and inadequate to do a particular task or take on a responsibility, for example, saying, "I am better with numbers and computers than you. I can get it done faster and more efficiently"

- Accusing you of being paranoid if you call them controlling

- Alienating you from your friends and family by demonizing them and making excuses about why the two of you should never see them

- Keeping you up all night fighting until you give in.

As I explained in the last chapter, people with BPD can act very differently from each other. For example, some want treatment very much (the conventional type), and others can't imagine it because everything is your fault (the unconventional type). People of the conventional type turn their pain inward, may self-harm, and often feel suicidal, while those of the unconventional type project unwanted attributes onto other people. So not every person with BPD has all these things in common. Some people with NPD (mostly those of the vulnerable type) do not cause the conflict that those of the grandiose type do.

Partners Share How the Toxic Environment Affects Them

My self-esteem has dropped so low that I am struggling at work and drinking a lot. I am spending more and more time away from home so I can avoid his criticism and rages.

—Sam

He is criticizing me to the point that I can't even make small decisions for myself anymore. All I can do is react. I'm starting to lose who I was before we got married. I feel trapped, even though I want to be here.

—Monique

I tell people who are new to the support group that after five or six years, the behavior you don't like will have you feeling miserable, trapped, and helpless. You'll know you're getting close to losing your mind when you can't make decisions for yourself, you feel like you have to tiptoe through your day, you take every comment to be an insult, you cry for absolutely no reason, and you know there's something wrong, but that's not enough for you to leave. You still love them and think you can fix them, and you feel so downtrodden and worthless that you are convinced it will all get better if you just try harder.

—Deanna

Walking on eggshells has given me migraines, stomachaches, depression, and anxiety and has caused me to seek relief in sweets and shopping.

—Judy

Living this way has caused me to isolate myself from the outside world for long stretches of time. It's no way to live. I have to have a core spiritual belief in my value as a human being to avoid succumbing to it and all that goes with it.

—Tyrone

High-Conflict People

The term "high-conflict person" or "HCP" was coined by Bill Eddy, coauthor of this book. High-conflict people have a pattern of high-conflict behavior that increases conflict rather than reduces or resolves it. This pattern usually happens over and over again in many different situations with many different people (Eddy 2018). Whatever the conflict is about is not really the issue; what is at issue is the HCP's personality, which he defines as a predictable pattern primarily including:

- All-or-nothing thinking (also known as black-and-white thinking or splitting)

- Unmanaged emotions

- Extreme behaviors

- Blaming and criticizing others

HCPs also tend to have personality disorders or traits from the "cluster B" category in the DSM-5, which includes borderline, narcissistic, antisocial, and histrionic. The majority of HCPs appear to have borderline or narcissistic personality disorders or traits.

All-or-nothing thinking (black-and-white thinking or splitting). Just like I mentioned above, HCPs tend to see conflicts in terms of one simple solution rather than taking the time to analyze the situation, hear different points of view, and consider several possible solutions. Compromise and flexibility seem impossible to them, as though they could not survive if things did not turn out absolutely their way. They often predict extreme outcomes if others do not handle things the way that they want. And if friends disagree on a minor issue, they may end their friendships on the spot—an all-or-nothing solution.

Unmanaged emotions. HCPs tend to become very emotional about their points of view and often catch everyone else by surprise with their intense fear, anger, yelling, or disrespect for those nearby. They may blow up after receiving comments over the internet—or any feedback. Their emotions are often way out of proportion to the issue being discussed. This often shocks everyone else. They often seem unable to control their own emotions and may regret them afterward—or defend them as totally appropriate and insist that you should too. On the other hand, there are some HCPs who don't lose control of their emotions but use emotional manipulation to hurt others. They may trigger upset feelings in ways that are not obvious (sometimes while they seem very calm). But these emotional manipulations push people away and don't get the HCPs what they want in the long run. They often seem clueless about their devastating and exhausting emotional impact on others.

Extreme behaviors. HCPs frequently engage in extreme behavior, whether it's in writing or in person. This may include shoving, hitting, or other forms of domestic violence, or spreading rumors or outright lies, trying to have obsessive contact and keep track of your every move, or refusing to have any contact at all, even though you may be depending on them to respond. Many of their extreme behaviors are related to losing control over their emotions, such as suddenly throwing things or making very mean statements to those they care about the most. Other behaviors are related to an intense drive to control or dominate those closest to them, such as hiding your personal items, keeping you from leaving a conversation, threatening extreme action if you don't agree, or physically abusing you. This intense drive to control is becoming known as "coercive control" and can be a basis for a restraining order in some courts.

Blaming and criticizing others. Like I mentioned above in referring to people with BPD/NPD, HCPs stand out because of the intensity of their blame for others—especially for those closest to them or in positions of authority. For them, blame and criticism are highly personal, and the HCP feels like they might not survive if things don't go their way. So they focus on attacking and blaming someone else and find fault with everything that person does, even though it may be quite minor compared to their own high-conflict behavior. In contrast to their blame of others, they can see no fault in themselves and see themselves as free of all responsibility for the problem. If you have been someone's target of blame, you already know what I'm talking about.

Frequently Asked Questions

We recently solicited questions from partners of people with BPD/NPD. Here are their questions along with our answers.

Q. Why does my partner deflect and blame me when it's so obvious they were at fault? How do they justify that to themselves? Why don't they want to talk about what they did?

A. Because they are splitting, seeing people in black and white (see the previous "Splitting, or Black-and-White Thinking" section). They can't accept accountability for anything negative or they will be "all bad" because of their intense shame. There is nothing you can do about this. They don't have the ego strength and security of their own self-worth to admit to their worst behaviors. They block it out, even dissociate it away. They don't need to justify it because that's what they really feel, which is to say, that's what they think. Because to them, feelings equal facts.

Q. When my partner splits, he is vile to me. He feels justified in "speaking his truth," and it's usually some nasty thing he has to say regarding sex. He just doesn't stop. Why?

A. See the answer above. Never accept them saying nasty things to you, especially regarding sex or any other sensitive area. (See chapter 8, "Setting Limits Without Fear.") One woman says, "I block my husband's phone number when he gets nasty to me over text. That really upsets him. I remind him that whether he gets blocked or not is up to him." Someone with BPD/ NPD cannot handle the intensity of their shame. They project those feelings onto you.

Q. If they are so afraid of abandonment, why do they keep abusing me, pushing me away, and leaving?

A. The borderline trait of feeling engulfed is one reason. More importantly, they always fear being left. They "know" that one day you will see that they are garbage and toss them aside. This causes unbelievable stress. They leave to control the inevitable.

Q. How can he complain about the dysfunctions of other people and their relationships but not see his own?

A. People often wonder how anyone who is smart in other aspects of their life can be so obtuse when it comes to themselves and their own relationship. Intelligence has nothing to do with BPD/NPD. When it comes to their psychic survival, people with BPD/NPD use blame, deflection, and other strategies so that they are never accountable.

Q. Why does my husband want to be intimate with me when he's just blamed me and put me down?

A. For people with BPD, once the fight is over, it's over. This is part of the abandonment-engulfment theme. Also, they do not recognize how their behavior affects you. They are too much into themselves and their strategies. Never have sex when you don't feel like it, no matter what they say or threaten. I have come across people in my research who do not realize they are being raped when they say no and their partner doesn't take no for an answer.

Q. Why does my partner blatantly lie or gaslight me when I have the evidence that she is wrong?

A. See the other answers above. It is because of splitting, shame, and lack of accountability. Accept that part of BPD/NPD may be lying and be cautious.

Q. Do they really not remember the vicious things they do or say?

A. Not remembering is more likely a trait for someone with BPD, not NPD. Some don't remember because they were in a state of high emotion. Sometimes they do. Someone with NPD is likely to remember but believe you deserved the tongue lashing.

Q. Have you ever seen anyone with BPD recover and become a healthy partner?

A. BPD is like a chronic illness that has treatments that improve it, but it takes work to keep the illness managed. I have seen people of the conventional type work very hard, especially in dialectical behavior therapy classes, and get much better. They need to use skills they've learned, however, when they get emotionally triggered. Recovery is completely up to them. But if a person of the unconventional type refuses help, they will probably never change.

Q. Do a majority of people with BPD have a desperate need to do everything together with their partner, including making every tiny little decision?

A. People with BPD do not like to be alone, and they like to have control.

Q. How is it possible for my partner to shut off all emotions, discard me like I never mattered, and then come back into my life like nothing happened?

A. This sounds like a narcissist. The discard is part of the idealization, devaluing, and discard cycle. You are no longer the person with the magic touch who is going to give them everything they need. They usually come back because their current narcissistic supply is not enough or has gone, so they go back to their old hunting ground hoping you will still be of some use. Do not go back to them. They will act the same way they did before, no matter what they promise. Block them on social media, change your number (and locks if they might have a key), and ignore them if they try to provoke you. You don't owe them an explanation. Just say no.

Q. What do you do when you truly love someone who is a mile deep in denial that they have BPD and you know they won't get better without treatment?

A. Write down what makes you happy; what you want in a partner; your values, wants, and needs; and what you dream about. Ask yourself if you can get this with your BPD/NPD partner. Only you can determine the answer and what you want to do about it.

Q. Why does my wife criticize me for the compassionate things I do for others?

A. If she can't blame you for something you did to her, she has to criticize and blame you for something, even if she has to make it up. See the answer to the first question.

Q. Is it possible that someone with BPD/NPD could be so scared of losing everything that they will change?

A. People change when the pain of things being the way they are is greater than the pain of changing. If you really feel like leaving, if it doesn't get any better, and if you're really willing to leave, you can tell them, "I will no longer be staying in this relationship without the following changes." If they don't make the changes within a predetermined time, leave. When it comes to limits, you must always follow up with the consequences to their actions or inactions.

In the rest of this book, I will use the term "high-conflict person" or "HCP" rather than "borderline" or "narcissistic." When I need to note a difference, I'll specify with either "BPD" or "NPD."

By now you're probably wondering how you got into this mess. In the next chapter, I'll go over why some people seem to be attracted to people with these personality disorders. I'll also cover what kinds of people attract those with BPD and NPD.

CHAPTER 3

What Drew You to This Relationship

Growing up, my mother was sick a lot. She would take to her bed for months at a time. She said the highlight of her day was when I got home from school and told her entertaining stories about my day. They weren't always interesting, but I would try to find something to make her laugh. So when I met my husband and I could tell he needed a lot of attention, praise, and nurturing, I fell into that same role with him. I think it's his dream come true to have someone like me since it's in my nature to meet his needs and help resolve problems. But what about my needs?

—Patricia

I grew up believing that my deceased father was a wife-beater and that this trait, or even worse, was in my genes and waiting to get triggered. I believed I was inherently bad, and being bullied just reinforced this. Who would want to be with me? But then I met Gloria. Suddenly there was someone who looked up to me and thought I was a terrific catch. She often told me how lucky she was to be with me. Her attention and admiration were like water to a man who wandered the desert for forty miles. It took time to see she was a broken woman. I felt it was my job to fix her, just like it had been my job to cheer up my mother.

—Chris

There are so many reasons why I was attracted to my narcissistic husband. First, there were the obvious ones. He was attentive, charismatic, and attractive. It wasn't until we were married that he stopped being attentive, said abusive things, and concentrated only on himself. I felt like the maid, just keeping the household running. My husband pulled me in at the beginning with his charm, but emotionally

abandoned me—just like my dad emotionally abandoned me when
I was six when my mom and dad divorced. How did this happen?

—Karen

High-conflict people have many positive attributes, and they are often good at disguising their negative attributes. If you haven't felt validated, appreciated, or loved in your life, the way they put you on a pedestal and love-bomb you at the beginning of the relationship can feel wonderful. HCPs have problems with intimacy (as I said in chapter 2), but they are very good at intensity, which is very different. This is a big reason why you may have been attracted to your HCP and pursued the relationship.

The intensity at the beginning of the relationship is glamorous. It's Valentine's Day every day: chocolate, flowers, and heartfelt declarations of love from someone you've known only a few weeks or months. The fact that you don't really know the person is overlooked in the intense rush of dopamine and oxytocin (the "cuddle hormone") that gives us that "in love" feeling that is celebrated in movie after movie, song after song. In the musical (and movie) *West Side Story*, Tony and Maria fall in love after one dance and a song at the balcony.

Intimacy, on the other hand, takes time; usually years. It grows gradually over time as two people come to know, understand, and trust each other. If your relationship is intimate, you would agree to the following:

- My partner accepts me as I am.

- I can trust my partner with anything.

- I share my innermost thoughts with my partner.

- My partner validates my thoughts and feelings.

- I know my partner would never deliberately hurt me, and if they did, they would deeply apologize.

- I can be vulnerable with my partner without fear.

- My partner and I are open and honest with each other.

If you disagree with many or most of the statements above, there's a good chance that your relationship is unhealthy and you're not getting the love, acceptance, and intimacy you deserve.

When I met my girlfriend, I was in a bad place. It was six months after a bitter breakup. I had moved to a new city for a job that didn't turn out to be what I thought it was going to be. I was ripe for a whirlwind love affair. By the time she started to devalue me, I was already hooked.

—Ben

Many times, relationships with HCPs are not about being emotionally close to someone, but about the fantasy and hope of being heard, seen, and responded to. On the one hand, you may long for it desperately. On the other, you may fear that you are not good enough to be accepted as you are, and that if someone really knew you, they would run away. This is another reason why you may have been attracted to your HCP: they were willing to keep the relationship in shallow waters, not the deep part of the lake where you feared you couldn't swim. One thing's for sure: the more time you spend with someone who cannot be truly intimate, the less time you have to spend with people who have that capacity.

Anyone can fall for the performance of an HCP during their mating dance. But once the HCP stops idealizing their partner and starts devaluing them in a way that can only be called abusive, most partners of HCPs usually leave within two to four years. People who stay in toxic relationships tend to fall in one of the following categories:

- They had a parent who was an alcoholic or had a personality disorder.

- As a child, they were given too much responsibility for caretaking their parent or siblings.

- They grew up in a chaotic household with caretakers who didn't meet their needs.

If we grew up in any of those environments, and if our early caretakers failed us in some critical ways, then our adult relationships are influenced in ways we don't understand. That's because the power of these experiences lies in our unconscious (or subconscious) mind, which influences our choices in life in a way we aren't usually aware of, and if we are, we underestimate.

The Power of the Unconscious

Our brains are structured in three parts: the brainstem (which keeps us alive), the cerebral cortex (the conscious part of the brain that plans, makes decisions, and talks to us all day long), and the limbic system, which seems to have evolved long before the cerebral cortex. The limbic system effects our emotions and our instinctive reactions, which is why it has been called the "emotional nervous system" (Encyclopedia Britannica 2023). The only thing your limbic system seems to care about is whether a particular person is someone to (1) nurture, (2) be nurtured by, (3) have sex with, (4) run away from, (5) submit to, or (6) attack. In a certain sense, the limbic system has no concept of linear time. Everything that once was, still is today, tomorrow, and yesterday. There is no past, present, and future (Hendrix 1988).

When you meet someone who reminds you of someone significant in your life, your limbic system tells you how you feel about the person, depending upon the nature of your relationship with the original person. If the new person reminds you of your high school bully, you may have a negative feeling about this person for unknown reasons. If it reminds you of an old girlfriend who you still have feelings for, you may feel positively—again, for reasons you can't explain (Hendrix 1988).

Most people are attracted to mates who have their caretaker's positive and negative traits, and, typically the negative traits are more influential... We marry our parents in an effort to better master the situation and break the cycle. Instead, the cycle breaks us. Famed clinician Harville Hendrix, author of *Getting the Love You Want: A Guide for Couples,* believes that when we look for a mate, we find someone with the predominant character traits of the people who raised us. This is called repetition compulsion. He writes (Hendrix 1988):

> Our old brain, trapped in the eternal now and having only a dim awareness of the outside world, is trying to recreate the environment of our childhood. And the reason the old brain is trying to resurrect the past is not a matter of habit or blind compulsion but of a compelling need to heal old childhood wounds.
>
> You fell in love because your old brain had your partner confused with your parents! Your old brain believed that it had finally found the ideal candidate to make up for the psychological and emotional damage you experienced in childhood.
>
> [Even] if you were fortunate enough to grow up in a safe, nurturing environment, you still bear invisible scars from childhood, because from the very moment you were born you were a complex, dependent

creature with a never-ending cycle of needs... And no parents, no matter how devoted, are able to respond perfectly to all of these changing needs. (14–15)

Hendrix's theory, which has been very influential, is that while the logical thing to do would be to marry people who compensated for our parents' inadequacies, the logical part of the brain isn't in charge of our choices. Those belong to the "time-locked, myopic" old brain, which bends toward the familiar and whose goal it is to recreate the conditions of our upbringing, returning to the scene of the crime, as it were, to resolve our unfinished business with our parents (Hendrix 1988, 35). Unfinished business refers to intimate interactions, emotions, beliefs, and behavior patterns that were developed in childhood that you continue to follow with your high-conflict person in the present—even when they don't work. Our families of origin are our template for how we live in relationships now, unless we consciously change that.

For example, if your childhood was filled with abuse and fear, you may choose a partner who flies into rages—in an effort to "get it right" this time and obtain the unconditional love and approval you never got as a child. This is why it hurts so much when your HCP takes those qualities away after those crazy, first love, delicious days, and why you try so hard to get it back when other people would have cut their losses and left the relationship. You don't want to be swindled again. You will try everything humanly possible to get back to that early, nurturing state that was promised to you when you made a commitment, even if it kills you. You will give up your needs, withstand abusive behavior, and damper down your suspicions that your children are being emotionally harmed by their parent or their toxic home environment.

Why Did My BPD Partner Choose Me?

I have borderline personality disorder, and I can tell you what I look for in a romantic partner. From the moment I meet you, I'll be making instant assessments of everything about you, from your facial expressions to your charisma. I will already be having a "happily ever after" fantasy. So I'll come on to you like no one has come on to you before. I'll want to know everything about you. You'll relax, open up, and share stuff way before you normally would. You'll be really nice to me and say really nice things about me. You'll find yourself in the company of someone who's fun, passionate, and engaging. I'll be so taken with you that you'll feel you're walking on air.

The thing is, I really am into you. I'm being totally sincere. But since my overriding belief is that I am a worthless piece of trash, and because you're a really wow person who likes me, I'm terrified you're going to discover that I hate myself and dispose of me. That would make me shatter. So if I catch a whiff of dissatisfaction with our relationship, I will perceive it as things coming to an end, and soon after, I will fall into a deep depression. I will be cold and distant and might even look elsewhere for another partner—a plan B. I chose you because I thought you were perfect. Intellectually I know that no one is. But I thought you were different.

—Shauna

Why Did My NPD Partner Choose Me?

My wife chose me because she knew I wasn't going to give her trouble. I wasn't an assertive person. I was quiet, kept to myself, and was content to listen instead of constantly being the talker. She saw me as someone who had been severely injured by another woman, and she promised to never do that to me. She saw my weaknesses, deepest fears, and regrets and used those against me.

She spent a year getting to know me and observe how I treated other people, including her family members. She saw that I was an open book. She saw that I like to help people. She found out I wouldn't say no to people because I would feel guilty. She saw that I am a people pleaser, which meant that I would fake a smile and suffer through uncomfortable moments if it meant that she would be happy.

She didn't want a loving, nurturing adult who implements rules, structures, boundaries, and consequences. She was looking for a parentified child, a servant, an enabler, an emotional wet nurse, housekeeper, cook, breadwinner, emotional (or physical) punching bag, a day laborer, scapegoat, and personal assistant who has neither power nor a voice in the relationship. She saw that I was strong, but I wasn't strong enough to say no to her.

—Tom

Are You a Caretaker?

Caretakers and people with BPD/NPD go together like peanut butter and jelly. Sid, a caretaker, says, "I have been married for seventeen years to my HCP. From the time of our first fight when we were dating, which led to her slapping me and saying some very hurtful things, I knew there was something wrong with her. I set out to both avoid conflict with her and shield her from any stress. I adapted, giving her everything she wanted. In return, she idolized me. Looking back, it wasn't healthy, but it was what I did to get the high she that she gave me."

In her book *Stop Caretaking the Borderline or Narcissist*, Margalis Fjelsted (2013) coined the word "caretaker" to describe people who spend most of their time and energy tending to the needs of their partner with BPD or NPD—almost as if they were a child with full-time needs. Fjelsted says that caretakers are:

- highly intuitive of the needs of the HCP

- intelligent enough to learn the distorted and contradictory rules the HCP needs to function

- observant enough to keep track of all the nuances of the fast-changing emotional family environment

- creative enough to find ways to calm and appease the HCP

- willing to forgo better treatment, more consideration, or equal caring from their HCP

Caretaking differs from being a supportive, loving spouse. While supportive people help loved ones with things they cannot do for themselves, caretakers take on the job of trying to please the HCP by protecting them from their own behavior, such as covering up their rude behaviors and the hurtful things they say. Caretakers try to save or rescue the relationship (and avoid being attacked) by relieving their partner's emotional distress, doing exactly what the HCP wants, and pleasing them as much as possible. Being supportive, on the other hand, is offering help (usually upon request) to someone who is ill, in over their head, or otherwise can't do something for themselves. Being supportive usually feels good, while caretaking often causes resentment and the feeling that you're being taken advantage of.

Caretakers possess empathy, compassion, and nurturing hearts. In her book *The Covert Passive-Aggressive Narcissist,* author Debbie Mirza (2018) says this about people who choose narcissistic partners:

> They are the ones who hold things together, often the heart of the family. They do almost everything in the home as parents. These are people on which you can rely. They are loyal, faithful women and men. They are often the dreamers, the optimists of the world, seeing the best in others. They are loving, kind, and pure-hearted. They trust the word of others because they are trustworthy and it is difficult for them to believe that someone they love would lie to them since it is not in them to behave that way. Lying, controlling, and manipulating go against how they are intrinsically made. They were made to love and be loved; that is when they thrive.
>
> They are self-reflective women and men who are interested in growing and bettering themselves. They look to see where they can improve. They don't blame others; they take responsibility for their own behavior.

Male caretakers are particularly prone to the myth that they should be able to fix things. Lenny, a college professor, says: "I am a hard worker who believes he can fix everything. I can do landscaping, plumbing, tile work, carpentry, and painting. I am entirely self-taught. I always believed I could fix anything, like so many things I have done in life. I felt that the more I read and studied BPD, the better I would understand my wife's erratic behavior and that our relationship could be salvaged as a result. My counselor pointed out that I could only be 100 percent responsible for my 50 percent of the relationship, and that if my wife didn't seek help of her own free will, nothing would change. It didn't matter how much effort I put into the relationship because my wife refused to seek counseling because 'I was the one with the problems.'"

Identifying Your Caretaker Type

Identifying the type of caretaker you are will help you overcome the urge to control a situation you can't control. It will also help you figure out where you are, where you want to be, and how to get there. The categories overlap a bit, and you can be more than one type of caretaker.

Romance or Relationship Addict

*She was the Juliet to my Romeo. I couldn't believe a woman
so beautiful would fall in love with me. She's my soulmate, my
princess. I am completely devastated by her change in personality.
I desperately miss the woman I met. I keep trying to get her to
fall in love with me all over again, but so far, no success. But
I'm not giving up until I have exhausted everything.*

—Evan

These people live for the neurochemical rush of new romance. The partnership becomes the most important thing on earth, and they are in a near-constant state of preoccupation with the person, romance, intrigue, or fantasy. To a higher degree than the other types, romance addicts project their version of the person they want their partner to be rather than who that person really is. They marry or get into long-term relationships believing that they can have security, only to be disillusioned and embittered when they realize it was all a fantasy and the person never was who they thought they were. This group has a lot of crossover with two of the other caretaker types: the greatly enmeshed and frustrated fixers.

The solution for these caretakers is to comprehend that the love-bombing stage was just that—a stage. You can't go backward and get that again because the HCP is now in the devaluing stage. If you weren't with them, they would go through the stages again and love-bomb someone else. It may be torture to realize that your love back then was not unique. Facing the facts isn't easy. It may be hard, but try to stop obsessing over the past and live in the present. You need to see the situation the way it is now, not years ago.

The Greatly Enmeshed

*I wanted to go to my parents' house, but he didn't want me to. He
says they don't like him. I really miss my friends and family.*

—Danielle

The greatly enmeshed caretakers have a hard time separating themselves from their partners, even within the relationship. They generally don't have limits because they don't understand the concept of separate minds and wants. They are very likely to think in terms of asking permission for things. They have a very difficult time taking care of themselves. They are stuck, but can't really describe how, because thinking badly of their spouse would seem disloyal. The thought of essentially "disobeying" their spouse would cause a great deal of anxiety and even fear. There is crossover with frustrated fixers and romance addicts caretaker types.

The solution is to begin to think, feel, and behave independently from your partner. Yes, you are similar in some ways, but you are not conjoined twins. You'll learn more about this later in the section about becoming your authentic self.

Survivor

We were in the car: me, my husband, and two kids in the backseat. My daughter wanted to hear a particular song, but I couldn't get the music playing fast enough. She started crying, and my husband started screaming at me that I was a lousy mother because I couldn't play the music on time. He went on like that, and I started crying. Then the children started crying. He just kept on screaming bloody murder. He woke up the next morning acting as if nothing had happened.

—Lucy

The survivor caretaker category is composed of people who live in fear and experience emotional, verbal, and physical abuse. This caretaker type could crossover with any of the other types. These caretakers do not feel safe with their spouse, whether or not their partner has physically, sexually, or otherwise abused them, or threatened to. They generally do not identify as victims of domestic violence. They are still consumed with understanding personality disorders and being good so that their partner won't get angry with them. Their life revolves around keeping their partner in a good mood. Even the children are expected to contribute to this effort. The HCP comes first, before the children and themselves.

Don't forget that men can also be victims of domestic violence, and sometimes it's hard to get them to take abuse seriously. Those who do not take it seriously often minimize the behavior of their partner, considering it just another price to pay for having a relationship with an HCP. Violence happens in same-sex relationships too. Some people may withstand pushing, pulling, kicking, and more and not consider that they are victims of domestic violence. They have it in their head that they can't be abused if they are physically stronger than their partner. But it's not just the physical abuse itself—for some men, it is extremely shaming to acknowledge something he believes is humiliating. If they do try to get help, often they are disbelieved, not taken seriously, or mistaken for the perpetrator.

Take abuse seriously. Seek help, and don't let shame or indifference hold you back. You also need to document abuse by keeping track of it, writing it down, and seeking help, so that in the case of a divorce, your children don't go home with your abuser. If your partner does it to you, what's to prevent them from doing it to your kids?

Frustrated Fixer

I went to a therapist, and she told me I was codependent. But I can't give up on my partner like my therapist wants me to. That would go against my conviction that everyone can be saved.

—Pat

The frustrated fixer believes they can save the relationship. It's their job to fix their partner. These folks often exhibit codependent behavior. While most codependency material is targeted to women, people of any gender can have codependent traits, which include:

- having an excessive and unhealthy tendency to rescue and take responsibility for other people

- deriving a sense of purpose and self-esteem through extreme self-sacrifice to satisfy the needs of others

- choosing to enter and stay in lengthy, high-cost caretaking and rescuing relationships, despite the costs to you or others

- regularly trying to engineer the change of troubled, addicted, or underfunctioning people whose problems are far bigger than your ability to fix them

- seeming to attract low-functioning people who are looking for someone to take care of them so they can avoid adult responsibility and consequences, or people in perpetual crisis who are unwilling to change their lives

- having a pattern of engaging in well-intentioned, but ultimately unproductive and unhealthy, helping behaviors, such as enabling

The solution for this group is to read about codependency, get professional help, and work on their schemas, which I will talk about later in this book. For men, the book *No More Mister Nice Guy* by Robert Glover is a great resource.

Conformer

It may be old-fashioned, but...

—Chris

The conformers believe in rules and stick to them when it comes to gender roles or divorce. They engage in black-and-white and all-or-nothing thinking. However, high-conflict people engage in so much black-and-white thinking that your own black-and-white thinking results in fewer options. Conformers tend to be inflexible and fall into three general categories.

1. People who believe that adultery and domestic violence are the only two reasons why a marriage should ever fail.

2. People who believe in traditional gender roles.

3. People who don't leave for religious reasons. But keep in mind, even the Catholic Church considers verbal and emotional abuse to be as serious as physical abuse and teaches that "no person is expected to stay in an abusive marriage" (United States Conference of Catholic Bishops 2002).

The solution for this group is to decide what is more important: your reason for staying or your very life and health. Assume that nothing will change. At the end of your life, will you feel as if you made the right choice?

Professor

Why don't you tell me how you feel, and I will paraphrase so you know I heard you. Then we will do the opposite. That way we can make sure we hear each other.

—Taylor

Professors simply cannot get over the fact that their high-conflict partner is intelligent and perfectly capable of attaining a PhD, running a company, or performing brain surgery, but can act like a six-year-old. Professors are convinced that it's simply a matter of getting through to their partner by finding the right therapist, having the right conversation, or finding the right words.

The solution for these caretakers is to remember that HCPs run on the assumption that "feelings equal facts." They don't want to understand you. While you want intimacy, your partner wants control or to win. They fear intimacy and build walls.

Childhood Schemas (Lifetraps)

When you chose your HCP, there was more going on than choosing a stand-in for your parents. One way to describe a particular way of looking at ourselves and the world is "lifetraps," which is based on schema therapy, a type of treatment devised by Jeffrey E. Young and Janet S. Klosko. Lifetraps, also called schemas, have a lot to do with why you selected them and why you stay.

When our core needs are not met in childhood, we tend to develop a certain way of looking at the world and ourselves that creates longstanding difficulties in our emotional life.

A lifetrap, or schema, begins to develop when we are children and our caretakers fail to meet our core needs. Perhaps we were abandoned, deprived, criticized, put in a parental role, abused, excluded, or deprived. Lifetraps and schemas can negatively affect a person's relationships, careers, self-esteem, life balance, and self-judgment, and lead to the feeling that something is missing. Schemas are like lines of computer code, giving you instructions for how to interpret things, how to feel about them, and how to react. They're extremely powerful because they create your thoughts, feelings, and actions. Recognizing and understanding your schemas is a big step to figuring out what's happening in your life and why you react the way you do. Once we are consciously aware of what our schemas are, we can change them.

According to Young and Klosko (1994), some of the most common maladaptive schemas (in order of importance) are:

- unrelenting standards

- subjugation of needs or emotions

- defectiveness or shame

- self-sacrifice

- enmeshment or underdeveloped self

- approval- or recognition-seeking

Unrelenting standards. People with this schema believe they must always strive harder to meet their high standards. For them, there is a right and a wrong way to do everything, and often they like this about themselves. These caretakers are sure that once they solve the mystery of their HCP's behavior, they can change it by working with their partner. When their HCP complains about them, they try to make them happy, and when they fail, they blame themselves.

> *As a kid, my mom encouraged me to do anything I wanted and that my only limitation in life would be my own self-doubt. It instilled a strong work ethic. But it translated into poor relationship decisions. After working on myself in therapy, I realized my work ethic allowed me to stay in relationships far beyond their expiration date. I believe that I will be the one to help, fix, or heal my partner's problems, and it drives me to keep trying—I just need to do it right, and I haven't found the way yet.*
>
> —Sally

Subjugation of needs or emotions. People with this schema think, *I can't stand up for myself. If I don't submit to other people, there will be negative consequences— they will get angry and reject me, and I will lose their love.* People with this schema are givers, and HCPs are takers. This compatibility is why you were drawn to your partner and they were drawn to you. An HCP wants to do things their way without fully considering the needs of others, and people who subjugate their needs and emotions make it easy for them to do so.

> *I hate conflict and will often do things he tells me to even though I know that they are not going to solve the problem. I do this to keep him feeling useful. I found he has to feel like he's done something to help in order to stay content. He gets hateful or distant when he's wrong, and I do anything to avoid this. I avoid adding fuel to the fire, so often I will just not speak up.*
>
> —Sandi

Defectiveness or shame. You think, *I am flawed, inadequate, and a mistake. If I let people get close to me, they will realize what a bad person I am. No one would ever have me except for my HCP.* The emotion most connected to this schema is shame, which happens when you feel your internal, unseen "defects" are on display. This is so painful that people will go to great lengths to avoid it. People with this schema expect to be treated badly, and the HCP obliges by giving them what they expect.

My father physically abused my mother, and I believed that this trait, and worse, was in my genes waiting to get triggered. I thought I was inherently bad and the only way I could be loved was to suppress my feelings and make sure the badness didn't break out. Being bullied at school and in the army reinforced this message. I was defective. I was bad. I didn't deserve respect. Who would want to be with me?

Then I met Karla. Suddenly, there was someone who listened to what I had to say and who satisfied my lust (in the short term, anyway). She gave me the opportunity to stop focusing on my failings and to prove to myself and everyone else that I was not bad and that I could "save" this broken woman. Of course, the reality was I couldn't fix her. Worse, every time she berated me, every time she became depressed, I believed it was proof I was a bad husband. I believed I deserved verbal abuse, and if I did what she wanted me to do, I would be a better husband. Ultimately, I got to the point where I thought I was worthless and that everyone would be better off if I wasn't there.

Self-sacrifice. If you have the self-sacrifice schema, you think, *My own needs are not important, my partner is suffering too much. When I sacrifice my needs for others, I feel good about myself.* People with this schema believe they don't deserve respect, nurturing, understanding, or empathy, and HCPs are naturally drawn to someone who doesn't demand these things from them. People with this schema rarely express their own feelings, needs, and wants, and often don't even know what they are. They are a perfect match for an HCP because they take the blame for things that aren't their fault and assume responsibility for other people's behaviors.

I was a caretaker. I had been since I was a little boy trying to take care of my sick mother. My wife needed saving. Nothing was more important to me than that. The success or failure of my life was tied to my ability to save my wife. The manipulation, the shame, the verbal abuse, the crises, they were all "badges of honor" in my journey to eventual success. But success never came. I thought my need was to "fix Susan." Slowly but surely, my mental health suffered because self-care wasn't important—it was something that would come after I fixed Susan. It was inevitable that I would crash and burn. I learned the hard way that the best way to be there to support your loved ones is to be there for yourself first.

—Lonnie

Enmeshment or undeveloped self. People with this schema think, *I feel empty. I don't know what I want to do or what I would like to do. I don't have permission to do the things I know I do like. If I weren't coping with my HCP's drama, I don't know what I would do with myself.* A surprisingly high number of people who have left their abusive partner say they miss the chaos, difficulty, and drama they struggled with during the relationship. It filled the empty places where confidence in the "self" should be. Without their HCP keeping them occupied and telling them who they are, they feel empty and uncertain.

> *I entered this relationship six years ago with no identity of my own. I feel empty. I don't have my own hobbies or friends, just those of my wife. I have no clue what I enjoy doing. I would rather not spend all my time with my wife (she's better in small doses), but I don't really know what I want.*
>
> —Mark

Approval- and recognition-seeking. People with this schema think, *I don't tell people what I really think because they might not like me for it. I hate it that my HCP thinks the wrong things about me and I spend incredible amounts of time and energy getting them to change their mind about me.* People with this schema spend a great deal of time and effort trying to justify and defend themselves because they absolutely need their HCP to understand they didn't do anything wrong. They do this again and again expecting a different result each time, which gives their HCP power and control.

> *I remember clearly that when I was a teen, my mother shattered all my dreams of being an actress. She wanted me to go to college and get a "real" job. I was guilted or shamed into making decisions that were really her decisions. When my "shame brain" kicks in, it is hard to feel okay. I only feel good about myself when I get recognition or when people like me. It makes things difficult, and I have a hard time saying no for fear of being rejected.*
>
> —Dick

Ways People React to Schemas

People have different ways of dealing with their schemas: surrendering, avoiding, and healing.

Surrender. When you surrender to a schema, you give in to it and let it run your life. You accept the schema as the truth, not a distortion, and act and react in ways that confirm it. You stay in your comfort zone because you feel helpless and hopeless. Surrendering extends your childhood situation into your adult life.

Avoidance. You shut out upsetting information, become numb to minimize the pain, and avoid facing the fear of trying to change. You escape by trying not to think about or feel the consequences of having this schema. But when you've numbed out pain, you also numb out pleasure. Avoidant people often find some kind of numbing agent, such as alcohol, binge eating, workaholism, and so forth, that helps them shut out the thoughts and feelings.

Healing. The answer to the question, "How did I get into this situation?" is that you and your partner acted as magnets to each other. Your schema fit right into what your partner wanted in a mate. Your partner drew you into the relationship by passionately lavishing you with their devotion and attention. They made you feel like the very best version of yourself by giving you compliments, being a passionate bed partner, and putting you on a pedestal. Unconsciously, you thought your partner would heal the core wounds you developed early in life—something you are probably still trying to do.

Often, people who get (and stay) involved with HCP partners are "caretakers," or people who fight a losing battle to create real intimacy, trust, and mutual caring. They scout out all the landmines they and the children might step on; make things all better if their partner gets upset (usually by giving in); and ignore, deny, or rationalize the HCP's abusive survival skills. By continually appeasing their partner, they prevent them from feeling the consequences of their BPD or NPD behavior, which allows it to continue. In chapter 4, we'll take a detailed look at the inside of an HCP marriage, and I'll explain how this happens. I'll also explore "trauma bonds," a hidden reason why people stay in toxic relationships.

CHAPTER 4

Understanding the High-Conflict Marriage

My recovery started in 1979 when I sought help for an abusive, personality-disordered, alcoholic husband. I'd given up so much of myself in my relationship that I became isolated from friends and family. I didn't know that my self-worth was nil and was surprised to learn that I had a problem. I had stopped trying new things and couldn't take pleasure in activities by myself—even watching television! I lost touch with my feelings and never considered my needs. Bit by bit, I was dying inside, so slowly that I didn't notice.

I had a bad case of the "if onlys": "if only he would change." Instead of initiating, I reacted. Instead of setting limits, I accepted his blame and sought to understand and help him. I excused broken promises, rationalized, and continued to adapt. It never occurred to me to put my energy into developing myself; instead, I tried harder to make things work.

After seeking help, I discovered that I was the one who had to change. I steadily grew my self-esteem, became more assertive, and set boundaries.

—Darlene Lancer, *Dating, Loving, and Leaving a Narcissist*

High-conflict relationships proceed in predictable stages, and the issues in each stage in the relationship are remarkably similar from couple to couple, depending on which disorder predominates, BPD or NPD. In this chapter, I'm going to cover the similar paths these relationships take and explore some of the various issues. First, though, I'm going to explain what a healthy relationship looks like. Few caretakers were raised in healthy families, which often means they are unaware when they are being treated badly.

What Is a Healthy Relationship?

Ted, married to a woman with BPD, writes, "I had no idea my wife's and my relationship was not normal. When I would see other couples, I would wonder which one was like my wife, toxic and angry, and which one was like me, the target of blame." Ted is not alone. Many caretakers don't know their marriage is a toxic one. Or they only secretly suspect that their marriage is not normal. Most often, these caretakers had a chaotic or abusive childhood, or they had a parent who was a substance abuser or had a personality disorder.

The following are traits of a healthy relationship. As you read each trait, ask yourself how important it is to you and if it's present in your relationship.

Conflicts get resolved. Even the best relationships have their share of conflict and angst. But in healthy relationships, conflict is handled with love and mutual respect.

Respect. Respect is about treating each other in the way you'd like to be treated even when you're angry and frustrated. Couples need to compromise; that's true of every relationship. But it should be done with mutual respect, not putting one person down, belittling their choices, or demanding that "the compromise" always benefits one person. Signs of respect including caring about the things that are important to your partner, speaking to them as you would want to be spoken to, and recognizing that differences are okay.

Support and empathy. In a healthy relationship, both partners are there for each other with warmth and affection through good times and bad. Even when their opinions differ, supportive spouses try to see things from their partner's point of view. Without keeping track on paper and pencil, people in workable marriages attempt to be there equally for each other, and both partners give and take. Otherwise, partners can get burned-out or feel used.

Communication and sharing. Honest, direct, and respectful communication is a key aspect of any relationship. That includes someone's ability to listen as well as talk. Many couples fight and yell at each other, but they take the other person's feelings into account. The ability to share your thoughts, feelings, and desires in an open and honest way is essential to the level of intimacy and sense of connection the two of you share.

Mutual trust and honesty. Honesty leads to trust, which leads to feelings of safety—probably the most important ingredient in a happy marriage. Safety means that you know your partner would never take something you told them in confidence and deliberately hurt you with it. Trust paves the way for the confidence to share your feelings, emotions, and self with someone else, which promotes intimacy. Because trust provides the foundation for nearly every relationship, a bond is threatened when someone lies, is unfaithful, or does something else to blow apart the trust between them. Without safety, honesty, and trust, the relationship won't work the way it's supposed to.

Enjoying time together and apart. Couples also need space for other friends, time to themselves, and quality time with their partner. This is not threatening to well-adjusted partners—after all, they have their own friends and want some time to themselves too. When people don't have enough of their own space, they begin to feel trapped and suffocated. The quality of their life diminishes.

Fairness and equality. Relationships marred by power and control struggles start to lose their intimacy because you can't afford to be vulnerable with someone who might use it against you. When one or both of you are enmeshed in a power struggle, the simplest of decisions such as "What time should we leave?" become fraught with angst and conflict. The need to be the top dog and have power over the other person is a quality that high-conflict people have in abundance.

Emotional intimacy and connection. This happens when each partner feels loved and (mostly) accepted the way they are. The more intimacy you have, the more rewarding the relationship is. But as I said in the last chapter, don't confuse intensity with true intimacy. Intensity is hearts, chocolate, and flowers, while intimacy is when you can ugly-cry in front of your partner and feel safe that your partner will love and support you.

A mutually rewarding sex life. The fruit of trust and intimacy grows from a sexual relationship that works well and is satisfying for the both of you. This may mean striking compromises about frequency of sex, who initiates, and so forth. Neither partner should try to force the other to do something that goes beyond their comfort, although it's also a good practice to try new things.

The Stages of High-Conflict Relationships

Now that you know what a healthy relationship is, let's look at the stages of a high-conflict relationship.

Stage 1. The Love-Bomb

At the beginning of the relationship, HCPs split their partner into "all good" and "all bad" (splitting). The HCP genuinely believes that their new soulmate is going to meet all their needs, all the time. People with NPD believe they have found a perfect source of endless narcissistic supply, and those with BPD believe they've found someone perfect to love them like a mother and never abandon them despite their feelings of worthlessness.

Caretakers usually bandy about phrases like "soulmate," "prince," or "princess," and thrive on the HCP's adoration. No one has ever loved them like this before. Both the caretaker and their partner assume they can fast-forward over the "really getting to know you" part of a relationship, which takes time. Things proceed at lightning speed; one man married a woman with BPD sixteen days after they met.

People who are most vulnerable to love-bombing are those who have experienced a recent loss, especially people just out of a relationship. But the loss could also be the death of a loved one, a job loss, or other significant stressors. People with family-of-origin issues, such as abuse or neglect, are also vulnerable. Caretakers usually have the schemas I discussed in the last chapter and long for someone to give them approval, acceptance, and a feeling of belonging, and they fear being alone. Caretakers are nice, naive, nonconfrontational, and dismiss red flags.

Stage 2. Mild Devaluation

During this stage, the HCP believes some of their shiny new silver is becoming tarnished. In the beginning, the caretaker was perfect, and now they appear to be just as filled with flaws as the rest of the human species. HCPs begin to make suggestions for how the caretaker might improve themselves. HCPs reward the caretaker when they act in ways they approve of, and do something punishing when they don't (via rage, the silent treatment, and so forth). The romantic fantasy is still intact because the HCP believes that the caretaker may still be potentially perfect, just in need of guidance. Caretakers feel criticized and blamed. Hopefully, their partner's hurtful behavior is just temporary—caused by stress, a new job, or other life situations.

Caretakers try to make sense of why their prince or princess suddenly says they have so many faults. Caretakers try to fix themselves, but the goalposts keep moving. Nothing they do is right. Other times, they begin to suspect that something unusual is going on with their partner. But they are sure their perfect mate lies beneath all this complaining and feel committed to fixing this relationship (and usually the HCP) and to getting the relationship back to where it was in the beginning. To make things confusing, sometimes HCPs do something nice for the caretaker, which keeps them hooked in. This is critical, because without those every-so-often good times, you might leave. You'll find they do something nice just often enough to keep you hooked.

In the beginning, the rose-colored glasses were on, and I ignored the red flags. Passion was bursting at the seams. We wanted to be together as much and as often as possible. We shared, we laughed, we cried, we were very intimate. And that first kiss, I won't ever forget it—there were no boundaries, and that's where it went all awry.

At first, I chalked everything up to her oddities. I saw signs that were definitely intense and not ones I had seen with others before, but for me, they just made her more special. So I figured maybe she was different in a good way. I thought if I could get past her oddities, just as I had tried to do with all who came before, and if she could get past mine, this could really be something special. I didn't see her behavior as directly hurtful. After all, we all have our oddities.

And then it all changed, and I was already hooked. I kept thinking it will get better, and it did. But it also got worse. After a time, she got hostile to the point that I felt I was in real danger of potentially being harmed. I did everything in my power to resolve it. I was codependent, and at the end, it was nothing more than an unhealthy enabling scenario. It was the hope of love, and I believed it could happen with her. She will always be special to me, but her inability or unwillingness to see herself through my eyes became dangerous for me, and I had to accept it was not only bigger than I am but also that there was nothing I could do. Neither of us could get to the bottom of our individual problem and work through it together, so we fell apart. The struggle was real, but I was shaken and stirred. The relationship made me more aware of myself and certainly a whole lot stronger and wiser.

Stage 3: Severe Devaluation

In this stage, caretakers get further worn down, depressed, traumatized, and stressed because they never know what kind of a mood their HCP partner will be in when they come home from work. The HCP has shoved them off the pedestal with great force, and it hurts. People with NPD want more narcissistic supply, and those with BPD panic and agonize that once again, their partner is not constantly fulfilling their "reasonable" demands. This causes no end of drama. By the end of this stage, HCPs split their partner even more all-bad instead of all-good. Abuse is plentiful at this stage.

Meanwhile, caretakers reaffirm their desire to fix their partner and themselves so they can get things back to where they were in the beginning. They need the approval, desire, and validation they once had. They are sure that there must be something they can do to make it happen. Here, the words "I hope" become increasingly common. Many caretakers deny, rationalize, and minimize the person's toxic behavior. They become obsessed with fixing their mate and changing the trajectory of the relationship. They believe that they can get their partner to go to a therapist, embrace their disorder, and overcome it. Almost every caretaker plays the waiting game, sure that things will change one day. Their partner will wake up and be the person they once were. But the love-bombing stage comes only once.

Meanwhile, caretakers feel traumatized by the criticism, blame, and other survival strategies the HCP uses to make themselves feel good and avoid accountability. Caretakers become obsessed with justifying, arguing, defending, and explaining themselves (JADE) and convincing their personality-disordered partner to stop criticizing and blaming. They are sure that if they say and do the right things, or are given enough time, their partner will change.

I call this the "roller coaster of hope:" it goes up in those rare times when the HCP acts loving (or at least neutral) and plunges when they are using their abusive survival tools. Caretakers use "if only" thinking: *If only I do what they want (for example, give up my friends), things will be calm and we will get along better. If I admit I was a bad person, they will stop arguing with me. If I give up my need for traveling with my friends, I can still be happy in this relationship.* It's so much easier for caretakers to agree with their HCP or do what is demanded of them rather than think about what they really want. Taken one by one, each demand may not be significant. But added up, caretakers start to lose touch with who they are and what they want.

Stage 4. Resolution (Optional)

After a number of years, one of three things can happen:

The status quo. The relationship stays in the devaluation stage and worsens over time. Over the years, the continuing abuse eventually causes the caretaker to become deeply depressed. Their self-esteem has been so decimated that they become deeply wounded people who are numb and shuffle from day to day, trying not to do something they will be punished for. This isn't a relationship but a hostage situation.

They leave. The HCP decides to leave the caretaker—usually very abruptly—which causes many tears and utter confusion. Caretakers are shattered, not knowing what really happened. They try to figure out what they did "wrong." In reality, their crime is being an imperfect person and having their own needs. Many people with BPD leave because they are afraid of being left: they were looking for someone who could heal all their childhood wounds, and you turned out to be a mere mortal, not a loving mother who is willing to give up all their wants and needs to keep them happy.

Keep in mind that many caretakers are also looking for people who will heal their childhood wounds. Many caretakers have low self-esteem, and the former over-the-top admiration, displays of affection, and general love-bombing lifted them up. To accept that they can't do anything to bring those things back on a permanent basis generates huge feelings of grief and loss. Unwillingness to end the relationship and denial are two defense mechanisms that caretakers use to tolerate the devaluation. Rather than get out of the relationship, they continue to wait it out, hoping that the desert will turn into a lush, verdant valley.

The caretaker leaves. In general, caretakers decide to leave the relationship when the things they've been accepting are no longer acceptable. At this stage, they have been in the relationship long enough to realize that wishing for something to happen does not make it so. They have found that they are no longer willing to pay the price to avoid punishment. They may come to this realization over time, or their partner may do something that crosses a boundary they are unwilling to tolerate. I call this the "hitting bottom" stage. It occurs when the pain of being together is worse than being apart. You can find out more about hitting bottom in chapter 11.

CAN LOVE CURE AN HCP?

If a partner has BPD/NPD because of abuse in their childhood, the caretaker often wishes that they could fix the problem if they loved them enough. Sadly, this is as impossible as love curing schizophrenia.. During very early childhood, we first learn whether people are trustworthy or not. Many people with those personality disorders had needs that went unmet, and no matter how much love we give them, their basic personality was determined long ago. Here is what one woman with BPD says about this: "If you're going to get involved with a person with BPD, you should be aware that you cannot cure them no matter how kind, patient, loving, and understanding you are. It won't do anything to treat the disorder because you cannot give self-love to a person. When your borderline partner realizes that you're not able to provide this because no one can, they will often split you to the negative."

For people with NPD, love is just part of the narcissistic supply they come to expect, in the same way people expect their mail to come six days a week. And when they split you, they are apt to be angry or full of rage and take out their dashed hopes on you.

In *Stop Caretaking the Borderline or Narcissist*, author Margalis Fjelstad (2013) explains that people with BPD/NPD, because they divide everything into either good or bad via splitting, place the blame and responsibility for their overly intense, angry, and anxiety-laden feelings on someone or something outside of themselves. Essentially, they need a caretaker to be responsible for their negative feelings. According to Fjelstad, family members give into the BPD/NPD person's wants to avoid being subject to a "temper tantrum, rejection, or emotional or even physical attack" (2013, 20). Essentially, she explains, the family dynamics are designed to protect the BPD/NPD in order to make day-to-day life activities comfortable for them. People in the caretaker role tend to rationalize that the BPD/NPD's behavior is temporary, that the BPD/NPD can learn to be more mature, get over the current problem, realize how their actions affect others, and so forth. But in reality, the BPD/NPD has no desire to change because they have a caretaker.

Enmeshment

In HCP relationships, both partners become enmeshed. That means they take it literally when the marriage vows include "the two become one."

In an enmeshed relationship, both partners are expected to think, feel, and believe in the same way, whether that rule is spoken or unspoken. This is supposed to prove that the two people love each other. But that's not true. Real love is supporting the other person in becoming their authentic self. Enmeshment ultimately prevents true independence. There's usually an enabler in the relationship, who becomes dependent on the other to define what is normal and what is not.

Signs of enmeshment include:

- having trouble separating your emotions from those of your partner

- being punished in some way when you think for yourself; for example, your partner belittles you for being "stupid" when you say you're going to vote for a candidate they don't like

- feeling the need to fulfill your partner's desires instead of creating your own

- feeling like you can't make decisions on your own

- having a confused sense of identity

- having trouble connecting with your emotions, because your emotional state, self-esteem, and happiness are almost always dependent on what your partner is experiencing

- feeling anxious and responsible for immediately fixing things, so that your partner will approve when conflict arises

- avoiding conflict by agreeing with whatever your partner says

- forgetting about your needs and wants or no longer being able to identify what those are

In a relationship in which two people are living their authentic selves, the relationship is healthier because:

- Each person has privacy. Healthy people don't feel the need to tell their partner everything or have their partner approve of their thoughts, emotions, and actions.

- Each person gets to have their own beliefs and opinions, which are respected by their partner. At times, each person will argue their point of view, but it doesn't harm the relationship.

- Each person gets to feel however they feel without their partner telling them to feel a different way.

- Neither person gets to demand that the other person change to meet their narrow definition of what they want.

- Each partner gets to react in their own way to any situation, and the couple can work together to solve problems.

Caretakers can start to believe that enmeshment is what allows them to demonstrate their love and care for their HCP partner. From this perspective, anger and disagreement can feel like evidence of your individuality or worse, that you do not love one another. As Fjelstad points out, "enmeshment serves to bring you back into the Caretaker role; to merge and serve the needs of the BP/NP" (Fjelstad 2013, 68).

All Types of Abuse

Up until now, I've talked about HCP relationships as being "toxic" and spoken of abusive behavior. But now I'm going to get deeper to introduce a new concept: emotional, verbal, sexual, and physical abuse. Does your partner's behavior rise to the level of abuse? Often people with BPD/NPD partners concentrate on how they want things to be instead of what is. They sometimes don't take an eagle's view on the way things are *right now*. Let's forget about the past and the future and take a closer look at what's going on *right now*.

According to the United Nations (n.d.), "domestic violence" or "intimate partner violence" is "a pattern of behavior in any relationship that is used to gain or maintain power and control over an intimate partner. Abuse can be physical, sexual, emotional, economic, or psychological actions (or threats of actions) that influence another person. This includes any behaviors that frighten, intimidate, terrorize, manipulate, hurt, humiliate, blame, injure, or wound someone." Often, the abusive partner does not need to be engaged in actual physical violence for their partner to feel the power of their coercive control. The following examples of domestic abuse demonstrate and include this (National Coalition Against Domestic Violence; National Domestic Violence Hotline; Dugan and Hock 2006):

- making fun of you when you're upset

- withholding help (with money, chores, childcare)

- showing extreme jealousy of your friends or time spent away from them

- threatening self-injury or suicide

- threatening to hurt or kill you, loved ones, or pets

- making you feel like you need their permission to do something, such as making a decision or visiting your friends and family

- raging and yelling

- hitting you with objects

- pressuring you to have sex or perform sexual acts you are not comfortable with

- acting in ways that scare you

- preventing you from making your own decisions

- threatening to take away the children

- intimidating you to have sex because you fear retaliation or more abuse

- physically intimidating you with guns, knives, or other weapons

- humiliating or mocking you

- dominating you, or coercive control

- ridiculing, shaming, or belittling you, including with sarcasm

- making false accusations

- excessive blaming and criticism

- disparaging your ideas

- name-calling or insulting

- pushing, grabbing, slapping, pinching, choking, biting, hitting, or punching you

- intimidating you through threatening looks or actions

- destroying your belongings or your home

- preventing or discouraging you from spending time with friends, family members, or peers

- trivializing your needs and desires

- controlling who you see, where you go, or what you do

- dictating personal choices, such as what you wear

- stalking you

- gaslighting, or denying reality, usually by putting down your thoughts, feelings, and behaviors

Domestic abuse happens gradually, so the victim may be unaware when the abuser's behavior crosses the line. The abuser doesn't think they are crossing a line, and since they have all the power and control, the abuse doesn't stop until the caretaker takes back their power by instituting consequences for the abusive behavior. "Consequences" are actions the caretaker institutes to take care of themselves when the abuser is being abusive. The consequences will vary depending on the intensity of the abuse.

Usually, caretakers believe that someone is entitled to leave a relationship if there is infidelity or physical abuse, while verbal and emotional abuse is not "bad" enough to justify leaving. In fact, research shows that the effects of resulting mental health problems are similar regardless of whether the maltreatment is physical, psychological, sexual, emotional, or some combination (MHS 2021). Verbal and emotional abuse can get worse and worse as time goes by, and many physical abusers start out as verbal or emotional abusers.

The emotional effects of verbal abuse include:

- feeling trapped, on guard, and hypervigilant

- feeling lost, crazy, and out of control

- feeling small, unimportant, and worthless

- feeling uneasy or even paranoid without knowing why

- feeling numb or suicidal

- becoming fearful when thinking about the next attack and how to get away

- developing depression, an anxiety disorder, complex post-traumatic stress disorder, or some other mental health condition

The cognitive effects of verbal abuse include:

- You question your communication skills.

- Your thinking becomes circular and confused.

- You question whether everything your abuser said is true.

- You blame yourself for the abuse.

- You think you can't do anything right and rely on others to tell you what to do.

- You think you'd have nowhere to go if you left the relationship, and you question whether anyone else would want you.

- You think that one day the abuse will stop, although the abuser has shown no signs of wanting to quit.

Your quality of life can be affected in the following ways as a result of abuse:

- You lose your spontaneity and excitement for life.

- Your life goals, dreams, and desires go by the wayside.

- You think your life has no purpose.

- You have sleeping problems.

- You want to escape and run away but aren't sure what you want to escape from.

- You have unexplained physical problems.

Abuse has the following behavior effects:

- You may turn to shopping, drugs, alcohol, sex, or any other addictive behavior.

- You might reward your abuser for temporarily stopping the abuse, which only encourages more abuse.

- You keep the abuse secret from family members and friends who could support and help you.

- You isolate yourself from others.

Complex Post-Traumatic Stress Disorder

You've probably heard of PTSD (post-traumatic stress disorder), especially as it affects people in the military. People can get PTSD from one traumatic event, such as surviving a plane crash. Complex PTSD (C-PTSD), on the other hand, can occur when a person is exposed to lesser trauma in smaller chunks over a period of years, such as ongoing domestic violence. It is not unusual for caretakers to have symptoms of C-PTSD, especially if the abuse is intense or long-standing. The signs and symptoms of C-PTSD include (National Health Service; Kreger, Adamec, and Lobel 2022):

- feelings of shame or guilt

- feelings of meaninglessness

- being preoccupied with the relationship between yourself and the abuser

- impaired memories

- difficulty controlling your emotions

- cutting yourself off from friends and family

- irritability

- changes in beliefs and feelings about yourself and others

- difficulty concentrating

- periods of losing attention and concentration (dissociation)

- relationship difficulties

- destructive or risky behavior, including substance abuse

- self-harm or suicidal thoughts

- reliving the traumatic memory

- avoiding situations or places that remind you of the traumatic event

If this describes you, seek help from a trained professional right away. Complex PTSD is very treatable, and treatment techniques like trauma-focused CBT and EMDR (eye movement desensitization and reprocessing) can work relatively quickly.

Gaslighting Is a Form of Brainwashing

Gaslighting means manipulating someone by repeating lies and untruths until the survivor starts questioning their own sanity. The word comes from the 1938 British play and later, American film *Gaslight* (1944), in which a man psychologically manipulates his wife into believing that she is going insane by dimming the lights and pretending it's not darker. He does it consciously for money, but it's not always conscious. Remember, HCPs look at the world differently than the rest of us, and one of their survival strategies is to be the one to define reality. They do this though constant repetition, sometimes over years. "Repeat a lie often enough and it becomes the truth" was statement about propaganda often attributed to Nazi politician Joseph Goebbels, and that's how it works here.

Survivors of gaslighting are always left wondering whether their own perceptions have any worth, which spirals into self-doubt. Survivors feel confused, anxious, isolated, and depressed.

Gaslighting is insidious and is one of the worst forms of abuse. Over time, it can break people down until they no longer trust themselves—their instincts, their sense of reality, or their values. This keeps them stuck in the relationship, which is one of the purposes of gaslighting. Survivors become so numb and confused that they just going through the motions of life.

Common gaslighting phrases include:

- "That never happened." (There are some instances in which a person with BPD believes this.)

- "You are just being…(too sensitive, dramatic, insecure, paranoid, overly emotional)."

- "You are…(making this up, imagining things, unable to take a joke, misunderstanding my intentions, exaggerating, overreacting)."

- "The problem is with you, not me."

- "You and your beliefs are wrong."

- "I never said that."

- "You need to change to meet my standards." (While they won't change at all.)

- Insults such as, "You're bad in bed," "You're not caring," "You don't show love," "Too much this and not enough that."

Robin Stern (2018), author of *The Gaslight Effect*, writes:

The problem is, gaslighting is insidious. It plays on our worst fears, our most anxious thoughts, our deepest wishes to be understood, appreciated, and loved. When someone we trust, respect, or love speaks with great certainty—especially if there's a grain of truth in his words, or if he's hit on one of our pet anxieties—it can be very difficult not to believe him. And when we idealize the gaslighter—when we want to see him as the love of our life, an admirable boss, or a wonderful parent—then we have even more difficulty sticking to our own sense of reality. Our gaslighter needs to be right, we need to win his approval, and so the gaslighting goes on.

If there's even a little piece of you that thinks you're not good enough by yourself—if even a small part of you feels you need your gaslighter's love or approval to be whole—then you are susceptible to gaslighting. And a gaslighter will take advantage of that vulnerability to make you doubt yourself, over and over again.

People who are especially vulnerable to gaslighting include:

- people who are needy and depend on others for their self-worth

- people who feel uncomfortable if they're not in a relationship

- people whose childhood left them feeling unworthy or broken

- people who are trusting

- people who are willing to look at themselves to see if they are acting appropriately

- people who lack the confidence to maintain a steady, realistic appraisal of themselves

- people who were gaslighted previously, including by their parents

Brainwashing

When abuse of any kind is intense and longstanding, sometimes the result is a type of brainwashing that you might find in cults.

Elements in the brainwashing process that apply to caretakers and HCPs include the following (Davies 2017; Layton and Hoyton 2023):

Controlling the environment. Most particularly, HCPs try to control whether or not you get enough sleep. They wake you up if you try to go to sleep during an argument, which they have already stretched out to consume hours. There is often the threat of physical harm, rages, threats, and so forth, which makes it more difficult for you to think critically and independently.

Stripping you of your identity. HCPs can break down your identity until you fall apart. Partners of HCPs tell me they have become exhausted, confused, disoriented, depressed, or numb. In this state, their beliefs about themselves waver, and the caretaker no longer knows what is true and what is false. The good news is that the brainwashing victim's old identity is dormant, not erased by the process. Once the new identity stops being reinforced, the caretaker's attitudes and beliefs will start to return—especially if they spend time with people who love them.

Constant criticism and blame. The HCP repeatedly and mercilessly attacks the caretaker for any "sin" they have committed, large or small. They may criticize the caretaker for everything from the way the caretaker chews to their extreme "badness," which makes the caretaker feel a general sense of shame. The caretaker begins to believe that nothing they do is right. They're not sure what they have done wrong; they just know *they* are wrong.

The possibility of salvation. There are times when HCPs act normal and even loving. They intermittently show the good parts of themselves, promise to go to therapy, or perform some act of kindness towards the caretaker. The caretaker hops on the "roller coaster of hope." When the HCP shows the caretaker some kindness, the caretaker questions their decision to end the relationship because their HCP partner has sown seeds of doubt.

Accepting the HCP's beliefs. Now that the caretaker knows what is wrong with them, HCPs give them an opportunity to redeem themselves by believing in the correctness of the HCP's beliefs, doing what the HCP wants, and feeling the way the HCP wants them to feel. This gives the caretaker a way to escape their "badness." All they need to do is apologize for their countless "sins" and promise not to sin again. If you say, "I'm sorry; I shouldn't have done that," in every conflict just to stop the argument, they will use that admission to shame and blame you. At this point in the brainwashing process, the caretaker is in the same position as a person who has been interrogated by the police for hours and not allowed to go to the bathroom. They will agree to anything to stop the suffering. They reject their old beliefs about themselves and adapt the HCP's way of looking at everything. They pledge allegiance to the new belief system that is supposed to stop the HCP from abusing them. The HCP will test the caretaker many times to assure their new belief system is holding.

All of this takes time, and it happens so gradually that caretakers are not aware it's happening. In her book *Brainwashing: The Science of Thought Control*, author Kathleen Taylor (2004) writes, "Human brains are good novelty detectors, but they have thresholds below which they cannot detect a change, and they have to make special effort when tracking perceptions over long periods of time. This means that they are bad at detecting long-term, cumulative change if each step of that change is very small. From the start, the abuser may exploit this weakness by testing his partner's tolerance in small ways, perhaps with a snide remark here or there. A victim of abuse may initially register each individual put-down as trivial ('He's tired, had a bad day, didn't mean it'), and unless she has made that special effort and conceptualized the remarks *as* part of a whole (as a concerted campaign, whether or not planned by the abuser) she will not keep track of them—or the cumulative effect on her self-esteem" (87).

Trauma Bonds

Trauma bonding is a psychological response to abuse, and it occurs when the abused person forms an unhealthy attachment bond with the person who abuses them (National Domestic Violence Hotline "Identifying and Overcoming Trauma Bonds"). We form attachments as a means of survival, starting when we are babies. Adults form attachments to others who provide comfort or support.

If your main source of support is your partner, and that partner alternates between treating you badly with rare acts of compassion, a trauma bond can develop. An abused person may even see out the person who caused their suffering and look to them for comfort. An abused person may turn to the abusive person for comfort when they are hurt, even if the other person was the one who caused it. Trauma bonds are very strong and can keep people in abusive relationships for far too long. If you don't know why you stay in this relationship even though it's abusive and you know it's not good for you, you probably have developed a trauma bond.

For example, Liza has a high-conflict partner, Peter, who has raged at her and abused her for twenty-five years. But every once in a while, he treats her with kindness, such as making her soup when she is sick. She gets a glimpse of the man she thought she married. This, combined with the gaslighting, makes her wonder if the relationship is really that bad and whether her husband is right about all the nasty things he says to her. Then Peter goes back to his abusive self, and Liza feels ready to leave the marriage, only to be waylaid by unexpected kind behavior. She is confused again and dismisses the abuse that normally goes on so she doesn't have to take the risk of upsetting the relationships.

In 1997, a psychology researcher named Patrick J. Carnes coined the term "betrayal bonds" to describe the ties that keep people in abusive relationships. Signs of betrayal bonds include:

- continuing to believe in promises to change when lasting change has never been forthcoming

- covering up the abuse or keeping it secret from loved ones

- having repetitive, destructive arguments that no one wins

- not having an emotional reaction to abusive behavior that horrifies others

- obsessing over showing their partner is wrong about you or convincing them they are mistreating you

- feeling stuck in a toxic relationship

- overlooking destructive, exploitative, or degrading behavior because of your partner's positive qualities

- feeling addicted to a relationship that is slowly destroying you

In my experience, it is extremely common for people with an HCP partner to try to block out the trauma by becoming numb. They intellectualize their situation and describe trauma their HCP has visited upon them as though it was happening to someone else. They look for reasons the abuse is justified so they don't have to deal with the fact that something needs to change, because the life that they're living is intolerable. When you numb your emotions, you numb them all, including the good ones. It is as if the trauma-bonded person is addicted to their HCP partner. Caretakers know the relationship is hurting them, but they maintain their addiction to this relationship.

This has been a difficult chapter to read. It's not easy to have the heart of your relationship spelled out in black and white. It's even harder to read what a healthy relationship is and realize that yours is far from it. But in my experience, it's necessary to really define the abuse so you understand that having a relationship with an HCP impacts your physical and mental health.

Please keep in mind that I am not saying that your loved one is necessarily a bad person. They didn't ask to have the disorder, and they are still a person worth much love and happiness. However, so do you.

Almost certainly, the content in this chapter has brought about lots of emotions. In the next chapter, we're going to explore those emotions and learn about techniques for coping with them. That has to be addressed before I can talk about anything else.

PART II

Skills to Improve Your Relationship

CHAPTER 5

Handling Your Turbulent Emotions

You can't cope with an HCP spouse if you don't take care of yourself. I see many partners struggle with this. If you fall apart, who will take care of the children and do everything else that you do? Even if it is just five minutes reading, meditating, or even coloring, you need that recharge time. The world won't fall apart in fifteen minutes. I recharge by taking care of my health. I go for a walk every day and eat healthy foods. I've lost fifteen pounds, which has boosted my self-esteem.

—Lee

Most people who are in a marriage or in a long-term relationship with an HCP are mentally, physically, and spiritually exhausted. They feel stressed, burned-out, exhausted, and bad about themselves, which are predictable side effects of being in a high-conflict relationship. You probably think you don't have time to take care of yourself. But your emotions will deal with you if you don't deal with them. In this chapter, I'll help you understand the importance of emotional self-care, including dealing with grief, stress, and trauma.

The first commandment for living in an abusive environment is don't make things worse. Be careful of the coping mechanisms you choose to use. "Worse" means coping with things by doing something that creates its own problem, like workaholism, alcohol and substance abuse, numbing your feelings, and sexually acting out. If your coping mechanism is creating a problem, seek help to quit the destructive coping mechanism and add methods that bring more positivity into your life.

Discover Your Emotions

Your emotions are there for a reason: to influence the decisions you make and the actions you take in your life, large and small. But most HCP partners short-circuit their emotions by becoming numb. Part of it is just exhaustion from dealing with their partner's heightened emotions and excessive demands. When it comes to your partner, you're always in crisis mode and paying attention to *their* feelings. Even when you sit down to relax, your head is spinning. It feels like it isn't safe to have emotions of your own.

And since most caretakers don't take care of themselves, being in touch with their emotions doesn't seem to offer any benefit. You might have to do something about the relationship, and that would make you feel scared, upset, and helpless. What if you don't love your partner anymore? These emotions stay locked inside your body.

As a result, your partner encroaches on your boundaries a little bit day after day until your life becomes unrecognizable and you've lost important parts of yourself. To make things more difficult, for many people, thinking and talking about emotions seems like a foreign language. If your spouse is an HCP and the emotional realm confounds you, I suggest you learn how to explore your emotions, perhaps by seeing a therapist or talking to someone who is emotionally fluent. Once you reclaim your emotions, you won't be so indecisive, ambivalent, and confused. You'll be better able to make your feelings consistent with your actions.

Identify Your Feelings

This exercise has been adapted from Steven Hayes and Spencer Smith (2005) and will help you release your emotions safely so they don't overwhelm or scare you. You don't have to lash out at others just because you're angry. You don't need to identify as a victim just because someone is victimizing you. It's safe to have feelings; you don't need to act them out.

At first, the following exercise may seem strange. But many people say it helps them start to think differently about, and be more accepting of, their emotions.

Step 1. Identify the Emotion

Do an internet search of "lists of emotions." Scan the emotions until you see one that you want to explore. You will see several emotions that qualify; take one at a time.

Step 2. Explore the Emotion

Make yourself comfortable and close your eyes. Say the emotion out loud and pay attention to your physical sensations and thoughts. Does this emotion feel true to you? How much or how little? Now imagine putting that emotion five feet in front of you where you can explore it without it overwhelming you.

Step 3. Give the Emotion a Form

Now that the emotion is out in front of you, close your eyes and answer the following questions: If your emotion had a size, what size would it be? If it had a shape, what shape would it be? If it had a color, what color would it be? Once you've answered these questions, imagine the emotion out in front of you with the size, shape, and color you gave it. Just watch it for a few moments and recognize it for what it is. When you are ready, you can let the emotion return to its original place inside you. Then, pick another feeling.

After the Exercise: Reflect

Once you've completed this exercise, take a moment to reflect on the experience. Did you notice any change in the emotion when you got a little distance from it? Did you notice any changes in your reactions to the emotion? What size, shape, and color did you give the emotion, and why? Did the emotion feel different in some way once you finished the exercise? Most importantly, have you repressed these emotions because you don't want to deal with them?

Dealing with Grief

You had great expectations for this relationship during the love-bombing stage. You thought you had found your soulmate. You had no idea how dysfunctional your partner was beneath the surface, and you're unprepared to deal with everything that's been thrown at you. In a very real way, you have lost someone: the person your partner was at the beginning of the relationship—the one you were expecting to be with the rest of your life. Take all the time and space you need to grieve your losses. You may also grieve for the pain your loved one is going through, the everyday family life you thought you were going to have, and your partner's lost potential. Everyone grieves differently, and there is no timetable. Be patient with yourself.

Famed researcher Elizabeth Kübler-Ross researched the stages people pass through when they learn that they are dying, and these stages can be adapted for those suffering a loss. The stages are denial, anger, bargaining, depression, and acceptance, although they are not always fixed to fit into neat categories and don't necessarily happen in that order. I'll go through each one and describe how it applies to an HCP relationship.

Denial

Denial comes to me in waves. I sometimes think of my wife as two people. She's the sweetest, most loving woman I know, and then there's a stranger that would do anything to get away from me. For a long time, I fooled myself into letting her nasty, passive-aggressive behaviors go. I was in the "denial" stage of denial, anger, bargaining, depression, and acceptance. I was arrogant enough to think I could handle anything, but mental illness is one thing I was unprepared for.

—George

In the denial stage, caretakers rationalize their high-conflict partner's behavior, brushing it off and convincing themselves that the real problem is that their partner is under stress, and as soon as their partner's workload decreases (or whatever) things will be back to "normal." Because of the nature of BPD/NPD, there are times when your partner acts like their old selves, so it's easy to get stuck in denial and believe the "good" partner is the real one and the "bad" one is just a fluke. In denial, you are buying time for things to get better without having to disrupt your life, make hard decisions, make someone angry, or challenge the unwritten rules.

Confusion is the mind's way of buying time. Staying in confusion is a place of nonmovement, not wanting to recognize that things aren't going well. Whenever you refuse to see that your partner is not interested, willing, or able to change, you're going back to this first stage.

Anger

Anger is a normal reaction to your partner's behavior. Without awareness of the personality disorders, you conclude that your partner is just refusing to do things that make you happy and to stop doing things that make you unhappy.

You don't realize that severe mental illness lies in their resistance to change. You're also angry at yourself because you can't "fix" your partner, and some of your self-esteem hinges on being able to do that. Sometimes you may blow up at your partner.

But anger is an uncomfortable feeling for most caretakers, so they often slip back into denial or experience other feelings instead, like hurt, frustration, shock, disbelief, and confusion. Caretakers believe that if their partners understood them better and were more mindful of their suffering, they would stop acting in hurtful ways. The fact that they don't leads to anger. But your partner responds with more anger, and you feel ashamed and hurt.

The positive thing about this stage is that you are recognizing that you deserve to be treated better and the relationship is not what you thought it would be. But at this point, changing the relationship feels impossible and overwhelming. It takes everything you have to manage day to day, and your focus on changing your partner instead of yourself—your only choice—limits your vision for what needs to happen.

Bargaining

I'm not going to leave this relationship until I have literally tried
everything I can imagine to change my husband. I don't know how to
do that because nothing has worked, and I've tried for two decades, but
I'm sure it will happen eventually. I can't accept any other answer.

—Meg

Bargaining is the stage of no longer being in denial, but a stage of magical thinking. The bargaining stage is an "if only" stage, as in, "If only I say the right thing in the right way, they will see the light," and "If only they will go to a therapist, they will get better." Caretakers exhaust themselves trying everything they can think of to move the dial for years or even decades. It is often confusing because sometimes the person acts like their old self—the person the caretaker fell in love with—and it's like an Alzheimer's patient suddenly remembering everything they've forgotten. But it doesn't last.

If you make a serious enough threat, they may change for a time—but it's not a permanent change. You ride on the roller coaster of hope up, down, and sideways until you get whiplash. But these good times eventually pass, and again and again, you're back at the beginning. One day, your spouse may see a therapist or show that they care about your needs or feelings. But it will come from within them; you can't control it.

This is a good a time as any to talk about "catfish hope" (Kreger 2022). *Catfish* is a reality-based documentary TV series on MTV that explores the world of online dating. A "catfish" is a person who creates fake profiles on social media sites with the intention of luring unsuspecting "hopefuls" into falling in love with them. At the behest of a hopeful, the show's two hosts investigate the potential catfish to determine whether or not the person is real. In almost all the episodes, the hopeful ends up crushed by the truth and cries when they find out that the photos—and the phantom internet person—they've told "I love you" to is a fake who has been deliberately fooling them.

For most hopefuls, the red flags about their "relationship" are everywhere. For example, if somebody doesn't want to meet you in person or talk on the phone in five years of online courtship, it's a good sign that they are not who they say they are. Deep down, each hopeful knows this, but they need this person to be real. They have planned a future with this person. They are emotionally vulnerable with this person. Most of all, they don't think they deserve better. So they miss or ignore all the red flags that most people would see. They believe the catfish's every excuse because their need for the relationship to be real is so deep.

After the big reveal, the hopeful is in much pain and anger. At first, they're angry at the catfish. But eventually they come out of their trance and wonder why they fell for the lies. They say things like, "Everybody in my life told me not to trust this person, but I went ahead and did it anyway." This is the essence of catfish hope: my story looks bleak, but, in the end, my situation will be the exception. I will live happily ever after. People who have an HCP partner can become the victims of their own catfish hope. So take a piece of paper, write down your hopes, and determine whether there is a basis for those hopes or not.

Depression

Depression is the next stage, but for most people, it's probably been present for a long time. Caretakers who stay with an abusive HCP long enough typically fall into a depression and no longer try to escape the abuse. They've tried everything, and a phenomenon called "learned helplessness" sets in. Nothing they've done has worked, so they give up. Many, if not most, caretakers are depressed to some degree.

If you are depressed, it's essential that you seek professional help right away—particularly if you are feeling suicidal or acting recklessly in ways that hurt you. If you have suicidal feelings, keep the number of the National Suicide Prevention Lifeline close at hand: 988 in the United States or 800-273-8255.

Acceptance: Accept Reality, but not the Behavior

Reality acceptance is a skill that helps keep pain from turning into suffering. While emotional pain is a side effect of being alive, you don't have to suffer. Suffering happens when you have a set of facts that you deny, rationalize, or minimize. Reality acceptance means accepting reality with your mind, body, and spirit. We do not accept reality when we try the same thing over and over again and expect a different result, because reality acceptance also means acknowledging that we have no control over certain facts. Denying the facts will not change them, only keep you stuck in thoughts such as, *This is unfair. Why me? Why now?*

In my experience, caretakers get stuck because they think that accepting reality means saying your HCP's behavior is acceptable. This is untrue. Acceptance does not mean approving what is happening or rolling over and becoming hopeless. It means not holding your breath until you, another person, or this situation is fixed. Acceptance is still challenging and painful, but focusing on what you can control versus what you cannot frees up all the energy you were using to fight reality. It helps you focus on how you can effectively cope with the situation and take care of yourself and any children you have. Reality acceptance prevents you from feeling bad about feeling bad. Here's how to accept reality:

1. **Change the things you can.** The serenity prayer goes, "Grant me the serenity to accept the things I cannot change; courage to change the things I can change; and wisdom to know the difference." In a way, that's what this whole book is about: giving you the wisdom to know what can and cannot be changed. You can't change your HCP, but you can change how you react, and that makes all the difference.

2. **Don't ruminate about the past.** Yes, you probably would have done things differently if you had a time machine. You might wish you would have paid more attention to the red flags. You might wish you didn't have children with this person. Maybe you wouldn't have made a commitment so early. All this thinking is useless, destructive, and lowers your self-esteem. Look to the future, not the past. Use the skills I am giving you in this book. There are so many that you could study them for weeks or months.

3. **Don't catastrophize.** Catastrophizing is looking at your situation and predicting disaster before it happens. By all means, think

ahead, make plans, and research problems, but don't be too pessimistic, because the worst may not happen. And even if it does, catastrophizing about things before they happen is not going to help you. Instead, face your fears and tell yourself, *Whatever happens, I will deal with it.*

We need to feel like we have control over our lives, so you should take control of things you can control. Tell yourself, *I can't change other's actions or words, but I can choose how I respond.* Upcoming chapters will go over how to communicate, set limits, and respond to crises in a skillful way. Just know now that your partner does not hold all the cards—you control 100 percent of your 50 percent of the relationship.

Take actions that improve your self-esteem. Two opposite things can be true at the same time: you're fantastic just as you are, and there's always room to improve yourself. You're perfect, exactly as you are, even through all the changing and evolving.

Unlike your HCP, you can tell the difference between feelings and facts. If you're making assumptions about yourself or your HCP, you can grow and learn. The most common example of this is that caretakers take things personally when it's really the disorder.

> As my exploration of myself forged on, I learned to understand how invaluable my emotions are. Once I allowed myself to throw a number of pity parties and felt as if my crying was through, I also learned that I had the power to change my emotional states anytime I wanted. All I had to do was accept that, yes, something in my life might suck at any particular moment, but I didn't have to attach to that negative emotion. I could choose to be grateful for my life, my ability to walk, my eyesight, my children, for the sky, the moon, the ocean, birds, and air. Instead, I could learn to allow myself to have faith that eventually whatever was happening in the moment would pass and that soon one day my life would absolutely improve.
>
> —Lisa

Get Help for Trauma

Earlier, I explained that C-PTSD can result if a person experiences prolonged or repeated trauma over months or years. Traumatic experiences often involve a threat to life or safety, but any situation—even if it doesn't involve physical harm—can result in trauma if it makes you feel overwhelmed and isolated. Trauma is subjective, not objective. You may be traumatized by something that someone else could take in stride, and vice versa. If you're already in a difficult situation, feeling stressed, have been traumatized before, or have recently experienced loss, you may be more vulnerable to being traumatized (Robinson et al. 2023). Emotional and psychological trauma is caused by extraordinarily stressful events that shatter your sense of security, making you feel helpless in a dangerous world.

Signs You May Be Experiencing Trauma

The impact of trauma can be subtle, insidious, or outright destructive, with both physical and mental repercussions. Symptoms may result from changes in regions of the brain that deal with emotion, memory, and reasoning. Affected areas may include the amygdala, the hippocampus, and the prefrontal cortex (Leonard 2021). Famed psychiatrist Dr. Bessel van der Kolk (2015) explains that trauma literally reshapes the body and brain, compromising the capacity for pleasure, engagement, self-control, and trust.

How do you know if you're experiencing trauma? You may feel one or more of the following symptoms to one degree or another. These are normal responses to an abnormal situation (Center for Substance Abuse Treatment 2014).

Emotional Symptoms of Trauma	*Physical Symptoms of Trauma*
• denial	• headaches
• anger	• digestive symptoms
• fear	• fatigue
• sadness	• racing heart
• shame	• sweating
• confusion	• impaired memories
• anxiety	• insomnia or nightmares
• depression	• difficulty concentrating
• numbness	• feeling jumpy
• overreactions	• being startled easily
• guilt	• aches and pains
• hopelessness	• muscle tension
• irritability	• hyper-alertness
• feeling disconnected	
• an inability to trust other people	

Trauma is more common in people who are under a heavy stress load, have recently suffered a series of losses, or have been traumatized before—especially if the earlier trauma occurred in childhood. Childhood trauma can result from anything that disrupts a child's sense of safety, including an unstable or unsafe environment; separation from a parent; witnessing domestic violence; or sexual, physical, or psychological abuse (National Child Traumatic Stress Network).

Healing from C-PTSD

Recovering from trauma involves seeing a therapist who is trained to treat people who have been traumatized. However, it is difficult to heal from C-PTSD while you are still in a relationship with the person who is traumatizing you. If you don't want to leave (or aren't ready), I strongly suggest taking some time away from your partner so you can see what life is like free from abuse. The idea is to get away for hours or days. You can do it alone or (preferably) with people who love you and can show up in a way that lifts you up. Turn off your phone to get the full experience. I suggest reading the chapters on communication and limits before doing so.

Remember that borderline HCPs fear abandonment. Arrange the time away way in advance and prepare your partner. You can leave them letters to open while you are away, give them a gift, like a stuffed animal, or arrange specific times you will call or text them. Don't communicate with them outside these times. Do not make yourself available 24/7. Narcissistic HCPs will want you around to take care of the things that are "below" them and to always be available to give them narcissistic supply. It is a sign of strength to get that time away even if they object or call you selfish. By now you certainly know your partner has biases and finds it threatening when you act independently. Usually, you can't take care of their feelings and yours at the same time. For once, take care of your feelings and take some time away, even if you have to tell a white lie to do so. Partners who have done so say it has given them a whole new perspective.

Form a Diverse Support System

I used to think that I was strong and I could handle anything on my own. I learned that isn't true. I need support because I can't do this on my own. I finally told my family the truth about my marriage, and I have a solid network of friends from high school and college that I can call on in a moment's notice. When my ex-wife and I separated, I called on my network of family and friends for support, and they were there. I considered my attorney and therapist as part of my support system.

—Ray, previously married to an HCP spouse

A solid support system can help alleviate the effects of difficult emotions and help us cope with stress. The most important function a good support network provides is a peek back into reality amid the gaslighting and brainwashing. We all get caught up in our own little worlds, so to speak, and a good network will look into your world and tell you if it's normal or not. You should be able to call on a support system that brings you back to reality and keeps your mind stable, so you are not pulled back into the crazy world of an HCP. There are many different types of support and support networks.

Friends and family. Choose family members who you feel safe with, who love you, and who are willing to keep your conversations confidential. Close friendships with others "increase your sense of belonging and purpose, boost happiness and reduce stress, improve self-confidence and self-worth, help you cope with trauma such as divorce, serious illness, job loss or the death of a loved one, and encourage you to change unhealthy lifestyle habits" (Mayo Clinic 2022).

Do not isolate yourself because your partner wants you to. If your partner is putting pressure on you to cut people out of your life, tell them, "No, not under any circumstance." Meet your friends someplace other than your house. Typically, men's friendships are based on doing things, so finding a friend to talk with can be harder for them. You may need to take a risk and really talk with a best friend from high school, work, or college. Tell your friend that you don't need them to solve anything; you just want someone to listen to you. Tell them this is a confidential talk. Don't talk to anyone who might repeat the conversation to others.

> One of the biggest things I wish I knew was to not feel so ashamed of
> the fact that my marriage was falling apart. I should have reached
> out to more people; I should have asked for help. But I didn't. And
> I know now that it is not a reason to feel ashamed. I was being
> emotionally abused. I was so depressed, so not myself. I wish I had
> opened up to more people; maybe I wouldn't have felt so alone.
>
> —Jonie

It's extremely common for caretakers to keep their partner's behavior a secret, barring friends and family from knowing that anything is wrong. Caretakers do this for a multitude of reasons, all of which benefit the HCP and keep the abuse going. Partners of HCP may keep secrets because:

We know that we shouldn't take the abuse, and we don't know how to explain why we do. You probably stay because of trauma bonds. This is one argument for trusting a friend! Exploring why you stay is something friends and family may be able to help you with. If you worry someone will try to shame you for staying, tell someone else. If you aren't looking for advice, but just to talk, tell them up front.

We love our spouses, and we don't want others to view them poorly. Your job is to protect yourself and your children, not your partner. It's that lack of self-preservation that leads people to get in abusive HCP relationships and stay in them. If you don't want your partner to worry that something might be cast in a negative light, and therefore keep it a secret, you're enabling them, allowing the abuse to happen with no consequences. This keeps the behavior going. You reward them by saying nothing, minimizing the chance that anyone will help you.

We have enough stress without the added stress of people being worried about us. Would you want to know if a loved one was having the same experiences? Of course you would. You wouldn't think that supporting them was an extra burden; you would be happy to do so. So give other people the chance to listen, and if for some reason you don't get what you need, reach out to someone else. You are loved, and people want the best for you. Don't shut them out.

It's almost impossible to explain. That's completely understandable. No one really grasps what you are dealing with unless they've been there and experienced the chaos. But they don't need to completely understand you to support you. Ask the friend or family member beforehand for some time and take as long as you need to share your feelings and experiences. You don't have to explain what BPD and NPD are if you find it complicated or exhausting. Just talk about the behavior that bothers you.

Often people blame us or trivialize what's happening. If this happens, find someone else to talk to. Cross this person off your list.

They might tell our partner what we say, resulting in retribution. Only talk to people you trust absolutely. That may be a therapist if you can't trust friends and family.

We're afraid they won't believe us. If they don't, find someone who will.

We just don't want to deal with the judgment and scrutiny that comes with it. This takes us back to "We know that we shouldn't take the abuse, and we don't know how to explain why we do." Talk to nonjudgmental people, people in the same situation, or a professional. Find other people who are going through the same thing, whether that's online (such as my online Moving Forward family support group) or in person. People in your situation will understand and will not blame you.

We've become isolated from friends and family. That's not surprising. Now is a good time to get back in touch with those people and tell them the truth about why they haven't seen you or heard from you. You may not have seen them, but you haven't forgotten each other. Some people are good friends with people they don't see often, thanks to Facebook and other online opportunities. You can start to get in touch with people there.

It's painful to talk about, and we feel like we can't go into it without breaking down. It's okay to cry. It's much better than repressing the thoughts and the emotions that go with it. Again, people love you and want to support you. If you really you don't want to cry in front of someone, cry before you talk to them.

Mental health professionals. You may be afraid to seek counseling—perhaps because you are afraid of being judged, learning something painful about yourself or your partner, or having your partner find out. A professional can determine if you need medication, can help you work on your schemas, give you an outside perspective, and treat trauma. I recommend choosing a psychotherapist who specializes in trauma and abuse, if possible. One great place to find a therapist is http://www.psychologytoday.com. Many local therapists advertise themselves here. It is highly searchable, and you can read what the therapists say about themselves and their practice. There's even a photo of the therapist.

As in any profession, not all therapists are good ones, and not many are well-versed in the latest information about BPD and NPD. If you've spent a few months researching BPD/NPD, you may have more recent info than some. But they know about healing from an abusive relationship. You should feel as if your therapy sessions are a safe place and the therapist has the experience and training to help you. Each therapist is unique and brings themselves and their experience to the table as well as their training. So look for a good match. If a therapist doesn't understand your issues or isn't helping you, find another therapist.

When people who knew my situation suggested getting a therapist, I thought, Why? My wife is the one with the problems: therapists, psychologists, psychiatrists, prescriptions, and doctors. I don't need a therapist.

But at the same time, I was very passionate about coaches, mentors/ mentees, self-help books and programs, and the like. I didn't realize this: coaches who have the education, skills, knowledge, and other resources that can help us learn, protect ourselves, and grow are called "therapists." I wish I had started sooner. It was the missing piece of my foundation of good food, exercise, sleep, and good people.

—Chuck

Online or in-person support groups. There are few, if any, in-person support groups for people with a BPD/NPD loved one. But it's essential that you listen to the stories of other partners who have a carbon copy of your HCP. Telling your story to people who know exactly what you're dealing with is very therapeutic. To join my online support group Moving Forward, go to my website http://www.stopwalkingoneggshells.com. Moving Forward offers a weekly Zoom support meeting just for partners. Other resources include the National Alliance on Mental Health (NAMI), Al-Anon, and in-person or online support groups for codependents.

If you are a religious or spiritual person, many churches will be able to support you, although most spiritual leaders aren't informed about BPD and NPD. Spiritual leaders tend to give standard marriage advice that doesn't work with HCPs. They can't grasp that you are dealing with mental illness, and they assume your partner is flexible and has the same goals that you do. If you feel invalidated, stop using that resource. That's good advice for all resources, not just therapists.

Handling Stress

I'm stressed. You're stressed. Who *isn't* stressed? But the stress involved in having a high-conflict partner is stress on steroids that can make you physically and mentally sick. Stress is your constant companion when you have a partner with BPD, either because something just happened, something is happening now, or something—God knows what—will happen in the future.

When you experience acute stress—that is, you see a prowler or a bear—chemicals flood your body to prepare you for fight, freeze, or flight (the "stress response"). The stress response is supposed to be temporary. Once you've fought off or run away from the bear or prowler, the response is supposed to dissipate.

But when you have a high-conflict partner, every day is a "God knows what crisis will happen today" kind of day. You're hyperalert and feel like you're walking on eggshells. Essentially, you live in a perpetual stress-response state. When stress-response chemicals, such as cortisol, are constantly in your bloodstream, they can contribute to or worsen stress-related illnesses, like heart disease, obesity, diabetes, depression, anxiety, immune system suppression, headaches, back and neck pain, sleep problems, and more. That's a lot of illnesses.

Stress can have severe mental and physical effects, including (Mayo Clinic 2023b, Kreger 2022):

- muscle tension or pain
- sleep problems
- restlessness
- social withdrawal
- chest pain
- drug or alcohol misuse
- angry outbursts
- fatigue
- anxiety
- change in sex drive
- headaches
- irritability
- feeling overwhelmed, unmotivated, or unfocused
- sadness and depression
- memory and concentration problems
- changes in heart rate or blood pressure
- getting sick more often
- bad moods
- gastrointestinal problems
- racing thoughts
- constant worry

As long as you are in a crisis situation, you will need to manage stress. I suggest you learn more about what works for you. Below are some ways to deal with stress. There are many books and articles about dealing with stress that go into more detail than I can here.

Belly Breathing

Belly breathing, or "diaphragmatic breathing," is an all-purpose tool, like a multi-tool pocketknife. You can belly breathe when you're anxious, stressed, needing to sleep, meditating, in the car, about to do something difficult, or in need of a break from a stressful day. For example, when you're going to have a difficult conversation with your partner, first soothe yourself and your own emotions by belly breathing. Belly breathe a few times during the conversation.

Here's how to practice it (Kreger et al. 2022): First, find a comfortable position, either lying on your back or sitting. Place one hand on your stomach and the other on your chest. Imagine your stomach is a balloon, and sip in air so your belly button rises toward the ceiling or the wall you're facing. Then let the air out. Take a few breaths as you normally would. Your belly should rise and fall with every breath in (inhale) and every breath out (exhale). Your chest won't move. Then repeat the process. Do this for as long as feels good to you or is helpful.

Belly breathing fights the stress response and anchors you to the present moment. It will calm you down and slow the pace of the interaction, so you have more time to think about which technique you want to use and what you want to say. Practice this tool until it becomes second nature. Try it at work when you become frustrated, impatient, or angry. Try it at the dentist's office when they're drilling. (I tried it, and it helped.) Then you'll be prepared during a crisis.

Mindfulness-Based Therapy and Meditation

Research says that mindfulness is one of the best ways to reduce stress. Researchers who reviewed more than two hundred studies found that mindfulness-based therapy was especially effective for reducing not just stress, but anxiety and depression too. There is some evidence to suggest that mindfulness may even boost the immune system (American Psychological Association 2019).

Mindfulness is paying attention to the present moment without judgment. It reduces stress and helps you become relaxed and nonjudgmental. You don't think about the past or the future, which eliminates much fearfulness, regret, and so forth. Notice your feelings in the present moment rather than blocking them or pushing them away. It is a skill that requires practice, since most of us live with "monkey mind," with a dozen thoughts going through our head at any moment.

Mindfulness Exercise

Sit down at a table and put a small amount of food in front of you, like a raisin, grape, or one spoonful of anything. Then observe the food. How does it look? Does it have a smell? What color is it? Try not to make judgments about it; just observe. Now eat the food, paying attention to the taste and mouthfeel. Write down your observations. If stray thoughts come into your head like, *This exercise is stupid*, or *This reminds me I need to pick up laundry detergent at the grocery store*, pretend they are clouds and let them float on by. Stick with what you're doing.

The following exercise is adapted from one Jon Kabat-Zinn uses in his course on Mindfulness Based Stress Reduction. It is based on an acronym to help people remember how to be mindful: STOP.

"S" stands for *stop and take stock*. Step out of your immediate reaction and emotional response to a fact, event, or situation and pause for a moment.

"T" stands for *take a breath* or *tranquility*. Bring yourself fully into the present moment. Belly breathe for a few minutes, observing your thoughts and letting them go. If you're having trouble thinking of nothing, focus on imaginary changing colors. Stand outside yourself and notice the story you are telling yourself that may distort "what is."

"O" stands for *open* and *observe*. Observe what is happening with curiosity rather than critical judgment. Accept what is happening in the moment as best you can. What physical sensations are you aware of (touch, sight, hearing, taste, smell)? What are you feeling right now? What assumptions are you making about your feelings? What is the story you're telling yourself about why you are having them?

"P" stands for *proceed* and *purpose*. Choose to proceed with more awareness, compassion, and intentionality. Make a conscious, intentional choice to incorporate what you just learned.

Proceed with a next step that you see fit after pausing and checking in with yourself.

STOP is a very simple practice that grounds you in the present moment. It helps you tune into your senses of sight, sound, taste, touch, and smell. At first, it's probably easiest to physically stop for a few moments, but once you are used to the practice, you can do it while you're doing dishes, walking the dog, or stuck in traffic.

Loving-Kindness Meditation

To build your mindfulness skills and reduce stress, I recommend that you practice some form of meditation daily for at least five minutes. Meditation can improve your outlook tremendously. Research has shown that mindfulness meditation reduces rumination (obsessively thinking about something), boosts working memory, improves focus, makes us less emotionally sensitive, allows us to think more flexibly, and helps our relationships be more satisfying. It is also commonly reported to reduce stress, insomnia, anxiety, pain, depression, and high blood pressure (Davis and Hayes 2012). Loving-kindness is one type of meditation, and here's how to do it.

1. Sit in a chair in a quiet, private place and belly breathe. Focus on the present moment using the mindfulness skills you learned in the previous exercise and let everything else fall away: your burdens, problems, and so forth. Imagine sunshine flowing down like honey through the top of your head, continuing down through your facial muscles and neck, relaxing each part of your body down to your toes. Continue belly breathing.

2. Close your eyes and place your hand on your heart. Call up the face of someone whom you love or loved; this could include someone who has passed away. Call up that love and compassion and let it flow through you. Imagine that person right beside you, sending their love. Use them to help you call up your self-love, if you can. Say the following aloud:

   - *May I be safe.*
   - *May I be happy.*
   - *May I be healthy.*
   - *May I live with ease.*

   I know this may be difficult. Just sit with yourself as you would a dear friend and give yourself the kindness you deserve. Have patience with yourself. Trust your wisdom and goodness, no matter what your partner says. You can't trust their perceptions, and you don't have the same goals.

3. Now call up a picture of your partner and repeat the phrases.

   - *May (name) be safe.*
   - *May (name) be happy.*
   - *May (name) be healthy.*
   - *May (name) live with ease.*

4. If you feel bold, try this step while thinking of someone you don't like and repeat the meditation. You may feel well afterward. You can also name friends or a group of living beings, such as people in your city or the world.

5. Open your eyes and come back down to earth.

Take your time and savor the meaning of the words. Whenever you feel lost, return to the phrases. Often people find it difficult to wish loving kindness for themselves. If you have trouble, work up to the meditation in small steps. For example, you can make one wish in your head. Do what you can and try again the next day. No judgments! Keep track of your moods in a journal to see if this practice is helping reduce your stress. You might be surprised. Distractions, including other thoughts, will enter your mind. Notice them, let them float away, and return to the meditation.

Get Enough Sleep

Lack of sleep triggers the body's stress response. Sleep deprivation has long-lasting effects on the body, and caretakers rarely get enough sleep—partly because their partners keep them up fighting until late at night because their feelings must be dealt with now. Walker (2017), author of *Why We Sleep*, says:

I was once fond of saying, "Sleep is the third pillar of good health, alongside diet and exercise." I have changed my tune. Sleep is more than a pillar; it is the foundation on which the other two health bastions sit... There are more than twenty large-scale epidemiological studies that have tracked millions of people over many decades, all of which report the same clear relationship: the shorter your sleep, the shorter your life (164).

I'll add that one of my readers told me how her sleep-deprived father got into a fatal car accident after several sleepless nights caused by his HCP partner. Take this seriously.

Other Beneficial Evidenced-Based Activities for Stress Reduction

Here are some other ideas for reducing stress (Kreger et al. 2022).

Art and other creative endeavors. Just forty-five minutes of a creative activity can reduce stress and distract you from your problems (Scott 2020, Kaimal et al. 2016). Paint a picture, knit, dance, plant a garden, or do batik.

Decluttering. Clutter can make you feel stressed, anxious, and depressed. Decluttering can help you improve focus, process information, and increase productivity (Sander 2019). Organizing and decluttering is also good exercise and can give you a sense of accomplishment.

Exercise. Moving your body improves mood, sleep, and your ability to do everyday activities. Exercise boosts energy, can be fun, strengthens your muscles, combats health conditions and diseases, and improves your sex life (Mayo Clinic 2023a). Choose something you like so you're more likely to do it.

Gratitude. Taking time to think about all the positive things in your life rather than ruminating on the negatives is the single most positive thing you can do for your happiness.

Nature. People who spend two hours a week in nature can see a boost in mental and physical health (White et al. 2019). Go for a walk in the woods. Visit a park. Take a long bike ride on a city trail. Listening to nature sounds can have a similar effect .

Treat Yourself with Self-Compassion

Research shows that a better and more effective path to happiness is not higher self-esteem, but more self-compassion: compassion for your failings and imperfections. People who practice self-compassion experience greater well-being than those who constantly judge themselves (Neff 2011).

Self-compassion involves recognizing your pain and treating yourself in the same caring way that you would treat a friend going through your circumstances. How would you emotionally support them? If your friend put themselves down because of a perceived flaw, what would you say? The question is this: do you deserve the same compassion that you give to others? Yes, you do!

In her book *Self-Compassion: The Proven Power of Being Kind to Yourself,* author Kristin Neff (2011) writes:

> I remember talking to my new fiancé Rupert, who joined me for the weekly Buddhist group meetings, and shaking my head in amazement. "You mean you're actually allowed to be nice to yourself, to have com-

passion for yourself when you mess up or are going through a really hard time? I don't know… If I'm too self-compassionate, won't I just be lazy and selfish?" It took me a while to get my head around it. But I slowly came to realize that self-criticism—despite being socially sanctioned—was not at all helpful, and in fact only made things worse. I wasn't making myself a better person by beating myself up all the time. Instead, I was causing myself to feel inadequate and insecure, then taking out my frustration on the people close to me. More than that, I wasn't owning up to many things because I was so afraid of the self-hate that would follow if I admitted the truth.

What Rupert and I both came to learn was that instead of relying on our relationship to meet all our needs for love, acceptance, and security, we could actually provide some of these feelings for ourselves. And this would mean that we had even more in our hearts to give to each other.

The following is a list of valuable components of self-compassion adapted from the work of Spencer Greenberg (Greenberg 2021):

- **You matter!** You have your own unique needs, wants, and values. They matter just as much as anyone else's.

- **Self-talk.** Banish the inner critic and talk to yourself in a gentler, kinder, more considerate way.

- **Connectedness.** Keep in mind millions of people are going through the same thing you are. You are not alone in your pain.

- **Change.** If you are dealing with feelings that are difficult at this moment, they will subside. This too shall pass.

- **Self-empathy.** When you are in pain, empathize with yourself. Orient toward yourself with tenderness, understanding, and compassion.

- **Self-acceptance.** After twenty-five years of helping people in difficult relationships, I can tell you that everyone fixates on the things they don't like about themselves. You can fully accept yourself, flaws and all, and still aim to continuously improve. That is an example of a "dialectic": two opposite things being true at the same time. We can accept ourselves the way we are and still work on ourselves.

- **Self-patience.** As I have said before, change takes time, and everyone relapses. You will be no different. Being patient with yourself allows your struggles to pass more quickly than they would by punishing yourself.

- **Reflection.** When you make a mistake or obsess over a flaw, ask yourself what someone who loves you would say about your struggles. Listen to their voices, not your inner critic.

- **Self-forgiveness.** So what if you did something you regret? So what if you have flaws—of course you do! While reading this book, you may be kicking yourself for not knowing this or that or not doing something differently. Welcome to the club called humanity. Self-forgiveness is a powerful way to reduce or even eliminate shame.

Proving to yourself that you're not the things your partner says you are is a form of self-compassion. If you answer yes to the following questions, it is likely the blame or criticism doesn't belong to you, but to your partner.

- Is my partner projecting their own stuff onto me? In other words, do your partner's complaints actually apply them and not to you?

- Is there a nugget of truth that your partner has widely exaggerated, or is their complaint based on something that is over and done with because it happened years ago? This is typical HCP behavior.

- Is this criticism based on your partner seeming to read your mind and accusing you of having the wrong motivations, or telling you what you're trying to do, as if they knew your mind better than you know yourself? Mind-reading can be an abusive act. You can't prove what your thoughts are, so this is a popular sign of abuse. Do not agree with your abuser just to get them to stop talking. Instead, try to stop feeling the need to control the way they think of you.

- Has no one else besides your partner made this accusation? If one or two other people disagree with your spouse, or you do, the blame or criticism is likely bogus.

- Is your partner using something you told them in a private moment to make you look bad? This destroys intimacy and trust. When your partner sets out to hurt you, question whether this relationship is in your best interests.

- Does your partner know what qualities are important to you, and is your partner using that information to hurt you? The best example is them telling you that you are selfish. When this happens, congratulate yourself—you're starting to pay attention to your own needs.

Activities that show compassion for yourself include:

- Getting a new haircut, manicure, or pedicure.

- Volunteering for a person or organization that will really appreciate you.

- Leaving a boring, dead-end job and finding a better job, especially one that is known to have a positive work environment.

- Accomplishing something you've been wanting to do for a long time, like writing a memoir, learning a new activity, or taking a class. Write down the enjoyable things you've done in the past and consider doing them again.

- If you are a perfectionist, taking up an activity you're not going to be the best at but will enjoy. Remind yourself no one is perfect.

- Dressing up one day and listening to the compliments you get.

- Making a list of the things you "have to do" or think you should do and asking yourself how necessary these activities are. If they're not necessary and you don't enjoy them, quit, and do something fun with your time that gets you interacting with others.

- Planning a special outing for you and a child. Take them to a fun event, especially a new one.

- Obtaining a list of events and activities in your community and trying them. Bring a friend.

- Trying new ethnic cuisine or going to your favorite restaurant.

- Starting a fun activity that gets you moving, like biking, gardening, dancing, or photography.

- Making a doctor's appointment for any weird aches and pain. Schedule a mammogram or colonoscopy if needed. Pay attention to your physical health.

- Looking for beauty in unexpected places

- Spending as much time in nature as you can.

In this chapter, I've attempted to convince you of the importance of emotional self-care. I hope I've succeeded, because learning and practicing the tools in the next four chapters will need your full concentration. *It is not selfish to take care of yourself.* Put relaxing and enjoyable activities in your calendar and review this chapter to see which of my recommendations fit your interests and lifestyle.

CHAPTER 6

Changing Your Mindset

The Universe totally supports us in every thought we choose to think and believe... What you choose to think about yourself and about life becomes true for you. And we have unlimited choices about what we can think...

Every thought we think is creating our future. Each one of us creates our experiences by our thoughts and our feelings. The thoughts we think and the words we speak create our experiences...

No person, no place, and no thing has any power over us, for "we" are the only thinkers in it. When we create peace and harmony and balance in our minds, we will find it in our lives.

—Louise Hay, *You Can Heal Your Life*

Chances are that you feel powerfully stuck, waiting for your partner to change. In other words, you're trying to control things you can't change, and you're not taking control of things you *can* change: your thoughts and actions. In this chapter, I'll talk about changing your thoughts. You might not realize the power that your thoughts have over your life, but I assure you that they do. In fact, there is an extremely popular field of psychotherapy called cognitive behavioral therapy (CBT), which is based on the theory that our thoughts lead to our feelings, which in turn lead to our behaviors. As an added benefit, changing your thoughts will help you in everyday life.

Judgmental thinking is one example. Learning to become aware of when judgment is present in your thoughts is one powerful way to change your mindset. Practicing nonjudgmental thinking can free you from focusing on "bad" things in your life, help you treat yourself and others with compassion, reduce stress about the future, help you deal with difficult emotions, and help you view the world with a more positive outlook.

Examples of Judgmental and Nonjudgmental Thinking

Judgmental Thinking	Nonjudgmental Thinking
My HCP partner is sick and needs to be fixed.	My partner is the way they are from some combination of nature and nurture, and they deserve to have their own recovery journey in their own time frame.
I am a caretaker, it's my fault, and I feel disappointed that I've let my partner treat me this way.	I am the way I am from some combination of nature or nurture, and I have taken the best actions and made the best decisions with the tools I had at the time. This is part of life. I can always make new choices.
I can't stand feeling pain, anger, worry, fear, and guilt.	Pain is part of life, just like joy, happiness, and love are. I may feel pain, but I don't have to suffer by making judgments and feeling bad about feeling bad.
It's not fair that I have to take responsibility for changing the relationship.	I have the opportunity to make changes in myself that may change the relationship. I am glad that I have control. It may be hard, but I have trust in myself that this is something I can learn.
I didn't plan for my life to go this way. Life should not be this hard. I hate where I am right now.	Life is a journey, and this is the road I've been traveling, making the best decisions I could with the tools I had at hand. I won't focus on the past; I will focus on the present moment. I will make good and careful choices, and I will be at another stage on my journey.

The Power of Our Thoughts

Let's say, for example, that you're on your way to a job interview when you come across a detour that is going to make you ten minutes late. In scenario number one, your harsh inner critic puts you down for not leaving earlier in case of the unexpected. Your critical father was right—you are a mess-up. By the time you get to the interview, you are feeling intense self-loathing and a few tears have spoiled your makeup.

In scenario number 2, once you realize your mistake, you vow to leave earlier in the future. Then you flip into problem-solving mode. It's not the end of the world. You call the interviewer, letting them know you'll be late and why. The two different thoughts—you're a mess-up versus you made a forgivable mistake—create two different realities, two different responses, and two different actions: one that serves you well and one that doesn't.

Now let's go through two real-life examples of HCP relationships that show how changing your thoughts can change your feelings and behavior.

- Your partner says you're stupid. In reality, you graduated from college and work as a teacher. You can choose to take in the insult and feel bad about yourself or realize "shaming and blaming" is just part of their disorder. You don't need to justify, defend, or explain yourself.

- Your partner tells you you're selfish for joining a gym and working out three times a week. You critically evaluate their comment and realize you are far from selfish because you're always trying to meet the needs of your family. You think, *That's the mental illness talking. I deserve to do something just for myself because it's part of self-care, which I need to do.* Or you can take the bait and argue with them—a move that will make things worse. You realize it takes two people to argue, and you decline their invitation. You know what is right, and no argument is going to change their mind. On the other hand, you can choose to believe that, indeed, taking care of your health is selfish and cancel your gym membership.

These are examples of attempted gaslighting or brainwashing by your HCP. Even if there is a grain of truth in their comment, they've made a mountain out of a molehill. Your partner's feelings equal facts, and you can't argue that they shouldn't feel a certain way. Do not justify yourself, get into an argument, or defend or explain yourself, aka JADE. When you JADE, you're suggesting that reality is a fact open to debate (you'll read more about JADE in chapter 7).

> One thing that shook my wife to the core was when she screamed at me, "You don't make me happy anymore!" I simply responded "What does happiness look like to you? Please describe it to me." She was speechless.

Steadfastly remind yourself you are not causing your partner's thoughts, feelings, or behaviors no matter how much they try to blame you. You cannot cure nor control their disorder. But it is up to you to accept the fact that you can't make them happy. You can only create an environment in which they have the opportunity to choose to be happy.

Don't Try to Control Their Opinions About You

One of the biggest hooks that keep you in a gaslighting relationship is your need to control what your partner thinks of you. As a self-reflective person, you may be all too willing to take their accusations seriously. *But you can't control what they think about you.* They're mentally ill, stuck in one way of reacting, and when they put you down, it serves to make them feel better about themselves. When you let go of your need to be right, it will set you free and eliminate most of your arguments. And all you've done is change your mindset.

Besides, your happiness depends less on asking yourself who's right and more on asking yourself if you appreciate the way your partner treats you. Instead of wondering, *Am I really selfish?* ask yourself if you want to be with someone who continually makes harsh accusations based on "alternative facts." Become comfortable with the idea that your partner is entitled to their point of view, no matter how improbable it seems to you. And of course, you are entitled to your own opinions as well. Do you want to believe the mentally ill person, or do you want to believe the person who knows you best (you!), including all your reasons, motivations, and emotions?

Practice Compassionate Detachment

Compassionate detachment means stepping back and stopping obsessive worry about the choices your partner makes and not rescuing them from the consequences of their choices. When you detach, you distance yourself emotionally from the actions, words, and feelings of your partner. You stop waiting for them to change, to get better, to be happy, and to be healthy, and you no longer take their survival strategies personally. Compassionate detachment allows you to take a step back and regain your emotional health so you can be authentic and let others be responsible for their own choices.

For example, one day your partner may blow up at you, then try to initiate sex at night. Rather than worry about disappointing them if you say no, feel free to say, "I don't want to right now." You don't have to explain why and invite them to blame you for the fight. Just say no. If they had wanted to have sex, they should have treated you better. They won't hold themselves responsible for their behavior, but you can. That is the essence of compassionate detachment.

Compassionate detachment does *not* mean that you stop loving them—in fact, it means that you love them enough to let them learn from their mistakes. Eventually, they will learn that their actions have consequences. That creates an environment of recovery because some of your responses will act as a sort of punishment, and when they treat you nicely, it's a type of reward because you continue to pay attention to them. It motivates your partner to start doing the things they're rewarded for and disincentives them to act badly—all without talking about it. And as an added bonus, it means that you love *yourself* enough to stop letting their behavior crush you again and again.

Ozzie Tinman, the pseudonym of a man who had an HCP wife, talks about detachment in his book *One Way Ticket to Kansas*. He writes: "Detaching is a conscious choice to give less emphasis to the emotional impact another person has on us. Some people think detaching and think of 'checking out...'" That's not what I mean. I mean granting less accessibility of your emotional state, long term, to the control or effects of another. Keep in mind they are often trying to make us feel badly. They manipulate our feelings to moderate their own pain. Other times they are out of control, unable to consider our well being, and flail at us in very hurtful ways. Detaching is accepting as an ongoing premise that 'I won't care as much about this as I did before.' Now the question is 'How much detaching?' It all comes down to what our ultimate obligation is. And I believe our ultimate obligation is to care for our own spirit" (Tinman 2005).

Silence Your Inner Critic

It's not enough to escape your partner's gaslighting. You need to silence your inner critic and stop gaslighting yourself. Your inner critic is the voice in your head that tells you something is wrong with you, you're not good enough, and so forth. The voice may belong to your parents, your partner, or your old football coach. One way to silence your inner critic is to make a list of what makes you a worthwhile person—the things you like about yourself—and evict the insults that are living rent-free in your head.

> I don't think my husband was intentionally brainwashing me, but yes, I ended up taking responsibility for the emotional turmoil he went through because I couldn't ever meet his (unreasonable) expectations. It took me a few years of distress, feeling like a failure, and struggling to keep on top of every demand or expectation he had of me. Finally, I realized that it wasn't me, that there was something not quite right with his logic and not quite okay with the magnitude of his emotions in response to the situation that was occurring. I guess I knew this on some level for quite some time, but when the split was over, I had a difficult time recollecting what actually occurred. I think because my life is so opposite of our old life together. My brain needed time to recognize the anomaly.
>
> I think what finally made me realize something was amiss in the relationship was when I was not okay with brushing a splitting episode under the rug like nothing happened, because doing so was taking a major toll on my emotional life and physical body. Learning about HCPs and reminding myself daily that the reactions of others have to do with what is happening inside of them and not with me has helped me significantly. And daily mindfulness practice and learning about my own triggers has helped too.

In reality, you're incredibly kind, generous, nurturing, understanding, and responsive to your partner's needs. I have yet to meet a caretaker who didn't have these wonderful qualities. Just don't go overboard with them with the wrong person. Feelings do not equal facts, and your inner critic is a form of self-sabotage, holding you back from what you want to achieve in your life. Positive affirmations can help. It may sound simplistic, but affirmations work because of repetition. Post affirmations like the following somewhere only you can access:

- "I am getting better every day."

- "I am lovable and loved."

- "I am an amazing person."

- "I don't have to be perfect. No one is."

- "My mistakes help me learn and grow."

- "I can control my own happiness."

- "I believe in myself and my goals and dreams."

- "I can be anything I want to be."

- "My confidence grows when I step out of my comfort zone."

- "I am in charge of my life."

- "I can get through anything."

The first few times I tried to think and do things independently, my husband got mad and gave me the silent treatment. I cried and fell into a deep depression. I realized he did not care that I was crying and sad, which confused me and caused me to be even more devastated. Then I started to become more accustomed to not asking permission to do things. I was still upset but started finding things to do with my daughter, like go on ride bikes, go on drives, that sort of thing. My husband became more and more like a roommate and less and less like a partner. I stopped trying to plan things that involved him because he became too undependable with his moods.

—Sharon

Overcome FOG: Fear, Obligation, and Guilt

Feelings of fear, obligation, and guilt (FOG) keep caretakers confused and feeling stuck in the caretaker role. First, let's talk about fear.

Fear

The number one source of fear is being unable to predict your partner's moods and actions. When you see them next, will they be furious, loving, critical, sincere, or demanding? Will they have sudden bursts of anger, make irrational demands, or give you the silent treatment? You may try everything in the book to please them. But since their feelings come from someplace inside them, it's best to depersonalize their tantrums, which have little to do with you.

Take actions *you* think are best. Your opinions are the ones that matter most because you have to live with the outcome. Remember to belly breathe and plan carefully so that no matter what mood they're in, your plans are not affected.

For example, if you have plans to go on a family outing and your partner insists you cancel them because they're mad at you, take the kids and go anyway. Your partner has no power over you that you don't give them.

Obligation

Feelings of obligation come when you see your partner suffering, particularly if they had a bad childhood. You may be the one keeping the family going. You may have made promises to them you no longer want to keep now that you know the extent of their mental illness. And if you're a caretaker, you'll probably believe that abuse isn't a good enough excuse to overcome your feelings of obligation. Remember from the last chapter that verbal and emotional abuse can be just as bad or even worse than physical abuse and can cause stress-related illness. You control your feelings of obligation, not your partner.

Guilt

You also control any feelings of guilt, which is almost always misplaced. In her excellent book *Stop Caretaking the Borderline or Narcissist*, author Margalis Fjelstad writes (2013): "You may have believed the BP/NP will be hurt, feel rejected, attempt suicide, become deeply depressed, or fly into a rage all because of what you do and say. But haven't you seen the BP/NP do these things even when you were trying your level best to do exactly what the BP/NP wanted? Just as you can't change or stop the BP/NPs behavior, you also can't cause his or her behavior. Therefore, you are not responsible for the BP/NP's feelings or behaviors. The BP/NP uses guilt to manipulate and keep you trapped in your own belief that you are essential to the BP/NP. This belief of your omnipotence in the BP/NP's life keeps you from facing the real struggles of the final stages of your own growing into adulthood—that is responsibility for yourself" (76).

When you find yourself feeling fear, obligation, or guilt, consider what thoughts are going on in your head. You'll probably find some of these thoughts that supercharge FOG.

- *I'm not good enough.*

- *I don't deserve it.*

- *Other people are more important than me.*

- *Expect pain in relationships.*

- *Don't ever make mistakes.*

- *My partner is responsible for my feelings.*

- *Being selfish is bad.*

- *Others always come before me.*

- *I shouldn't stand up for myself.*

- *It's my partner's job to make me happy.*

- *I can't say no.*

- *If I leave this relationship, it means I am a bad, selfish person.*

- *My partner's world will fall apart without me.*

- *If my partner is in a bad mood, I'm in a bad mood.*

- *I'm responsible for my partner's happiness.*

- *I have no choice.*

- *I'm afraid of anger in myself and others.*

- *I shouldn't ask people to take actions that are hard for them.*

- *Never upset anyone with your own needs.*

In that moment, step back, assess what triggered the feeling, and take action to stop that feeling before you find yourself being pulled into your partner's drama.

When Being a Caretaker Makes You Feel Like a Good Person

When you feel unworthy and damaged, being a caretaker can elevate your self-esteem. Supporting someone makes you feel less unworthy and unloved. When you want to feel worthy, you may pick being a caretaker—putting everyone and anything before yourself and putting yourself last—over feeling unloved.

But it is possible to be a loving, compassionate, loyal, kind person without being a caretaker. You have many, many good qualities that have nothing to do with caretaking, and if you don't know what they are, I suggest you ask your friends. I did this myself: I wrote to my closest friends and family and asked them to tell me what they thought made me a worthwhile person. I was incredibly touched because people took time out of their day to think about me, which said a lot. They came up with all sorts of things they admired about me—things I never would have thought up by myself.

Supporting someone is a great thing to do. When you support someone, you help them with things they don't know how to do for themselves. But when you caretake your partner, you enable high-conflict behavior. Supporting truly helps, while giving in to demands that are unfair, or that you don't like, keeps your partner stuck in their high-conflict behaviors. Being a caretaker might not be a problem if you were married to someone who was healthier and more giving. But a high-conflict partner will exploit this tendency, and you'll find yourself being pulled deeper and deeper into the HCP's alternate reality.

Stop Needing Your HCP's Approval

It's always great to get the approval of others. But the more you need your partner's approval, the more you open yourself up to being controlled and manipulated. Your partner will give you approval for the wrong things, such as caretaking them, putting yourself last, being hypervigilant so you can fulfill their every need, putting them before the children, giving them narcissistic supply, and neglecting your own friends and interests so they worry less about being abandoned.

In short, they will approve of you if you think, feel, and behave in ways that are probably unhealthy for you. If you give in to your partner's demands, they will demand more. If you take the blame, they will blame you even more. If you attempt to smooth things over by agreeing to things you don't really agree with and apologize when you haven't done anything wrong, don't assume that will end the conversation. They will use your apology or agreement as a sign that you're the problem person in the relationship, and they will bring up your "crimes" again and again. Be aware of how your own fears, such as fear of conflict, lead to needing approval. Seek your own approval instead. Look to your friends and family for validation, not your HCP.

Stop Predicting Disaster

What will happen if you follow the suggestions in this book? Are you imagining the worst and discounting that these methods will work for you? If so, you've given up before you've even started. "Disaster-vision" leads to anxiety, uses a tremendous amount of energy, and doesn't come up with real, workable solutions to the problems that arise in a relationship with an HCP. It doesn't lead to making good decisions. Aim for flexible thinking, managed emotions, and reasonable behaviors. When you use the suggestions in this book, you'll be throwing something new at your partner, and they don't like change. They're used to specific responses from you, such as: doing what they tell you to do, *not* doing what they don't want you to do, agreeing with them, not participating in self-care, not having any boundaries, not seeing friends and family, asking permission for things, doing all the housework, and so on. In other words, they approve of things that benefit them, not you. Needing their approval comes at a great cost. What's important is approving of yourself.

Realize You and Your HCP Are not the Same

Right now, you may assume that you and your partner are both using the same operating system. But one of you is a PC and the other a Mac. Let me give you some examples:

- You can deal with things you can't control. Your HCP gets anxious when things are out of their comfort zone.

- You can clearly see what makes you feel a certain way, but your partner believes their emotions are caused by someone else.

- Their facts are based on feelings. Yours are more firmly rooted in reality.

- You see past, present, and future, while your partner lives in an ever-present now. You may have made dinner four times this week, but if you ask them to make dinner the fifth night, you're *always* asking them to make dinner.

- Your partner assumes your thoughts, feelings, and perceptions are identical to theirs. When they see a difference, they feel threatened and try to sway you over to their alternate reality.

- You may not like change, but for them it becomes a major crisis.

- You can tolerate being close to people and at a distance. But when someone tries to become truly intimate with your partner, or you move far away, your partner becomes uncomfortable. They're threatened by closeness and distance—especially partners with borderline personality disorder. This is one reason why your relationship has so many ups and downs.

- You may have low self-esteem, but HCPs have deep feelings of inadequacy and being undeserving of love. When someone loves them, they assume that person has something wrong with them. You can't convince them otherwise.

- As I mentioned previously, I believe that people with BPD are emotionally at age two, and people with NPD are emotionally at about age six. They don't really grow up. Like children, they only consider their own needs and emotions, not anyone else's. When you aren't focused on them, they feel nonexistent. When you're not there, someone with BPD may have an emotional crisis, while someone with NPD may feel angry that you're not feeding their ego.

- You can be logical. They can sometimes, but not other times when you really want them to be. The more you expect them to be logical, the more frustrated you will feel. If you switch into caretaker mode and try to teach them to be logical, you will simply irritate them and waste their time—and yours.

Solve Your Own Problems

So much heartache could be resolved if you allowed your partner to solve their problems and you concentrated on your own problems. As a general rule, the person who wants things to be different is the one who owns the problem. When you expect your partner to change to meet your wishes, you're expecting them to solve your problem of dealing with their difficult behavior. When you expect others to solve your problems, you will get angry and frustrated when they don't. When they expect you to manage their emotions and poor self-esteem and you take that problem on and attempt to solve it, you reinforce whatever they're doing. If someone else is solving your problem for you, why change? If you try to solve their problems, you deny them the opportunity to grow and encourage behavior you want to stop.

Before you attempt to solve a problem, determine whose problem it is. If it's your problem, work on it. If it's their problem, give them the opportunity to solve it in the same way you let a child take on more and more responsibilities. Let's look at some common examples.

Things that are your problem include:

- **Abuse.** If you are experiencing abuse, get away from it permanently or temporarily rather than trying to change the abuser.

- **Exhaustion.** If you're tired and your partner is keeping you up, sleep in another room or check into a motel.

- **Needing emotional intimacy.** If you want intimacy, find it with other people rather than trying to change your partner in ways the disorders won't allow. Or realize you're going to have to go without it and make decisions based on reality, not hopes and dreams.

- **Housework.** If your HCP expects you to do all the drudgery, you have a few choices: you can hire someone to do the work, do it yourself, bribe the kids to do it, or let the work go unfinished and lower your expectations.

- **Your partner makes impulsive decisions.** Insulate yourself from the outcomes of those decisions. Make sure your bank requires signatures from both of you before withdrawing money or else have separate accounts. If your partner invites people to dinner, expecting you to serve something special, let them know they'll have to make dinner themselves or take their guests to a restaurant.

Things that are their problem include:

- **Fearing abandonment.** They will get upset and jealous of the time you spend with others. When you try to solve that problem for them by ending your friendships, you create problems for yourself and encourage them to look at you as someone who is going to solve their problems (feeling fear) for them. They may not want to go to therapy, but that doesn't mean they can rope you into becoming their therapist. Let them deal with their challenges on their own and keep your social life.

- **Stroking their ego.** The only way your NPD partner will stop using you inappropriately to meet their needs is if you do not to play their games, ones like "I'm better than you," "Give me strokes," and "Promises I don't intend to keep." What's keeping you playing these games isn't only them, but also your desire to control their thinking about you. But here's the thing: even if you play these games and try to please them, their need to always be right means they *want* to look at you as though you were beneath them, and so they will. There is no way to win their games, other than not to play.

In this chapter, I've talked about how changing your mindset can change your life. The amount of power you have over your own life is amazing and much more than you ever thought possible. In chapters 7 and 8, I will talk about communication and limit-setting techniques. In chapter 9, I'll talk about how changing your behavior can free you from the life you're living.

CHAPTER 7

Communicating Without Apology

My borderline wife would express upset over Thing A. I would respond (defensively) to Thing A. She would get more upset because I wasn't getting the point (that had nothing to do with Thing A). I would respond with more vigor to Thing A. She would abandon Thing A and accuse me of Thing B. I would get spun around and begin defending myself against Thing B. Sometimes I would insist that we stick to Thing A. Either way, she would now insist on an apology for the horrible way I was treating her, which would now become Thing C to argue over. I would spend a couple days furious that she seemed to seek out confrontation over pathetically unimportant issues. She would recover much sooner and wonder why I was still upset. Days later, she'd bring up Thing A again, and the cycle would start over.

—Robert Page, *BPD from the Husband's POV*

Communicating with an HCP is exceptionally difficult. People with NPD typically have very little capacity for empathy, and when BPD people are emotionally aroused (about a six out of ten, where ten is extremely emotional), they have trouble accessing empathy. HCPs look at issues in black and white and can be paranoid. If they acknowledge your emotions or take them seriously, they see themselves as "all bad." They may make threats or rage at you, call you names, try to punish you, or give you the silent treatment. In this chapter, I'm going to explain how to stay safe, reduce the number of arguments you have, and teach you specialized communication techniques designed for HCPs.

Understanding Fights with HCPs

Why do HCPs fight like it's a life-or-death situation? Because to them, it *is* life or death. That's why they will try to get you to participate in an all-night-long argument even as you beg them to let you sleep. Susan, who self-identifies as having BPD, explains:

> *People with BPD react so strongly because when you express your side of an issue, even if it's a simple disagreement, we are triggered by the most shameful, most difficult parts of ourselves. We already hate ourselves, so our overreactions and refusal to see your side of things come from a deep place of pain and fear.*
>
> *As a comparison, imagine a group of casual swimmers swimming in the ocean when one gets stung by a (seemingly) deadly jellyfish or gets bitten by a shark. Then they yell out and try to swim to safety for themselves, not really capable of concerning themselves with the other swimmers because they are so enveloped with their own pain and dread. In short, moments like this, which spark these tantrums, feel like life or death for us. This is why it seems like we have no empathy. That's why we fight to the death: it feels like we are losing you, which somehow feels worse than death.*

People with NPD have a bit of a different perspective. They need to be in control at all times (also true for people with BPD to a lesser extent), and when you disagree with them by expressing your own opinion, they will gaslight you so they can regain control of your shared reality. When you disagree with them, they feel like they've been slapped in the face. They worry that this is the first step to losing you as a source of narcissistic supply, which they would have to replace—and it's not easy to find someone to give up all their needs and be consumed with satisfying them and giving them strokes. Besides, they want to win. Winning is everything because otherwise, they are a loser.

Given the destructiveness of HCPs, the way to prevent setting off your partner is to refuse to justify, argue, defend yourself, and explain (JADE) and use the tools in this chapter. Believe it or not, you can reduce the number and intensity of arguments by using the tools in this chapter. Your partner can't argue by themselves.

Use Positive Self-Talk

During an argument, what you are telling yourself is just as important (if not more so) as what your partner is saying to you. The first step is pausing and taking several belly breaths (see chapter 5). Then remind yourself of what you've learned in this book. Here are some phrases that you might want to tell yourself as you breathe.

- "Their upset is really about their feelings of worthlessness and shame. This has nothing to do with me."

- "Inside, my loved one is really hurting. I am seeing their pain come out as anger."

- "I am loved. I am powerful. I am (name what is important to you)."

- "My loved one is sick, not bad."

- "My loved one is a child in an adult's body." (Look at pictures of them as a child so you can easily recall their child image.)

- "I will not let them intimidate me."

- "There is a clear, strong, plastic dome above me that protects me from them. I am safe."

- "This is unpleasant, but I am not going to die."

- "Their emotions are intense and come from a place where they feel inadequate and undeserving of love. I cannot change this."

- "For someone with NPD, negative attention is as good as positive attention. Fighting back just gives them what they want."

- "Having a different point of view triggers their shame, which, in turn, can trigger rage, sadness, and everything in between. If I want to have a discussion, I will wait until they are not emotionally aroused."

- "Don't expect more than they can give."

- "They may look at fights as an opportunity to win, while I want to solve a problem and increase intimacy. If we don't have the same goals, there's not going to be a meeting of the minds."

- "I'm not going to expect them to be logical."

- "I will not fall for FOG (fear, obligation, and guilt)."

It is necessary for me to remain calm when my husband picks a fight. If there is any sense of aggression from me, the rants escalate. We have had some terrible fights over the years, and I felt for a long time that not engaging was a sign of weakness. In my mind, I was being attacked and I must defend myself, which led to law enforcement getting involved. It was only when I understood that the attacks were really about him, how he perceived me, and how he interpreted me that I was able to choose to remain calm. It took me many years to understand that I had a choice. At this time when he begins to spiral, I remain calm and attempt to redirect him to explain why he is angry or ask him what he is feeling. Is it really because of something I actually said or did, and if he thinks it is, is it true? Sometimes I have to walk away and say we can discuss this when things are calmer. It doesn't always work; however, I always have the choice not to feed him the ammunition he needs to continue.

—Cathy

Do Not JADE: Justify, Argue, Defend, Explain

Just because someone invites you to an argument, you don't have to accept. The best way to decline is to avoid "JADEing": justifying yourself, arguing, defending yourself, or explaining. Meg writes:

Why justify my actions and thoughts and feelings to him? He doesn't really care about my view. He only cares about his own. Why argue about anything with him? He always "wins," and if he doesn't, it's someone else's fault. Besides, only one viewpoint is right—his. Why defend? He automatically thinks everything is my fault. He tells me I'm stupid for the way I did something or I should have done it his way. So now I say, "This is the decision I have made." Why explain? He doesn't hear anyway. All he does is cross his arms, stare at me with a smirk on his face as if he's thinking, Blah blah blah. Then he'll say, "Oh, so that's your excuse? Your whole life you've made excuses."

One of the ways HCPs try to sway people to their point of view is to constantly question your reasoning. For example, "Why do you want to do that?" or "Why do you feel that way?" The hope is that when you try to explain yourself, they will obtain information they can use to prove you are wrong about your choices, feelings, wants, needs, and values. It's like trying to have a conversation with someone who wants to change your beliefs about something like politics or religion. They're not interested in what you have to say as much as they're interested in learning what tactic to take to oppose you. The way to counteract this is to avoid JADE: justifying, arguing, defending yourself, explaining. Not giving a reason or explaining your decisions gives you control over your own thoughts, feelings, and actions. You can state who you are, what you feel, and what you're going to do without getting into a debate about right or wrong. You are refusing to participate in manipulative conversations in which everything about you is "wrong," invalidated, and rejected. The following is an example of a JADE conversation.

Let's say that a few coworkers invite you out for a drink after work. You call your partner, and they don't want you to go. We'll look at how they might use the information you give them to convince you that staying home with them is your only choice.

Your justification: I will have a really good time at happy hour with my coworkers, and it will make me happy.

HCP response: You mean you're not happy with me? I stay depressed and you go out and have fun? You have no compassion, and now I know you don't even want to be around me.

Arguing: I can love you *and* go out and do things on my own.

HCP response: It sounds like I'm just one big burden to you. Maybe I should just go kill myself or stay home all the time so I don't bother you!

Defending: Really, I deserve to have a night to do something I want to do.

HCP response: Next you're going to want separate vacations? You must hate me and hate spending time together.

Overexplaining: I don't have things my way most of the time. What about when you didn't want me to go to Florida to visit my sick father, so I stayed home?

HCP response: Fine, go. Forget about me. I don't have anything to say to you. (Later, the HCP gives you the silent treatment.)

JADEing is not a way to change things; it is a way to keep things as they are. When you JADE, HCPs use the information you impart to come up with counterattacks and reasons why you are wrong. The more information you give them, the more information they have to use against you, especially if they have NPD. Remember, your partner's mind is already made up because their facts are based on how they feel. The roller coaster of hope often gives you an itch you need to scratch—*certainly this time, they will come to see things your way if you explain it correctly.*

But they aren't interested in your true motivation, personality, actions, and so forth. Their goal is not to try to make you a better person but to make you out to be the bad guy—the one who needs to change—by taking things they don't like about themselves and projecting them all on you. Their complaints often have a little bit of truth to them, but the HCP exaggerates and makes things much worse than they sound. Most of the time, HCPs would rather get a root canal without anesthetic than accept any responsibility for their actions. Because of your schemas, you are primed to believe their distortions, which lowers your self-esteem, making you more likely to believe in their criticism and blaming, which lowers your self-esteem some more. Pretty soon you're spiraling down, wondering why this relationship is causing you so much pain.

Alternatives to JADEing

The first alternative to JADEing is to stand up for yourself without engaging in an argument. Another option is simply not responding. This works when your partner accuses you of something ridiculous. Instead of justifying yourself, arguing, defending yourself, or explaining, respond in the following ways.

Keep in mind it's okay that you have your reality and they have theirs. If you had to think the same way, that would be an example of an enmeshed relationship, where your thoughts, feelings, and opinions must be the same as your partner's. In these types of relationships, the caretaker can lose their identity.

Your partner wants to intimidate you and make you feel responsible for their feelings, especially anger. The phrases below acknowledge that you are not responsible for their skewed perceptions, but without calling them skewed perceptions, which would result in rage and DARVO (deny, attack, and reverse victim and offender).

The following phrases and tactics deflect your partner's manipulations without JADEing. They say, "I see you and your manipulations, and I'm not buying into them." This allows you to disengage and stay calm. These phrases also help you detach from your need to have your partner think a certain way. Some of them may not be easy to say because you are disagreeing with your partner, perhaps for the very first time. Some are easier to say than others. Try them out with friends and family before you try with your high-conflict partner so you can say them in a calm and gentle manner.

- "Really?"

- "I see."

- "I'm sorry you're upset. Yelling isn't going to solve anything."

- "This subject is off-limits."

- "I don't choose to have this conversation."

- "Some people would agree; some people might not; some people might say no. As for the others, who knows? You'd have to poll everyone."

- "What an interesting way to look at things."

- "How interesting."

- "That's an interesting point of view."

- "What an interesting comment to make."

- "Fascinating." (Channel the voice of Mr. Spock from *Star Trek* here.)

- Agree with part of the statement. For example, if your partner says, "Loading the kids up on Halloween candy, I see." Response: "Yes, I'm giving the kids some candy."

- "I'm sorry you're upset."

- "I don't accept your definition of me."

- "I need to go."

- "Let's agree to disagree."

- "I hear you, and I'm going to think about it. I don't want to keep talking right now."

- "I don't like the way I'm feeling right now, and I'm not willing to continue this conversation."

- "I love having intimate conversations with you, but not when you're putting me down."

- "I'm not comfortable with where this conversation is going. Let's talk about it later."

- "I'm not responsible for your perceptions of me or this experience."

- "I am permitted to have my own experience And I'm okay with the fact that we disagree. I am entitled to my own perceptions of this experience."

- "I'm sorry you are angry, but I'm not responsible for your feelings. It's okay that you're angry, but I am not the cause of your feelings."

- "I know you feel that way, but I don't agree with you. I see things differently. That is your perception, but mine is different."

- "That is certainly your opinion. Some people might agree; others might not."

- "That is one opinion. Everybody deserves to have their own opinion."

- "Whatever you say, dear." "Whatever you feel is true for you." "Whatever." (Feign ignorance of their negative intent.)

- Take what they say at face value. For example, "Are you wearing *that* to the party tonight?" Response: "Yes."

- "I'm sure you see it that way."

- "Please stop talking to me in that tone. I can't hear what you're saying as long as you're yelling."

- "I'm not going to continue this conversation."

- "Perhaps you didn't mean to hurt my feelings, but I'm too upset to talk about it right now. We can talk about it later when things calm down."

- "It may not be your intention to put me down, but I feel put down, and I'm not going to continue the conversation."

- "I don't want to continue this argument or conversation right now.

- "I hear you, and I'm going to think about it."

- "I don't want to talk right now."

- "You are entitled to your faulty perception of me."

- "Let's get back to the subject at hand."

Another tool is to also buy yourself time. Instead of answering right away, take time to consider their request. For example:

- "I don't have an answer right now. I need some time to think."

- "You've asked me an important question, and it deserves some consideration."

- "Before I answer, I need to talk to (whomever) or wait until (whatever)."

- "I'm not sure how I feel about what you're asking. Let's talk about it tomorrow."

- "I have to check our budget to see if we can afford this."

Getting Out of Unsafe Situations

When one of you is getting too emotional (probably them, but you may get overly emotional too), there is no use continuing the conversation. When an HCP is angrier than a six out of ten, their emotions have taken over, and there's not much you can do about it but get yourself and any children to a safe place. In the next chapter, you'll learn how to set limits ahead of time for that kind of behavior. But for now, important things to know about rage are:

You do not have to, and should not have to, be an audience to their rage. Continuing to engage won't help; they don't have the ability to self-soothe and respond in a calm, logical way. When they are having a tantrum, treat them like a child you love dearly. Say, "I love you, but things are too emotional for us to speak respectfully with each other now. When things are calm, we can speak again." Or, "I can't talk to you when there's so much conflict. I am leaving now and will be back in an hour" (make sure to tell them when you will be back). Keep repeating this no matter what they say (this is called the "broken record" technique). And then leave no matter what they say.

Don't answer the phone; don't text. They need to understand that there is a price to pay for abusing you. Take any children with you. Rage attacks are extremely damaging to them. If you leave *every time* they get into a relentless rage, there will come a time when they know what will happen when they raise their voice.

125

Remember their raging is not about you. Their rage is about the things they tell themselves, their skewed perceptions of events, the experience of feeling slighted, or a complete projection of how they are feeling about themselves at the moment. Anger may be a substitute for a less desirable feeling. Anger is an energizing emotion that can mask other emotions, such as shame, depression, or unworthiness. Think about what's going on in your partner's life. You may be able to surmise the feeling they are trying to cover up.

Observe without judging. Rage is part of the mental illness, and that's why it takes place. Rather than becoming one with the rage, detach and observe it, like a psychologist, or like you are watching a movie. Step back and get some perspective.

Keep in mind that rages can lead to physical violence. Stay near an exit. Call the police if necessary. Report injuries to the police. If you are confronting domestic violence, talk to the police in your district ASAP so they have some background on your spouse. If your spouse hits you, report it. If you ever decide to leave this person, or vice versa, documentation may be the difference between obtaining or losing custody.

Do not let your partner be violent to your pets. One woman with BPD was so jealous of her husband's cat that she hit the cat, who started showing major signs of anxiety. One narcissistic husband threatened to kill the dog if his wife ever left. If you want to stay in the relationship and your partner is abusing a pet, find them a new home.

Just say no. When your partner, as they likely will, forgets about their hurtful actions and expects you to be emotionally or physically intimate, say no if you don't feel like it (and you probably won't). They may not hold themselves accountable, but you can and should. Otherwise, they learn that rages are acceptable.

Don't try to control them. You may be exhausted from trying to arrange the world so they don't rage. But the causes of their anger attacks are *internal*, not *external*. That's why nothing you do stops them. Control yourself instead by taking the steps in this book.

Don't fall into a rage yourself. Chances are high that to minimize conflict, you have said what your HCP wants you to say, you have repressed your anger and other feelings, and you have apologized when you have nothing to apologize for. A person can only do this for so long. When they rage at you, it becomes almost automatic to rage back, which only makes the situation worse.

Don't debate who is right and who is wrong. HCPs never say they are at fault because it damages their shaky self-esteem.

Say "we" instead of "I." This shows you're in this together and you should pull together as a couple.

Now that we've reviewed some simple communication tools that can help keep conversations with your partner on track, let's look at some specific communication techniques to use with HCPs.

Validation

Validation is critically important when your HCP has BPD only. Validation doesn't work as well with people with NPD because they can manipulate your words and use them against you.

Validation involves listening to your partner's emotions while being fully present, reflecting the emotions back in your own words, and asking questions to make sure you fully understand their internal experiences. When you validate your partner's emotions (feelings, but not thoughts or actions), you radically accept not only the emotions, but your partner. You are saying, "I understand you have this very powerful feeling. This must be very difficult for you." And perhaps, "If I were in your position, I would feel that way too" (if it's true).

Validation is a key way to let your partner feel heard and understood by recognizing and accepting their emotions as understandable *to them*. In other words, if you grew up in your partner's shoes, or if you had BPD/NPD, you would probably feel the same way. You do this by listening mindfully, paraphrasing, and normalizing their feelings. (The emotions may not be normal to you, but they are for HCPs.) Validation shows acceptance, understanding, and compassion, all of which improve the relationship. It also takes the place of conversations in which neither party is listening but is instead feeling angry and defensive and trying to prove their point, which is useless and hurts the relationship.

It's important to understand what validation is not:

- Validation never means agreeing with or approving of what they said, felt, or did. In fact, for our purposes, validation isn't about thoughts or actions at all. It's about their emotions, and emotions are never right or wrong. They just are.

- It's not about pretending to agree or believe something when you don't. Telling your partner you understand why and how they're feeling is a way of communicating that the relationship is important even when you disagree on the issues.

- It's not about apologizing, giving in, saying things you don't mean, accepting the unacceptable, forgetting about your needs, or anything else that would make you betray yourself.

There are three steps to validation.

Step 1. Listen to your partner express their emotions while being fully present. Fully pay attention to them exclusively without glancing at your phone or having a conversation with someone else. Be mindful of your body language. Sit if they're sitting; stand if they're standing. Be aware of the expression on your face; it should show care and concern. As you listen, it is critical that you withhold any judgments. Your partner is letting you into their life, so be respectful. For example, if your partner is jealous, you can truthfully say, *"If you had been* flirting with someone at the party, it would upset me too. Perhaps to you it looked like flirting. I was really talking to her about politics." Notice that I did not use the words "but" or "however." These words have a way of erasing the first part of the sentence.

Step 2. After you have closely listened, reflect your partner's emotions back to them in slightly different language. (See below for a list of emotions.) You can ask questions to learn more and show that you are listening, such as "Do you want me to just listen, or to help you problem solve?"

Other questions might be (Kreger et al. 2022, 101):

- What happened then?

- What are you feeling?

- What exactly happened?

- Are you safe?

- Tell me more.

- Are you upset with me?

- I don't understand. Can you help me understand?

- How can I help you?

- Okay, this is my understanding, tell me if I'm misunderstanding anything...

- Have you ever felt like this before?

Step 3. Normalize your partner's emotional reactions without making them sound defective, keeping in mind that underneath it all, they feel shame and have low self-worth. Just like you see the world through your schemas, they look at their environment with black-and-white thinking, unmanaged emotions, and extreme behaviors. They distrust people and tend to see the negative in people and situations. And most of all, for them, feelings equal facts. So when I say, "Normalize their emotional reactions," I don't mean buying in to their perceptions—I mean recognizing and reflecting their emotions. After all, if you experienced the world the way they do, you might have the same feelings yourself.

"Validation" Doesn't Mean "Valid"

Even though the word "validate" has the word "valid" in it, it *does not mean agreement* with the person's thoughts or actions just because it has the word "valid" in it. It doesn't mean you would feel the same way if the same incident happened to you. What it means is listening to your partner's emotions (both those displayed and discussed) while being fully present with them, reflecting the emotions back in your own words, recognizing that their emotions are real to them, and saying it's okay to feel that way. You may not agree that your partner *should* feel that way, especially when it's about you. But they do have those emotions, and feelings don't have IQs.

Reach across your reality and grasp your partner's hand in comfort because they have a disorder and can't come to your reality without treatment. Ask questions to make sure you fully understand their internal experiences.

Normalizing reactions that come from such a skewed way of looking at the world is not easy. It is going to be difficult and will take practice. Just keep in mind you are validating their *emotions,* not their beliefs, thoughts, behaviors, or conversations.

Emotions vs. Thoughts

Many people have trouble with validation because they confuse emotions with thoughts or beliefs. For example, the following statement is wrong: "I feel like you're trying to make me the bad guy." The correct sentence is "I *think* you're trying to make me the bad guy." You're expressing a thought, not a feeling. A feeling is one word; for example, "I'm getting the impression you're trying to make this my fault, which makes me feel frustrated, angry, and hopeless." Three emotions, each one word long. Below are more examples of emotion words.

A Very Limited List of Emotion Words

happy	enjoyment	annoyed
sad	disgust	frustrated
angry	awe	bitter
afraid	excited	mad
confused	lonely	dislike
surprised	hopeless	offended
amused	miserable	horrified
contemptuous	worried	delighted
sympathetic	stressed	content

You can use these statements at any point during the validation process:

- "Wow, how hard that must be."

- "That's messed up!"

- "How (insert emotion here, like *frustrating*)."

- "What a tough spot to be in."

Common Validation Mistakes

Validation takes practice, and no one becomes perfect at this, as it's still hardwired to some extent in our brains to lash out when someone lashes out at us. But you can get better and better at it. Here are some common mistakes:

Not talking about emotions. Many people miss the point of validation entirely and skip right to responding. Instead, forget about the situation and listen like a detective for the emotions. Try to rephrase what your partner says so you're not using the same words all the time. You might want to use a thesaurus for frequently used emotions.

Thinking you have to validate things you don't agree with. Again, validation has nothing to do with thoughts, opinions, and behaviors. Validation is about your partner's inner reality, not the empirical truth. It's about showing you care about their feelings, which makes them feel heard and seen. That is extremely powerful.

Getting emotionally triggered and adding that emotion to the conversation. Sometimes your partner is going to be angry or upset with you. It takes practice to respond to their emotions instead of justifying yourself, arguing, defending yourself, or overexplaining (JADEing). If your partner is off base and says something like, "You don't love me," or "You're never there for me," try saying, "If I thought that were true, I would be very (emotion) too." You will have time to correct their impressions later, such as saying, "I do love you." For an easy rule, just remember to use the phrase "If that were true…"

Not using the right tone of voice. Be careful not to sound too mechanical, even though validation can be hard at times. You want to sound concerned and caring, even when your partner upsets you. Sometimes that will be difficult.

All it takes is practice to halt that urge and communicate in a way that calms things down rather than riles them up even more. When practiced with someone with BPD, validation is effective at getting what you want: a better relationship, a focus on problem-solving instead of winning, and avoiding another pointless circular argument.

Never Invalidate Your Partner

To "invalidate" someone means that you deny their emotions, tell them they have no reason to have those emotions, or do not take their feelings seriously. Here are some examples of invalidating statements:

- "Just calm down." (Don't say this to anyone; it's patronizing.)

- "You're making too big of a deal of this." (To them, it's a big deal.)

- "You shouldn't feel that way." (Don't tell someone how to feel.)

- "That's unreasonable." (Maybe it is, but don't label it so.)

- "What you're trying to do is…" (Don't assume you know.)

- "What you think is…" (Don't assume you know.)

- "You're too emotional." (Saying that will make them more so.)

- "That's illogical." (It makes sense to them.)

Adding a "Truth Statement"

When you feel confident that your partner has felt validated or is getting empathy and respect, you can add in a "truth statement." A truth statement communicates *I have a reality too, and it is XYZ.* Do not use the word "but." "But" negates anything that comes before it.

Let's say your spouse is upset because you are texting with someone in your choir about a special event you are planning to honor the choir leader. After validating their feelings ("I can see you feel…"), you could end with a truth statement: "I am helping my choir arrange a special event in appreciation of our choir leader, and I need to communicate by text with some of the other choir members." If they don't believe your truth statement, don't keep repeating it. You cannot fill the empty hole inside them. If they don't want to accept your truth statement, don't back down if they get upset; just keep repeating your validation and truth statement without judging them.

Self-Validation

You can validate yourself! Self-validation is recognizing and accepting your own thoughts, feelings, sensations, and behaviors as understandable, considering your situation. If you can validate yourself, you will feel empowered and stronger, less needy for approval, and you will not doubt yourself so much. Simply talk to yourself as you would a friend who is upset. The more you can do this, the better.

As you accept your thoughts, though, realize they may not be true in the same way your partner's thoughts are not necessarily true. If you tell yourself, "Everything is hopeless. I'm trapped. Nothing I do will make any difference," accept that that's how you feel right now. But it doesn't mean you'll feel that way tomorrow, and it's not true. This book will help you. The next tool is one used for people with NPD, although it also works for people with BPD.

EAR: Empathy, Attention, Respect

The equivalent of validation for narcissistic individuals is called EAR, which stands for empathy, attention, respect. It's a method that coauthor Bill Eddy developed for calming HCPs or anyone (as explained in his book, *Calming Upset People with* EAR). Empathy, attention, and respect is probably the opposite of what you feel like giving someone when they are verbally attacking you. But EAR statements give you a chance to calm them down and increase intimacy with your upset partner, whose impairments make it difficult for you to connect in other ways. EAR statements are valuable because your partner may not be getting EAR from anyone else; it's common for them to have alienated other people. They are often starving for it. Here's how to formulate an EAR statement.

Empathy. Empathy and sympathy are two different things. Having empathy for someone means you can feel their pain, anger, and frustration, while sympathy means you regret they have those emotions. You might never have painful feelings for same reasons as your partner, but you do know what it's like to have them. Statements that show empathy include (Eddy 2021):

- "I can see how important this is to you."

- "I can understand how this can be frustrating."

- "I'm saddened to see that you're feeling bad."

Attention. Phrases that show you are paying attention include:

- "I will listen as carefully as I can."

- "I will pay more attention to your concerns."

- "Tell me more about what's going on."

You can also show attention nonverbally:

- Maintain good eye contact.

- Lean in to pay closer attention.

- Nod your head up and down.

Respect. Even the most difficult upset person usually has some quality that you can respect.

- "I respect your role as _____."

- "I respect you because _____."

- "I respect your success at _____."

Giving yourself an EAR statement can help you manage your own emotions, too, because our own self-talk can bring us down or boost us up. For example, you can tell yourself, "It's not about me" when your partner blames or criticizes you. Another EAR statement you might give yourself is, "You're good at bouncing back from bad situations," or "You have a lot of good skills that will help you in the long run."

BIFF: Brief, Informative, Friendly, Firm

The next tool, BIFF, is stronger than a truth statement. Bill Eddy, who is also lead author of *Splitting: Protecting Yourself While Divorcing Someone with Borderline or Narcissistic Personality Disorder,* developed BIFF as a tool to respond to emotional, hostile emails from two coparents who were divorcing or divorced and forced to communicate with each other because of their children. But it can also be used as a verbal tool, as long as the person practices it until they become familiar with it.

When you need to remind someone of a limit, BIFF is there to help. When someone is more interested in being right than in coming to an agreement and is only listening just enough so they can argue with your point, BIFF can close the discussion. BIFF is a solution to responding to blame or criticism, which Bill calls "blamespeak." Here's a breakdown of the method, which is described in several BIFF communications books including *BIFF for CoParent Communication* (Eddy et al. 2020).

Brief. BIFF statements are short so your partner can't pick them apart and find something to argue about. They are also about one issue. If you were writing down your BIFF response, it wouldn't be more than one paragraph of two to five sentences. The more you say, the more likely you are to trigger another blame-speak response.

Informative. We use BIFF because we have information we need to get across: "I will be at the movies from two to five." Or, "I said it wasn't okay to talk to me that way. I'm leaving and will be gone for about an hour." Or, "It's evident that we disagree about this. I appreciate your point of view. But since this is my place of work, I'm going to do this in the way I see best."

Friendly. BIFFs are friendly and respectful, even though you may not feel like being friendly or respectful. So BIFF responses can be hard. You can start with something like, "Thank you for telling me your opinion on this subject," "I appreciate your concerns," "I look forward to talking to you in a few hours." Use the usual pleasantries, even if the HCP doesn't, such as "please," and "thank you."

Firm. Make your "truth statement" crystal clear so there is no room for interpretation. This might be a reminder about a boundary you have, a statement about what you will or will not do, or a final response to a conversation you wish to end. You want to let your HCP know that this is all you have to say about a subject, and you're going to stick to the "informative" resolution you described. If your partner objects to something (and it may be quite a vociferous objection), you can say, "This isn't a power struggle—it's about me making what I feel is the right decision," or "This isn't about me trying to control you, but about doing what I feel is right." Again, don't join two sentences by using the word "but."

Here is an example of BIFF. As you will see, it is brief.

Informative: "Like I told you yesterday, I'm not going to keep conversing when we're not problem-solving anymore."

Friendly: "I look forward to talking to you later..."

Firm: "...when a few hours have passed or whenever we can talk about this without fighting."

Before you use BIFF with an HCP, practice writing a few BIFF statements, either in response to an email or social media message.

Use the SET-UP Communications Method

SET-UP stands for support, empathy, truth, understanding, and perseverance. The SET-UP method was developed by Jerold J. Kreisman (2018) and appears in his book *Talking to a Loved One with Borderline Personality Disorder: Communication Skills to Manage Intense Emotions, Set Boundaries, and Reduce Conflict.* This three-part model can help when you need to think on your feet and want to avoid being dragged into emotional and unproductive interactions.

SET-UP acknowledges the reality your loved one lives in but brings them into your reality. It says: "I care about you, and I empathize with you." Through your understanding of validation, you know how important that is. But unlike validation, the "T," the "truth" section of SET-UP, also says, "I have a reality too, and it is XYZ." A truth statement can also imply, "This is how it is going to be," or "This is the way we are going to do things."

It's vital that you do the steps in this order, or else SET-UP is meaningless. First try practicing on friends and other members of your family until it becomes natural. Get feedback and become comfortable with the tool. Use it in low-stakes interactions until you become more comfortable with it.

Step 1. Support. A support statement usually begins with "I" and demonstrates concern and a desire to help. It should imply, "It's important to me to try to help you feel better," or "I care that this issue is important to you." Let's take the example of your partner wanting you to drive them to work because they're late and missed the bus, but you can't. You can say, "I see, you want me to drive you to work. I know your work is important to you, and I agree it's important that you get to work on time."

Step 2. Empathy. Express empathy, which is a signal that you can put yourself in their shoes and look at the world through their eyes. Then express the emotions you can see right in front of you. Empathy is a "you" statement. Continuing with the example, the partner continues: "I can imagine it feels frustrating that you missed the bus and you're worried about being late to work."

Step 3. Truth. Truth statements, which are the same as those I talked about earlier, address the practical options of what can be done to deal with the current situation and are best expressed in nonjudgmental ways. The truth point of the SET triangle will be the most challenging because it will confront their attempts to avoid the situation. It also demands practical problem-solving. You are stressing accountability, and that's not easy for someone with BPD because it puts shame on top of shame. That's why the "support" and "empathy" statements are so vitally important.

These three steps are done in an atmosphere of understanding and perseverance.

When You Get the Silent Treatment

The "silent treatment" is a passive-aggressive, manipulative tactic and can be a form of passive-aggressive abuse. Passive-aggressive refers to a type of behavior characterized by *indirect* resistance. Silent treatment falls into two categories: the silent treatment at home in your presence, or things like disappearing, not answering a text or email, or not returning a phone call. Your partner uses this to:

- put themselves in a position of control

- avoid conflict resolution

- silence your attempts to say something they don't want to hear

- punish you for some imagined reason

The silent treatment is difficult for caretakers to withstand. They tell themselves they've done something wrong and feel anxiety, fear, heartache, and loneliness. You might as well be in a state of oblivion. If this describes you, you've abandoned yourself and are relying on your partner for approval. We've discussed this elsewhere in the book, including chapters 3 and 4. Here are some common, but unhelpful, ways you may find yourself responding to the silent treatment:

- You beg them to stop this torture and engage in a productive conversation. So how do most HCPs respond to the silent treatment? This is like buying your child candy at the grocery store. Your HCP learns that whining works and will repeat the behavior.

- You try to fix whatever you did "wrong." You may apologize for things that aren't your fault (never do this). You make promises to change your evil ways. Again, your HCP learns that this works and will repeat the behavior.

- You beg, plead, suck up, try to fix it, bargain for peace, and otherwise do exactly what your HCP partner expects you to do. They enjoy your pain. It makes them feel powerful and right. When you don't beg them to get in contact with you, the silent treatment no longer produces attention, which reinforces the behavior.

- You respond in kind, giving them the silent treatment at home. This just puts you on their level and makes things even more uncomfortable. However, if their passive-aggressive behavior is the type that occurs outside the house (for example, they disappear and don't respond to you), stop texting, emailing, looking for them, worrying about them, and so forth.

- You acknowledge there's nothing you can do to change the situation, so you suffer in silence, outwardly pretending everything is fine. *No problem here.*

Whether or not the silent treatment causes suffering is entirely up to you. No one can make you feel bad without your permission. It's vital that you eliminate your need from their approval. That is one of the main messages of this book: it's important to disentangle yourself and be your own person. Do not talk to your HCP about the silent treatment, except to acknowledge it once and tell them you'll chat again when they decide they want to, and until then, you will give them their space. When you say you will give them their space, it makes it sound like you are partly in control. "I see you don't want to talk. That is fine—I will give you your space." It's perfectly fine to fake it before you make it. You'll get better with practice.

When you respond to the silent treatment in the way I recommend, your partner will get no satisfaction. From your partner's perspective, the silent treatment has failed to teach you a lesson. Instead, you taught them a lesson: their silent treatment no longer controls you. You're not begging any more. When you don't reinforce the silent treatment, it makes it less likely they will use it in the future.

Above all, do not become overwhelmed and needy and take actions that let the silent treatment work, or else it will be repeated. What does it mean for the silent treatment to "work"? It works when you beg your partner, "Talk to me, won't you just talk to me, we have to work this out." Your HCP already has it worked out. They want control, and that means taking control from you. So don't beg, plead, try to negotiate, have a talk, or anything like it.

Have you complained that you have no time for self-care? Without constant caretaking, you have that time now. Read a book, listen to music, call a friend. Bake a yellow cake with colored sprinkles over chocolate frosting. Think about what you did before you had this person in your life. Do you remember how you used to enjoy spending time on your own? Put on some music or the TV if you don't like the quiet.

Keep in mind this is *their* silent treatment. You are free to act normally, and you should so things can slip back to normal without a big fuss. Say, "Well, I'm going to carry on. Dinner is at six, you're free to have some or not, and then I'm going out with some friends. Have a nice time at home." It's okay to say things like "hello" and "goodbye" because not doing so feels unnatural and actually takes effort. You can always leave notes or texts about where you will be and when you're coming home.

If the silent treatment lasts for more than a few days, it's a perfect time to get out of the house if you can, even for a few days. One of the most powerful things you can do to reclaim your life is to spend a few days in the company of non-disordered people, having ordinary conversations and treating each other with common politeness, with no major crises or upsets. If you have children, it is especially helpful for them to see this.

Folks know that the silent treatment is a reflection of the other person, but the nagging question is how someone we love deeply can turn into an uncaring stone in the blink of an eye without warning. The best tip I have for overcoming the silent treatment it is to use this time to enjoy life without chaos. If you need to communicate something like, "I need the car this Sunday," go ahead and do it. If they don't respond, do as you see fit. In other words, don't yield your power to them and certainly don't go groveling for their attention—that's what they want.

—Nelson

WHEN "SORRY" SEEMS TO BE YOUR EASIEST WORD

Apologizing when you've done someone wrong is obviously a good thing. But most caretakers take it too far. The words almost become a verbal tic, they're said so often. When your partner is arguing with you, it seems like the expedient thing to do to get them to stop harping at you. Resist the urge to do this, and stand up for yourself, your needs, wants, and values.

The Gray Rock Method

The Gray Rock (GR) method is a temporary method for dealing with people who need to pull strings and provoke reactions—usually people with NPD. GR will throw people with BPD for a loop because they are so afraid of being abandoned, so I only recommend this if you are coping with a narcissistic HCP. The goal is giving your HCP so little material to work with that they can't put you down, argue, rage, and so on.

It is called Gray Rock because you attempt to be as boring, non-stimulating, and not sexy as a gray rock in a bed of identical gray rocks. Using the method, make no conversation except about innocuous things, like the weather, sports, what you had for lunch, and what you're going to have for dinner. Opinions, requests, explanations, or anything else that would trigger or interest someone with NPD are generally off-limits. Don't mention that you got a great job evaluation, because people with NPD usually get envious and irritable when hearing other people's good news. Here are three critical factors about Gray Rock:

- Gray Rock is not a punishment. The purpose of GR is to lessen the pain your HCP causes *you*, it's not to cause *them* pain.

- GR is not manipulation. It's self-preservation.

- GR is not a quick, easy fix for long-term problems. This is only a temporary solution.

Here are some guidelines for implementing GR:

- The first rule about Gray Rock is you don't talk about Gray Rock.

- Keep conversations short and impersonal.

- Don't ask questions.

- Try your best to avoid sensitive, interesting, or meaningful subjects.

- Expect your HCP to notice and try to get a rise out of you. Practice with friends or other family members first, having them say accusatory, critical, or blaming statements until you can be nonreactive and calm when it comes to your HCP.

- If things calm down as a result, it means GR is working. No matter how tempted you are to stop GR in the moment, stay with it.

The CARS Method

The CARS Method is designed to help you organize your responses to calm down your partner, to redirect their energies, and to focus them on positive future choices and consequences. CARS stands for connecting, analyzing, responding, and setting limits. CARS was developed by Bill Eddy as an overall method that can be easily remembered and used under pressure in any high-conflict situation. It's described in depth in his book, *5 Types of People Who Can Ruin Your Life*. You can use any or all of the four parts of the method, depending on what the situation needs. They can be used in order or out of order. Use your best judgment.

Step 1. Connect with EAR statements. The first step or skill is to attempt to calm the HCP's emotions by forming a brief positive connection with them. Of course, the first thing that most people feel like doing when they're blamed or attacked is to attack back—to say, "No, it's not all my fault. It's all *your fault!*" While this might get a reasonable person to stop and assess the situation, with an HCP, this response simply escalates their emotions and aggressively defensive behavior. In these cases, it is helpful to respond with a statement that shows empathy, attention, or respect—an EAR statement, as you learned above. This is especially helpful for the NPD HCP.

This may be very difficult to do at first. An EAR statement usually calms down HCPs right away, at least long enough for them to use their problem-solving skills for a while. However, don't linger too long with an EAR statement or the person may try to manipulate you based on your empathy. Be ready to move on to analyzing.

Step 2. Analyze options. After you have connected with your partner and hopefully de-escalated the situation, you need to consider your alternatives or options. Approach this process in three steps:

A.   Brainstorm several possible options for yourself and write them down.

B.   Check yourself for high-conflict thinking—remember, you are human too.

C.   Select an option and analyze it carefully.

Another way of analyzing options is to make or respond to proposals. You can almost always take a past problem and turn it into a proposal for the future. Whatever has happened before is less important than what to do now. Avoid emphasizing how bad the problem is. With an HCP, this just triggers more defensiveness. Plus, people never agree on what happened in the past anyway.

Picture a solution from your list and do it or propose it. Here are the three key steps for making proposals:

A. **Propose.** The person making the proposal will state who will do what, when, and where.

B. **Ask questions.** Allow the other person to ask questions about the proposal, such as: "What's your picture of what this would look like, if I agreed to do it?" "What do you see me doing in more detail?" Then, you answer the questions fully.

C. **Respond.** The other person will respond to the proposal: yes, no, or maybe. If the response is no, then it's that person's turn to make a new proposal.

This method helps keep the situation from escalating. It discourages arguing about proposals, which is what HCPs often do. Instead, you just ask for sincere questions and a response. Of course, the questions should be who, what, when, and where questions, such as sincerely inquiring: "How do you picture implementing that idea? What would my part be?"

Step 3. Respond to hostility or misinformation. Misinformation and intense blaming are very common in high-conflict disputes and are often the result of their distorted thinking (sometimes called "cognitive distortions"). Most often, HCPs don't realize their thinking is distorted. While we all have distorted thoughts occasionally, it's important to "check ourselves" to be realistic—for example, "Is this really true? Or am I jumping to conclusions?" HCPs tend to have a lot of these thought distortions and accept them without question. What's more, they often pass them along to others without realizing how absurd they sound.

And some of the time, they knowingly spread misinformation. They think they have to do so in order to protect themselves from the dangers they see around them—which are usually based on their distortions, but they don't realize that. They often truly believe that others are out to hurt them, and in their eyes, this justifies their extreme behavior. I will talk in more detail about distortion campaigns in chapter 12, "Leaving the Right Way."

Step 4. Setting limits. This may be the most important task. It generally helps to state the limit you are setting, then explain the consequence that will occur if the limit is violated. Keep in mind that you can't control what the HCP will do, but you can control what you will do.

For example, you might say, "If you keep talking to me that way, I'm going to have to end this conversation." Then, if they keep talking in that way, you can say, "You have chosen to have me end this conversation, so I am leaving. Let me know when you are ready to talk civilly."

Be Patient with Yourself and Everyone Else

How many years have you and your loved one been locked in the same conversational circles, stuck in your same positions? Have you been giving your loved one the benefit of the doubt, assuming they know more or are better at things than you? Have you been afraid to speak up because you feel afraid, obligated, or guilty? Have you been letting your HCP have their way because it's easier?

Change takes time. Learning skills, especially ones that go against your immediate urges, takes time because you have to unlearn all the old, "bad" ways. You will make plenty of mistakes. Great! That's what you're supposed to be doing. Each mistake gets you a little closer to where you want to be. Be patient and gentle with your loved one too. Don't expect too much. In fact, expect them to get ruffled at this change, because as you know, change is threatening.

These tools won't make things perfect. You can only change your 50 percent of the conversation. But measuring your responses and having a goal, rather than just rambling on, can help more than you would ever expect.

Let me leave you with words from the brilliant author Harriet Lerner (2014) from the *Dance of Anger*:

> It is never easy to move away from silent submission or ineffective fighting toward a calm but firm assertion of who we are, where we stand, what we want, and what is and is not acceptable to us. Our anxiety about clarifying what we think and how we feel may be greatest in our most important relationships...
>
> In the short run, it is sometimes simpler to continue with our old, familiar ways, even when personal experience has shown them to be less than effective. In the long run, however, there is much to be gained by putting the lessons of this book into practice. Not only can we acquire new ways of managing old angers; we can also gain a clearer and stronger "I" and, with it, the capacity for a more intimate and gratifying "we." Many of our problems with anger occur when we choose between having a relationship and having a self.

CHAPTER 8

Setting Limits Without Fear

The game changer that made a difference in our relationship was determining my boundaries and acting on them. I didn't even communicate the boundaries in advance because he would have seen them as a challenge and want to "win" by not giving in.

The consequence if he doesn't observe my limit is the way I react. Every time he started raging, using circular logic to trap me, or saying stuff like how selfish and horrible I am, I just said, "I'm not going to debate that; so I'm going now, and we can talk in a couple of hours when we both feel calmer." He may never hold himself accountable for his behavior, but I certainly can.

And then something miraculous happened. He rarely ever rages or argues anymore. He stops himself from saying hurtful things because he knows I will leave. And he started helping with chores without me asking, because I'm not nagging him. This way he doesn't "lose" by giving in to my nagging. Instead, he sees that if he helps with chores, then we can spend more time doing fun things together.

This has helped immensely, and the best thing about it is, it didn't require him to change his behavior first. Mind you, these things will only work if the partner still has a desire to be together and there is still love on both sides. If your spouse doesn't care whether they're damaging the relationship or their partner anymore, then you really don't have a marriage anymore. It's over.

—Pat

Setting limits causes anxiety for many caretakers. This chapter will show you how to successfully set limits by implementing consequences. Since the consequences are under your control, you don't need your partner to make any changes (although many do). More about that later. But first, the following are some overall benefits of having limits:

- Boundaries are an integral part of healthy relationships because they help maintain a balance between the two partners. Right now, things probably feel all out of whack, with their wants and needs dictating the way you live. This is not sustainable or healthy. When you set firm limits, you have a template for how differences are going to be resolved so you don't have to start from scratch each time.

- Limits are your values in action. But you have probably compromised some of your values along the way. For example, you may value honesty, but the only way to live a normal life is to keep things from your HCP, such as seeing people they don't like. You believe in treating others with kindness, empathy, and compassion, but your partner lacks all three. Living against your values, unable to reconcile the two, produces a state called "cognitive dissonance." People like to be consistent in their attitudes and actions, so living with cognitive dissonance causes a constant unsettled feeling. Limits give you the opportunity to settle some of these differences, such as setting limits about your children, who you know are hurting.

- Speaking of children, when you set limits, you serve as a role model for your children. They will also need to know how to set and observe limits with their parent—if not now, then sometime later. It is never too early to start showing them how. Kids as young as five have been known to take their cue from the non-disordered partner.

- Healthy boundaries help stop relationships from becoming "enmeshed," in which the partners are expected to agree with each other about everything. An individual choice or opinion is seen as a threat because it implies the other person is wrong. Limits allow you to stake out your own territory.

- Limits may be the only way to get your needs met. You probably have so many needs that are not being met that you've forgotten that you have needs at all. For example, without support, love, and compassion from your partner, you're living in a deprived state.

You need to find alternatives, many of which may involve setting limits.

- A belief in your ability to exert control over the environment and to produce desired results is essential for your well-being. Converging evidence from animal research, clinical studies, and neuroimaging work suggests that the need for control is a psychological and biological necessity (Leotti et al. 2010).

Setting limits and observing them is not in the nature of many caretakers. They tend to be afraid of anger and confrontation, which they assume is always a part of setting limits (untrue). Caretakers believe in self-sacrifice, subjugation of their needs, and not disagreeing with their partner—especially those in enmeshed relationships. Secretly, most feel defective and afraid of asking for what they want or need. They're desperately trying to argue and logic their way into getting their partner's approval (approval meaning both getting a pat on the head and permission to make their own choices). They're resigned to take what their partner is dishing out because they're frozen with fear, obligation, and guilt.

Stop Enabling

Before we talk any further about limits, I'd like to show you why limits are more even important than the reasons I just stated. One huge problem is that caretakers accidentally reinforce, or "enable," negative behaviors. When you set and observe limits, you no longer reinforce unwanted HCP behavior. It's true, you can't change their behavior. But you can create an environment that doesn't *reward* HCP behavior. You reward HCP behavior by letting them control your responses, whether that's letting them goad you into an argument or cutting off contact with friends and family. First, let's go over what enabling means.

At its heart, enabling is not doing for a loved one things that they can (or can learn to) do themselves. There is a huge difference between enabling someone and supporting them. In enabling, you are allowing the status quo to go on. Support means helping the person address their behavior and the consequences of their behavior. Our loved one can truly benefit from support rather than enabling. It can help them realize the severity of their behavior and may even lead to them seeking treatment. But one thing is sure: when we "enable" them, they have no reason to change (Hazelden Betty Ford Foundation 2021).

The following actions are signs of enabling.

Protecting someone from the consequences of their behavior. Let's say you want your partner to stop calling you at work twenty times a day, but you keep answering the phone to tell them not to call you. Pay attention to the behavior, not what is said. By answering the phone, you are enabling the calling to continue.

The same rule applies to cutting off all contact. If you have gone "no contact," you reinforce unwanted behaviors when you respond by paying attention to them when they call, text, or otherwise contact you. The action is what is most important, not what you say. Especially for NPD HCPs, negative attention is just as powerful as positive behavior. They are still manipulating and controlling you.

Keeping secrets about your partner's behavior. Your partner is counting on the fact that you aren't telling the truth about their behavior for the reasons we discussed (and demolished) in chapter 4. This helps allow the behavior to continue.

Refusing to follow through with consequences when they pay no attention to your limits. In this chapter, I'll explain that consequences are steps *you* take to protect yourself from HCP behavior. These consequences need to be observed each and every time your partner steps over the line.

Attempting to control something out of your control. We've talked about this often in this book. You need to be the catalyst for change, and you can't be as long as you engage in enabling behavior.

Can you see the enabling in Kristen's story?

Sleep was a huge issue in my marriage, and the lack of it contributed to me reaching my breaking point. My husband was a night owl, and he would guilt and pressure me into staying up late with him. If I went to bed before him, he would sometimes barrel loudly into the room and turn on all the lights, making it nearly impossible to sleep. Then he would act innocent as if he didn't mean to wake me up, but needed to see when he came in the room.

He rarely allowed me to take a nap. He would wake me up shortly after I fell asleep, or he would guilt me into not taking one. Eventually, I would drift off, and he would get upset that I fell asleep when he was talking but it was at least 2:00 a.m.

The main thing I remember from the sleep deprivation was how utterly useless I felt. I couldn't remember anything, I was delirious and unhappy and never felt like I was effective at anything, playing right into his theory that I wasn't working hard enough. I was sick all the time, and he would still not let me rest to recover, finally leading to a brush with pneumonia.

I think he did it because it was a lot easier to control me. I was constantly off balance, confused, and never quite able to connect the dots. I think that suited him just fine. When I was sleep-deprived, I could not make decisions. When I was so unsure of everything, he could easily gaslight me, which he did often because I was so unsure of my memory.

He is a lot better now but only because I began to set boundaries. I also have my own room now. It upset him at first, and he would be loud and rage and wake me up. He doesn't do that anymore but only because I put my foot down.

Enabling Substance Abuse

It can be difficult to understand how you may be enabling HCP behavior, so I'm going to share a story about enabling a child with a drug addiction to make it easier to understand. It's more extreme, but that makes it a good example. This is a true story. In this example, a mother, Frieda, enables her daughter to use drugs, even though she has the best of intentions to do the opposite.

Frieda's thirty-four-year-old child Nancy is an addict whose drugs of choice are alcohol and prescription painkillers. Of course, Frieda wants Nancy to stop taking drugs, but in the meantime, she wants to make Nancy's life as happy and safe as possible. It's the least she can do because she wasn't a very good mother in Nancy's formative years. She is afraid for Nancy, feels obligated to help her, and her guilt is off the charts (FOG: fear, obligation, and guilt).

Frieda lets Nancy live with her and feeds her because she doesn't want Nancy living on the streets. This enables Nancy to abuse drugs full-time without needing a job for living expenses. Now all her money can be used for drugs. When Frieda talks to Nancy about moving out, Nancy uses fear to stop her mother from kicking her out. "Do you want me to live on the streets and maybe get assaulted?" she says. Then Nancy presses the guilt and obligation button: "When I was in middle and high school, you were working sixty hours a week. You weren't really acting like a mother. You owe me."

Frieda drives Nancy to the liquor store to get booze because if she doesn't, Nancy will walk to the store on a busy, dangerous road or take the car and drive drunk. Frieda's biggest fear is Nancy dying, so she has strong motivation to drive Nancy. Frieda takes prescription painkillers for severe arthritis but gives Nancy half her pills because Nancy says she needs them. Nancy pushes the "obligation" button, saying, "Only a monster mother would deny her daughter pills she needs to keep from getting dope sick."

As you can see, enabling behavior can act as a reward. But don't tell that to Frieda. All her relatives have demanded that she throw Nancy out. But when she tries doing that, or not giving her money, or not driving her to the store, Nancy cries, complains, begs, and shouts at her mother for hours until Frieda gives in. This pattern has been going on for the last five years.

In reality, Frieda is taking care of *her own* feelings rather than doing what's in Nancy's best interests. Specifically, she's trying to lessen her FOG and not be subject to Nancy's tantrums, which means giving in. Nancy is addicted to drugs, and Frieda is addicted to Nancy, who serves as her own mood-altering drug since Frieda's happiness depends on how Nancy feels that day.

Enabling in an HCP Relationship

Now that you understand the basics of enabling, let's talk about HCP relationships. Here are some examples of enabling:

- Your HCP wants you to stop going out after work with coworkers. You argue about it again and again, but arguing doesn't bring you any closer to agreement. Afraid of what your partner might do in response to you not giving in, you come home directly and miss out on rumors of a reorganization. You rewarded your HCP, making it more likely they will try to make unreasonable demands in the future.

- Your borderline HCP wants you to be reachable 24/7. When you're not, they rage and make threats. In response, you carry your phone everywhere and rush to get it even when your HCP is interrupting important business. At night, if they're feeling angry, they wake you up at 3:00 a.m. to complain about something you did during the day. You wake up and listen, which is rewarding your partner for waking you up. Complaining about it has no effect. It's just like

Frieda telling Nancy to get a job while paying for her expenses. *Complaining and nagging will not work with HCPs. They just reinforce the status quo.*

- You and your narcissistic partner are dressing up for a New Year's party. They disapprove of your outfit and demand that you wear your sexy red dress with the sequins. You're not comfortable doing this. But you don't want to have a fight, so you wear the wear the red dress. Again, your HCP, knowing their demands work, is more likely to make similar demands in the future.

- You want to go to your high school reunion, and your partner refuses to go. You really want to attend, so you tell your HCP you'll go by yourself. Your partner gets upset and replies, "I know why you want to go without me—you want to hook up with your old high school sweethearts." This presses your fear, guilt, and obligation (FOG) buttons. You stay home (a reward for your partner), opening the door to all kinds of control tactics.

While you cannot directly change your partner, you have a chance of affecting their behavior *indirectly* by positively reinforcing wanted behavior and establishing limits with consequences for unwanted behavior. Here's how indirect control works. Let's say you're tired of doing all your partner's laundry because they never pitch in. You set a limit: from now on, your partner can do their own laundry. Your choice forces your HCP to make a choice. They can wear dirty clothes, wash them themselves, buy new ones once a week, or pay someone else to do the washing. You made the choice to stop doing their laundry to take care of yourself, and your decision forces them to change.

I had a chance to go to Canada on a week-long hunting and fishing trip with some friends, my brother, and my dad, who's not getting any younger. My borderline wife was not in favor, and finally, after trying every reasonable approach to no avail, I just said I'm going.

For the three to four months leading up to the trip, she acted like a four-year-old whose mommy was going to leave her in the middle of Times Square. I didn't back down, and the day that I left, she was crying. When I got to the last place that had telephone service before I was gonna be out of contact for about six days, I called her, hoping that she would calm down. She poured it on even worse. She almost ruined the trip for me, but I knew I had to stop the incessant caving into her emotional outbursts. A few days after I returned home, she was back to normal.

We caretakers can always just go ahead and do what they want us to do, or we can let our partner think what they want to think and just go ahead and do what we want to do. But there is some force compelling us to drag out the bag of tricks to try to get them to see things our way, the right way, no matter that it never worked before. Here comes Albert Einstein saying that the definition of insanity is doing the same thing over and over again and expecting different results. So what is that force? It's you trying to get things to the way they used to be. Do you want your validation, to be seen, to be understood? To be noticed, to be heard, to be loved, to get your needs met? It's also understandable, and we all deserve it. But I didn't and can't get that with an HCP.

—Heath

What Is a Limit and a Consequence?

Limits and consequences are *not* about controlling someone else's actions. A limit is a stop sign that says, "When you do this (or don't do it), it bothers me and makes me feel XYZ." A consequence is an action *you* take to care for yourself so your partner's behavior is less irksome. You can phrase this by following up with an "if-then" statements: "*If* you start raging at me, *then* I will leave the room."

In the example at the beginning of this chapter, Pat set a limit on arguing. When her husband tried to start an argument or started calling her names, she said, "I'm not going to debate that." And if he persisted, her consequence (a way she took care of herself) was to leave the room and perhaps the house. Then she reminded her husband she would come back, and they could talk when things were calmer. This decreased his raging and arguing because he didn't want her to leave. The best consequences are natural outcomes of a situation and things your partner cares about.

Pat didn't directly try to get him to stop raging and calling her names. She did so indirectly. There's no guarantee that your spouse will modify their behavior, but rewarding their behavior by going along with things you don't think are right will encourage them *not* to change.

Psychotherapist Beverly Engel (2002) explains how limits disappear in an HCP relationship. She says, "Most of us begin a relationship thinking we have certain limits as to what we will and what will not tolerate from a partner. But as the relationship progresses, we tend to move our boundaries back, tolerating more and more intrusion or going along with things we are really opposed to. While this can occur even in healthy relationships, in abusive ones, partners begin tolerating unacceptable and even abusive behavior and then convince themselves that these behaviors are normal and acceptable, and they believe their partner when they tell them they deserve such behavior" (118).

Here are the five basic principles of limits:

1. **Your limits are for you and about you, not against others.** They are about respect: respect for yourself, respect for others, and respect for the relationship. Your partner probably won't see things that way because they *feel* otherwise, and for them, feelings equal facts. Naturally, you'll have discussions and try to come up with solutions that work for both of you. But don't compromise on things you feel strongly about because your emotions, values, needs, and wants are just as important as theirs, if not more so. Stick to being your authentic self.

2. **Setting limits requires trusting your own perceptions, feelings, and opinions—most significantly, those about yourself.** During the limit-planning process, you will generate a list of limits that are important to you. Let's say you want to set a limit about spending: If either of you wants to buy anything over $100, the other one needs to be consulted. If your partner reacts with, "That's silly, it should be over $500," stick to your opinion: $500 is too high considering your bank account. You may end up compromising, but don't let your partner's determination to be "right" affect your convictions about what the financial limit needs to be. You need to be an advocate for yourself and your point of view, which is of the utmost importance.

3. **Different people will have different limits and consequences because each person has their own unique emotions, values, needs, and wants.** Normally, we talk about limits as being "wrong" or "right" according to some invisible measuring stick that must be inside the desk of a newspaper advice columnist. There is no stick. For example, is an online emotional affair with someone two thousand miles away as serious as a real-life affair? To some people it is; to others it isn't. You don't need anyone's permission or approval to set a limit.

4. **Some limits are easier to set than others, and some can't be set at all.** For example, let's say you want more intimacy in the relationship. Things like this require you to ask for what you need, and your partner is not obliged to give it to you. You need to be more specific as to what intimacy is for you. For example, if your partner takes personal information you've shared and then uses it against you in a fight, you can set a limit with a natural consequence: *if* they do it again, *then* you will stop confiding in them.

5. **Don't rescue your partner by excusing them for not observing your limits.** For example, you might minimize or deny by saying to yourself, "They had a bad childhood." "They're under stress." "They had a bad day." And on and on and on. You stop feeling like a victim by taking responsibility for your limits, and your spouse takes responsibility for how they react to your limits. You're solving your own problem, and your partner knows what they need to do (or not do) to avoid a consequence they don't like. So they can solve *their* own problem.

The Process of Setting Limits

This limit-setting process needs to be started a week or two before you actually set the limit, depending on how fast your process goes. Spend time with each step. You may wish to do this with a supportive family member or friend. Their outside perspective can be very helpful.

Step 1. Unplug FOG (fear, obligation, and guilt). Learn to trust yourself and your abilities to change for the better. When you truly realize that not having limits is causing chaos, negatively affecting your children, making you miserable, and leaving you out of control, you're ready to give up FOG and do what you need to do to make limits work for you. Tell yourself, "Whatever happens and however I feel, I can handle it." If fear is keeping you stuck, be specific about what it's about so you can address it.

Keep asking yourself, "Then what?" For example, "I tell him I am going to the reunion whether he goes or not." Then what? "He will make a big fuss and try to make me feel guilty." Then what? "That will make me feel uncomfortable. But whatever happens and however I feel, I can handle it."

Step 2. Clarify your limits to yourself. Think about what limits you would like to set. Brainstorm, perhaps with people you trust who may be able to see things you don't. A limit can be about what you want someone to do (or stop doing), what you're willing to accept, what you want to start doing (or stop doing), and more. Come up with bottom-line behaviors for yourself. Possible examples: "(1) I will not sleep with someone who calls me names. (2) I will not argue with someone who has been drinking. (3) I will take care of my own finances. (4) I will not have conversations with anyone when I feel desperate (or defensive, obsessive, or whatever)." Whatever your areas of concern, determine what you need to do to change and make those your bottom-line behaviors.

You also might want to start out by looking at this list of rights that you were given at birth. You have the right to:

- control your life and make your own decisions

- be good enough, just as you are, and be treated like an equal

- speak up when something doesn't feel right

- take care of yourself

- have privacy

- express your feelings

- say no without explaining yourself

- have your values, needs, and wants (VNWs) respected

- grow and change

- love and be loved

- express your opinion, even if others disagree

- not fix the problems of other adults

- control your life and make your own decisions

- leave the relationship

Questions like this can also get you started in clarifying your limits:

- What subjects do you try to avoid?

- What is best for your life, in the long and short term?

- What is best for those in your care?

- What do you want in this relationship?

- What do you need in this relationship?

- What makes you feel safe?

- What makes you feel uncomfortable?

- What makes you feel angry?

You may want to keep a journal for a while and pick out certain behaviors that make you uncomfortable. Writing things down is a good way to keep track, because you won't conveniently "forget" or dismiss what happened because it's too painful or it happens so often you've gotten used to it (or both).

Step 3. Calculate the costs of not having the limit and the benefits of having it. To maintain your limits over the long haul, you need to have the conviction that each limit is necessary and appropriate. After you write these down, memorize them to stay motivated, confident, and willing to observe your consequences. Conviction comes when you know how much it costs *not* to have the limit in place—especially when compared against the benefits. The longer you wait, the more it costs. The table below shows examples of behaviors that need a limit, the costs, and the benefits of setting a limit.

Behavior That Needs a Limit	Costs of Not Having a Limit	Benefits of Having a Limit
Calling you unpleasant names or making negative generalizations about you.	I feel depressed, mistrustful, and bad about myself.	I will be happier with myself and the relationship.
Partner has rules about what I can and can't do.	I don't feel like a competent person to make my own decisions, and the conflict is killing me. So I go along with what he wants rather than what I want.	I can do what I want to do. I will feel less depressed and more upbeat about life.

Behavior That Needs a Limit	Costs of Not Having a Limit	Benefits of Having a Limit
Partner has isolated me from friends and family. I don't see them often, and I keep secrets about my life.	I miss them, being around them, and having fun. I don't go out anymore. I get splitting headaches, and I am sick of trying to get my partner to change their mind.	I am an adult, and I can choose who I want to be with. I will have fun again, especially now that my parents have a family camping trip I want to attend.
My partner calls me twenty-five times a day and wants to know where I am every minute because they don't trust me.	Everyone deserves privacy, even me. I feel like my life is not my own, and I don't like telling white lies when I go to my Zoom support meeting. I'm less able to focus at work, and I'm feeling engulfed by my partner's oppressive needs.	Freedom! I can go anywhere I please without my partner needing to know where I am.

Step 4. Come up with consequences and rewards. In this context, the definition of a consequence is an action taken to take care of the self that may also be punitive to unwanted HCP behavior. Keep in mind that a consequence must matter to the other person. They need to want something that is being removed, dislike something that is added, or find your reward…rewarding. So, you need to know their needs and wants. Sit down for a couple of days and brainstorm. What are they getting from you right now that they do not appreciate or thank you for? What is important to them that you can withhold?

When coming up with limits and consequences, keep them doable. You will need to observe your limit and implement the consequences every single time (see the section on intermittent reinforcement later in this chapter). That includes late at night, after you come home from work, when you're watching a movie, or when you're out for a drive. Especially at the beginning, make your consequences easy to implement.

Boundary Violations in the Car

If your partner rages in the car or otherwise acts in a scary way and your limits have not stopped this behavior, do not get into the car with your partner. One woman I talked to was being traumatized in the car in an ice storm, and she and her children were sobbing as a result of the abuse. There was no way to stop because of the storm. Don't underestimate what your HCP is capable of. Many of them know that you can't easily leave and will take that opportunity to abuse you. Protect yourself and your children, even if it's a hassle. Download ridesharing apps or write down the number of a cab company and show how serious you are about not being abused. It may be a major hassle. But listening to abuse in a small, enclosed space without the option of leaving can be traumatizing, and no convenience is worth that.

Following are some examples of consequences to behaviors with limits. You will notice the consequences are not about getting your partner to change, but about taking care of yourself.

Behavior That Needs a Limit	Consequence of Having a Limit for This Behavior
Calling you unpleasant names or making negative generalizations about you.	Say, "You have a right to your opinion, and I have the option of not listening to you put me down. I'm leaving the room."
Partner has rules about what I can and can't do.	I will go out and do what I think is best. If my partner makes a fuss—or a major crisis—I realize that's because I've followed their rules so long that I never questioned them. It will take them some time to get used to the new me.
Partner has isolated me from friends and family. I don't see them often, and I keep secrets about my life.	I'm going to start calling people when I'm at work and apologize for being out of touch for so long. Then I'm going to have lunch. When I feel like talking about what's happening, I will confide in someone. After I get back in touch with people, I will tell my HCP I've rethought that rule and can't go along with it. I won't be swayed by FOG.

Behavior That Needs a Limit	Consequence of Having a Limit for This Behavior
My partner calls me twenty-five times a day and wants to know where I am every minute because they don't trust me.	I will not answer calls or texts unless my partner is in the hospital or there is a true emergency. If they fake the emergency, I will no longer answer when I am at work.

Whenever possible, the consequences should stem from the limit. These are called "natural consequences." For example, a natural consequence of leaving food out at a picnic is insects. The consequences for your spouse going over the number of texts or calls allowed might be that you stop answering them altogether for that day. Here are a few more examples of consequences:

- When your partner lies to you, withdraw your trust. You don't have to argue about whether or not it was a lie. From now on, when something is important, ask for proof.

- If they spend more than the agreed upon amount, take away or cancel the credit card.

- Stop waiting if they're late and go to a planned activity by yourself.

Ignoring someone with BPD/NPD can be very powerful punishment, so use it sparingly. The appropriate time to do so is when they are doing something to provoke you, such as rolling their eyes or repeatedly asking for something after you have said no. It does not apply to abusive or hurtful behavior, which should be addressed. Also, people with NPD like attention of any kind, and negative attention is better than none. So diverting your attention to something besides them may be effective in some instances.

Now let's look at rewards, or positive reinforcement. You may be wondering, *How do you give positive reinforcement?* You will seldom announce it, as in, "I'm giving you a reward now because you asked me about my day." (By the way, if your partner isn't doing anything right, reinforce neutral behavior.) Giving rewards partly depends upon whether or not you disclosed that you're setting limits. What is most critical is that you give the reward, or positive reinforcement, as close as possible to the wanted behavior. (This also goes for punishment, but it isn't always practical.)

One of the strongest rewards you can give is attention in any form, including body language, facial expression, tone of voice, and touch. It can be as simple as mirroring their body language, making sure you're not doing anything else when you're speaking with them, looking at them directly in the eyes, saying "uh huh" every once in a while, validating them (unless you've gotten into trouble about this with your narcissistic partner), or saying thank you ("Thank you for asking about my day.") When looking for rewards, in addition to brainstorming, you may wish to read *The 5 Love Languages: The Secret to Love That Lasts* by Gary Chapman.

Step 5. Consider possible outcomes. During the planning process, consider possible outcomes to your consequence-reward scenarios. Hope for the best; plan for the worst. For example, if you have travel plans, they might hide or destroy your passport. Put important documents in a safe place before setting that limit. If they will keep calling and calling you, turn off the phone. If you depend on your partner for a ride to work, have an alternate plan. Think through the likely responses, and then prepare for them as best you can.

Step 6. Implement the limit. You may be like Pat, whose story opened this chapter, who didn't say anything because her partner would see it as a challenge. After you have gone through the planning process, pick a start date. Have support people willing to encourage you and remind you of the costs and benefits.

If your partner reacts negatively, keep in mind this is just the beginning of a process. This is a change for you, and it's probably a change for them. You've had time to prepare for it, and they may not have. Even if you told them, they may have brushed you off, not realizing how serious you were. Remember that you'll have to adjust to changes, and so will they. If something doesn't work as expected, modify what you're doing and keep trying. If you make a mistake, try again. If you choose the wrong negative or positive reinforcer, change it. We are all works in progress. Learn from your mistakes and successes. The "Communicating Your Limits" section below gives further explanation about how to communicate your limit to your partner.

Communicating Your Limits

Step 7. Prepare yourself for countermoves. In her *New York Times* bestseller *The Dance of Anger: A Woman's Guide to Changing the Patterns of Intimate Relationships,* author Harriet Lerner (2014) addresses the neglected area of "countermoves," or the heightened actions your partner will take to see if you're really serious about a limit. The point of a countermove is simply to say,

"Change back!" (Lerner 2014, 14). Or in other words, "Keep to the status quo. I liked things exactly the way they were when everything was to my advantage." A countermove can be immediate and obvious, or it can be delayed and passive-aggressive.

For example, if your partner called you a "crazy bitch" before, now they will call you a "mother******* crazy-ass bitch who deserves to go to hell." Before, they didn't want you to go to the reunion; now they don't want you to see any of your friends and family. This makes countermoves rather predictable, something you can think through and plan for. Because countermoves are part of the human condition, Lerner (2014) warns against trying to stop your partner or telling them they shouldn't feel the way they do. That is invalidating.

Lerner (2014) says that in the face of a countermove, our top job is to keep clear about our own positions and not take countermoves personally. Countermoves aren't about you. They're about the disorder getting its needs met, which includes the survival strategies (discussed in chapter 2). The HCP is feeling threatened by your new level of assertiveness, separateness, and maturity and reacting to that.

Nobody likes having to solve their own problems and deal with their own feelings, especially HCPs. Their slogan is, "Don't make me accountable for anything." Well, by setting limits, you've now given them the adult responsibility of managing their own self-esteem and emotions. It's possible that by doing that, you've revealed how dependent they are on you. You may have even indirectly motivated them to seek help. When you're dealing with annoying countermoves, keep in mind that as difficult as limit-setting can be for you, it's probably harder for your partner. Try to have patience with them, but never accept abuse.

Don't expect a card of congratulations from your HCP. Lerner (2014) says, "Most of us want the impossible. We want to control not only our own decisions and choices, but also the other person's *reactions* to them. We not only want to make a change; we want the other person to *like* that change that we made. We want to move ahead to a higher level of assertiveness and clarity and then receive praise and reinforcement from those very people who have chosen us for our own familiar ways" (31). Don't expect your partner to praise you for your new limits and doing what's best for yourself. They also won't appreciate the fact that if you can successfully set limits, there's a much better chance for your relationship to improve.

Intermittent Reinforcement

Earlier I mentioned that you should communicate to your partner that you will observe your consequence (put it into motion) every single time. That's because of what science says about the power of "intermittent" reinforcement. Intermittent reinforcement is a concept that is larger than limits, rewards, and punishments. It involves the whole relationship. It's vital that you learn about it.

Thus far, all my examples of rewards have been on what behaviorists like B.F. Skinner call a "continuous schedule." An example of a continuous schedule is when a rat gets a pellet each and every time they press the lever. But the unexpected happens when we give the reward on an "intermittent" and "variable" basis: we give the reward every once in a while, at unpredictable times.

With this kind of intermittent reinforcement, the rat would get a pellet only on the 8th, 16th, 17th, 30th, and 43rd time they pressed the lever, for example. On this schedule, we might expect that the rats would become frustrated and eventually lose interest in the lever.

But instead, the opposite occurred. They found that the rats became obsessed with the lever. It was as if the rats said to themselves, "We know that a pellet is coming eventually. If we just keep at it, pretty soon, we'll get fed." So, in other words, the way to cement a behavior in place—in rats or people—is to give a reward on an intermittent and variable (irregular, unpredictable) schedule (McLeod 2023).

Now let's translate that to your relationship with your partner. Sometimes your partner intermittently reinforces you to star in the relationship, and sometimes you intermittently reinforce them. Intermittent reinforcement will lead someone to continue a behavior for a much, much longer time than they would if you stopped reinforcing the behavior on a continuous basis. For example, intermittent reinforcement is the glue that keeps people in their seats at gambling tables. If casinos stopped paying out completely, consumers would get wise to this and stop playing. The possibility of being reinforced maybe, eventually, is one reason why gaming chips jangle so loudly when someone wins and there are bells, whistles, and bright flashing lights (Cherkasova et al. 2018). In a way, intermittent reinforcement has kept an entire industry afloat.

Steven, a man whose wife has BPD, says:

> People who are married to an HCP want to undo whatever happened that caused it to all slip away. We stay locked in for just another glimpse of heaven. We know it exists because we've seen it and experienced it,

but we can't find it anywhere. Our high-conflict spouses promised us everything and then took it all away!

Occasionally, we are rewarded with a smile of approval, the smallest sign of affection, or the tiniest bit of mirroring and idealization. This triggers our emotional memories. Euphoria returns for the briefest of times. See, they are the people we fell in love with! But it is just so elusive.

We reason that enduring hell is not so bad after all for just one more glimpse of heaven, and we stay around much longer than we should, hoping and praying that the person we fell for will make another visit.

In summary, most of the time, life is "hell." But the reward—the "glimpse of heaven" when your partner makes you feel good about yourself again—-is so strong it keeps you in in the relationship, hoping and praying for a little bit of heaven.

Communicating Your Limits

Now that you've gone through the limits-planning process, let's take a look at how you communicate those limits to your partner, if you decide to do so.

Marsha M. Linehan (2014) developed a method for people to communicate their limits to their borderline loved one, or to anyone who is difficult to talk with. It will work for people with NPD too. The acronym for it is DEAR, which stands for describe, express, assert, reinforce.

Describe. Recount the situation as you see it in a factual and unemotional manner. "Yesterday when we were talking after work, you called me a few nasty names, including 'crazy bitch.' You said it in a loud tone of voice, loud enough so that the kids could hear."

Express your feelings. "When you called me that name, I felt as though you had slapped me in the face. More importantly, I was worrying about how this was affecting the kids—both listening to us arguing all the time and hearing their mother being called a name they shouldn't even know at that age. When you call me names like that, and you do on a weekly basis, it really takes away my trust in you in you and weakens our relationship. That's the opposite of what I want for us."

Assert your limits. Remember we do this with an if-then statement. "I know I've complained about this before, but I haven't really done anything about it. Looking at how this is affecting our family, I need to change that. I hope you decide to stop on your own. But if you don't, I feel resolute about my decision not to allow this name-calling to go on. It is too destructive to me, this relationship, and this family. *If* you call me names, I've decided that first, I will ask you to stop and remind you why. *Then* if you don't stop, I will leave the room or, if you follow me, the house. We need some time for things to calm down so we can speak with each other in a civil manner."

If you find this hard to do, keep a list of affirmations in a private place and look at them often, for example:

- I have the right to put myself first sometimes.

- I can forgive myself for my mistakes.

- My feelings are legitimate, and I am the final judge.

- I can change my mind when I need to.

- It's okay to ask for help when I need it.

- I can change what I don't like.

- My time is my own.

I've gained a great deal of confidence and self-esteem since I started to pay attention to protecting my values, needs, and wants with limits. Before I had limits, I felt resentful, stepped on, and victimized. So I told my husband that if I felt he was threatening me, I would leave the house and stay with my sister. He didn't like that one bit.

Sure enough, he busted through my boundaries anyway. But I was prepared because I knew he would challenge me to see if I really meant it. Once he tried to follow me, and I drove to a police station.

But after a few times, he realized I was serious. I was really going to walk out the door. He didn't try to stop me from leaving but called me every five minutes to rage. I knew it was him, so I just turned off the ringer and deleted the messages without listening to them. I didn't come home until after he calmed down. Eventually he learned, and his rages just got further apart.

Yes, it was a lot of work. But taking limits seriously and following through was worth it.

Reinforce the benefits of your limits. "I think this will make everyone in the family happier, especially the kids. I won't feel so frustrated and hurt, and maybe you will feel a little calmer yourself. I think this will really help our relationship. I know it will from my perspective."

When you assert yourself, the price you will pay in the relationship, at least for a while, will likely be rough. Underlying issues and conflicts will begin to surface (Lerner 2014). You may start asking yourself some serious questions:

- Who is responsible for making decisions about my life?

- How are power and decision making shared in this relationship?

- What will happen in this relationship if I become stronger and more assertive?

- If my choice is either to sacrifice myself to keep this relationship or to grow and risk losing the relationship, which do I want? What are the long-term consequences?

- Do you want to avoid conflict by defining your own wishes and preferences as being the same as your family member's wishes?

- Do you want to define yourself as your partner defines you?

- Do you want to sacrifice your awareness of who you are in your efforts to conform to their wants and needs?

Congratulate yourself for getting this far. You're declaring separateness in a relationship that may be enmeshed, which is an amazing accomplishment. Just like when you first set limits, have a support system that can keep you afloat during the countermoves period. Set up times to take care of yourself: browsing a bookstore, playing video games or watching sports with friends, a massage, or whatever feels good to you. You got through puberty. You can get through this. Validate yourself and be proud of your courage, flexibility, and determination.

CHAPTER 9

Reclaiming Your Power

Sometimes…we have no control over our lives simply because we have not yet chosen to take it.

—General Martok, *The Left Hand of Destiny*
by J. G. Hertzler and Jeffrey Lang

This chapter is about actions you can take to improve your life, centering on taking back the power and control you've given (no matter how inadvertently) to your high-conflict partner. In short, this chapter is about how to stop being a caretaker and start becoming a fully independent adult—one who makes their own decisions and stops being a punching bag for a childlike partner who uses harmful methods to get their needs met.

When you stop being a caretaker, you give your partner the opportunity to grow, learn from their mistakes, and become more independent. True, they probably won't appreciate these lessons—at least at first. But just like being a "helicopter" (overly involved) parent teaches children they can't cope without their parent, we harm our partners when we helicopter them by letting them use us for their survival. And we hurt ourselves because these survival strategies are abusive.

Note that none of the techniques I outline in this chapter (as well as in any other chapter) are going to make up for the fact that your partner has BPD or NPD. The fact is that you are in a relationship with a mentally ill and highly dysfunctional person. Nothing in this book or any other can change that. But these techniques go a long way toward improving your life as you begin to see your relationship for what it is, not what you want it to be.

The Problem Pyramid

In this section, I'm going to discuss one of the most important concepts in this book. It is about understanding when a problem is actually yours to solve and when it isn't. Once you understand the difference between the two, you will be freed from cleaning up other people's messes. Also, once you learn which problems are yours to deal with, you can take the needed actions to manage these problems.

The best way to identify if a problem is yours to solve is to ask yourself the following questions.

- Who wants or doesn't want the status quo?

- Who is uncomfortable with the current situation?

- Whose needs aren't getting met?

- Whose behavior doesn't align with their values?

These are important questions, because although you may be sympathetic to the person with the problem, it may not be a problem you should accept as your own.

In their book *Joint Custody with a Jerk*, authors Julie A. Ross and Judy Corcoran (2011) introduce the concept of the "problem pyramid." If you answered "I am" or "me" to one or more of the questions above, you're probably on top of the problem pyramid. Your partner may also top the problem pyramid. *Your job is to identify who's on top, solve problems that are yours, and let your partner take responsibility for their problems.* To illustrate the concept of the problem pyramid, I will talk about the plot and the characters of the 2013 teen movie *The Geography Club*. This will take some concentration, so read this chapter when you are fresh.

The Geography Club is a 2013 film based on the 2003 novel of the same name by Brent Hartinger. The movie is about a group of high school students who want to create a Gay-Straight Alliance at their school so LGBTQ students have a supportive place to socialize. But they are so concerned about the potential stigma of belonging to the LGBTQ community that they choose a boring name for the club, the Geography Club. (Keep in mind that the book was written in 2003, at least two decades ago.)

First, I will give you a broad outline of the film. It takes place at Goodkind High School. The main character is Russell, who is beginning to find out his sexual orientation. He has a crush on Kevin, a football player, who shares kisses with Russell but who is firm that he does not want anyone to know he might be gay.

Russell's best friend is Gunnar, who is an average student that has a crush on a girl at school. The girl will only go out with Gunnar on a double date, and Gunnar needs a friend to complete the date. He puts extreme pressure on Russell to go on the date. Russell doesn't want to go and fake being straight. But he won't tell Gunnar he may be gay. The pressure works, and Russell goes on the date, which ends up with him being outed at school.

A key plot point is that Russell participates in bulling a male student of the club. Russell is on the football team too, and because of peer pressure, he joins members of the football club in dressing a male student of the club as a girl. Russell becomes ashamed of his behavior and comes out at school and joins the newly named Gay-Straight Alliance.

Now I am going to talk about the four main characters in terms of who is on top of the problem pyramid. Try to remain nonjudgmental of the characters and be mindful instead.

Russell's want. Russell recently flirted with an anonymous person online. To his surprise, he finds the internet stranger is none other than handsome and football-obsessed Kevin, who goes to his school. Kevin helps Russell get on the football team. The jocks on the team make him a member of the elite popular kids. Russell's main want is to have an out relationship with Kevin. That puts him on top of the problem pyramid.

Kevin, however, is unwilling to get out of the closet because it would hurt his chances to play football. He does not want to be a pariah in school. Ultimately Russell and Kevin part ways because Russell won't be with someone who stays in the closet (his value), and Kevin is unwilling to go public (his value). Eventually, Russell joins the Gay-Straight Alliance and becomes a visible LGBTQ person in the school. This puts him in touch with his real values.

Kevin's want. Kevin wants to stay firmly in the closet, only having casual sexual experiences rather than an actual serious relationship. He believes that coming out of the closet would make it impossible for him to be on the football team and would make him a laughingstock at the school (he's not wrong). Kevin sticks to his values: he would rather lose Russell's friendship and pretend to be straight to protect himself from losing his spot on the team and losing his place in the popular crowd. He has no problem making this decision, so there is no problem pyramid.

Gunnar's want. Gunnar is a socially awkward boy who is good friends with Russell but is unaware of Russell's sexual orientation. He is a regular kid, not an elite football player. Gunnar wants to date a certain girl, but the girl will only go on a date with him if he can find a friend and make it a double date. He's on top of the problem pyramid. So Gunnar begs and pleads with Russell to go on the blind date and is bewildered by his friend's hesitation. Russell is not ready to come out of the closet, but he certainly doesn't want to pretend to be straight and mislead his date. But Gunnar insists, so Russell goes along with the date. In other words, Russell solves Gunnar's problem, which only leads to disaster.

Russell's lack of honesty has consequences. Riding high when he makes a crucial football play that helps his football team win, peer pressure incites him to go along with bullying a shy member of the Geography Club in a humiliating way. He has become part of the elite group and is popular for once. But whenever he goes against his values, people get hurt—including him.

Eventually, Russell bows to peer pressure and goes on the double date with Gunnar. At one point, his date wants to make out with him and moves to start kissing him, and Russell involuntarily jerks away. The moment is caught on camera. The next day, flyers appear all over the school with the picture of him jolting away from his date and declaring Russell to be the school's "number one homo."

Min's want. The Gay-Straight Alliance club is the brainchild of Min, who is ambivalent about whether the club should be called the Geography Club (the safe name) or the Gay-Straight Alliance (the scary choice). But as time goes on and a member of the group is bullied, she is a strong proponent of renaming the club as the GSA—even when her girlfriend walks out of the group because she doesn't agree. Min's behavior is aligned with her values and there is no problem pyramid.

Eventually, the group, renamed the Gay-Straight Alliance, becomes accepted and many students show their support for it. Russell eventually learns that acting in accordance with his values makes him happy, even if he doesn't get everything he wants (like Kevin).

Lessons from The Geography Club

So, what does this film have to teach us about the problem pyramid? Right off the bat, some of the things we learn from *The Geography Club* include the following.

Values matter. When the decisions we make are based on our values, we have better outcomes. For example, if you believe that each partner should be faithful to the other, acting in a way contrary to that (for example having an affair or tolerating your partner's affair) will cause you to experience cognitive dissonance. Cognitive dissonance is the discomfort we feel when our behavior doesn't align with our values. The problem most caretakers have is that they've become unfamiliar with their own values. Consider setting some time aside to learn about and define your values. You can find instruction, worksheets, and exercises from various sources for free online.

Values can conflict with each other. Sometimes two of our values may come into conflict, and you may, at some point, have to make a decision about which one tops the other. For example, you may value having an intact family with no divorce, but the behavior of your partner may be so outrageous that you don't know how you can stay in this relationship. You are the "wanter," so you're on top of the problem pyramid. This means you need to solve the problem, not your partner.

We can't always get what we want. Like Russell and Kevin, you may love someone who doesn't see the need to change themselves, and you may have to make a different choice if you want your needs fulfilled. For example, you may ask your partner to help out around the house, but if they refuse, you have many choices: do it yourself, hire someone, learn to tolerate messy rooms, have each family member do a better job at cleaning up after themselves, or some other solution. If you're the "wanter," you're on top of the problem pyramid.

Sometimes you have to make tough choices. Russell liked Kevin very much, but he made the tough choice to end the relationship—not knowing when the next one would roll around—because Russell wanted to be out and Kevin didn't.

You don't have to rescue your partner when they're at the top of the problem pyramid. Gunnar tops the problem pyramid when he needs to find a friend for a double date. But he turns around and tries to make it Russell's problem. Rather than say no and withstand Gunnar's pressure, he says yes, setting up a collision that lets everyone at school know he's gay before he's ready to come out. This is a situation caretakers know very well: being pushed around by an HCP who doesn't seem to care about their feelings, only their own.

What It Means to Be Responsible

At least 50 percent of the disagreements you have with your partner have to do with the fact that they want you to solve *their* problems for them and vice versa. If your partner was not an HCP, you could work on the problems together, communicating, negotiating, and getting to the root of the problem. But that's mostly impossible with your HCP partner, who dominates conversations, puts you down, refuses to compromise, and points the finger of blame at you. That's because in their black-and-white world, the only other option is taking some responsibility themselves. That is not likely to happen because they are shame-based. And you can't talk about the root cause of the conflict, which is that they likely have a mental illness. So you need to stop trying to solve their problems and concentrate on your own.

In their book *Joint Custody with a Jerk*, authors Ross and Corcoran (2011) say, "In order to take responsibility for solving a problem, we must first recognize what responsibility means. It means knowing that the choices we make in our lives have consequences and it means being willing to accept that what happens to us is a direct result of those choices. Taking responsibility gives us power and control, because when we recognize the relationship between our choices and their consequences, then the next time we don't like a consequence we can make a different choice" (49).

Let's take a look at how it works when your partner, the "wanter," tops the problem pyramid. You'll be using skills you learned in the "Communicating Without Apology" and "Setting Limits Without Fear" chapters.

When Your Partner Tops the Problem Pyramid

Situation	Their Responsibilities	Your Responsibilities	Discussion
Your partner is furious at 10:00 p.m., you know they want to argue all night, and you want to get some sleep.	They are responsible for their own overwrought emotional difficulties. If you take their problem on, you will encourage this behavior and not get a good night's sleep.	To be compassionate that they have feelings they want to share right now and validate them, but set a limit around the times you will and will not have a discussion. Your consequences might be having your own bedroom (which has a lock), spending the night at a motel or at a friend's, or coming up with other solutions.	It is a powerful change to hold your spouse accountable for their behavior. They won't like it and will press you even harder, like Gunnar pressured Russel to go on a date. When you withstand the pressure and implement your consequences, it's hard in the short-term, but over the long-term, you will make this behavior less likely to happen in the future. This is true of all the examples in this chapter.

Situation	Their Responsibilities	Your Responsibilities	Discussion
Your partner is blaming you for something you didn't do, or for saying something you never said.	Bring forth some kind of evidence that you did what they're accusing you of. If they just disagree with you, take another look at the responses in chapter 7.	Living in constant chaos will wear you down. So carve out a special place for yourself that is accessible, safe, and private. It can be inside or outside the house. It can even be a mental picture you can visit when you need to relax, comfort yourself, or get some space.	Always remember that your partner is responding to their own internal upsets. Something has triggered them, they feel bad, and since they don't own their feelings, you are a convenient scapegoat. When they feel bad, they search for an external reason for their upset. You are not perfect, but you are a convenient target.

Situation	Their Responsibilities	Your Responsibilities	Discussion
They want sex, and you don't.	Ask yourself if you feel the same way. If you do, have fun. If you don't, decline and do not let your partner pressure you to do something you don't want to do.	If your partner has just been rude to you, you may not feel like having sex with them. It is fully your right to say no.	One of the Moving Forward members had an HCP spouse who wanted sex three times a day, and she didn't have the boundaries in place to say no. Another member said that he always said yes because if he declined, his partner would make it into such a huge issue that it was easier to go along with it—even when birth control was not handy. Imagine an invisible shield all over you. Only let people in whom you have invited.

Let's take a look at how it might work when you want something, putting you on top of the problem pyramid.

Situation	Their Responsibilities	Your Responsibilities	Discussion
You want your partner to change something about themselves.	They may or may not agree that they should make those changes. If they don't take your feelings about this into account and purposely do things that hurt you, that is a significant indication you do not have their respect and this relationship is not good for your mental health.	Put a limit on the amount of time you're going to wait for your partner to change. Pick your date carefully. Or, you can pick something that will be a signal to you that the relationship is over.	Take another look at the difference between hope and "catfish hope" (see chapter 5).
You want to feel safe in your home.	To treat you in a way that makes you feel physically and emotionally safe.	To get yourself and any children to a place that feels safe.	I've already talked about safe places. You might also consider the home of a friend or relative, a domestic violence shelter, or a separate room with a lock.

Situation	Their Responsibilities	Your Responsibilities	Discussion
You want your needs met.	To meet your reasonable needs and care enough about your happiness to meet your needs.	Realize your partner may have a mental illness that can render them incapable of meeting your needs. Recognize that even if they are capable, they might not care enough to fulfill your needs. If you want to stay in the relationship, you'll need to find alternate ways to get your needs met or go without.	It is normal and natural to want to have your needs met in a marriage or long-term relationship. But the person you fell in love with may be limited in what they can fulfill. Knowing the difference between *can't* and *won't* can help you determine what to do—although ultimately, it doesn't make any difference.

Solving your problems and letting your partner solve theirs is probably the biggest step you can take to stop being a caretaker and have healthy relationships with others. The first and most important thing: you can stop waiting for your partner to change. That's their problem, not yours. And you can solve your own problem of getting your needs met.

Keep Your Communication Strategy Going

It can be tough to remember, but HCPs escalate their behavior when they get a strong reaction from you because the attention acts as a reward. But there is a fine line between being a doormat and ignoring provocative behavior. Stick with your limits each and every time—when it comes to limits, forget about intermittent reinforcement. But don't raise your voice, threaten them, or let them know how much they upset you (that would be reinforcing).

Ignore sarcasm, anger, or emotionally acting out. Reward cooperation and other behaviors you would like to see more of. When you walk away from rages, insults, and other unwanted behavior, remember you are not punishing your partner but increasing your self-confidence, taking care of yourself, and not rewarding acting-out behaviors, which gives your partner the opportunity to learn and grow. When you exit, don't do it in a dramatic way. Just remember that you left your drink in another room, you have to go to the bathroom, or some other normal reason.

Always pay attention to what your body language is telling them. Make sure it falls in line with what you want to say because facial expression, tone of voice, and body orientation are much more powerful than what you say. Keep in mind that although your way is to talk things out and resolve things, when one person is an HCP and thrives on conflict, this rarely works. When your partner becomes demanding and persistent, stay calm and say over and over again what you want and don't want. Exit as soon as you can. You might repeat the following statements:

- I am not going to have an argument over this.

- I am going to see my friend.

- I am leaving for _____ minutes (or hours). Then I'll come back.

- I do not want to criticize you or the other way around.

- Let's talk when things are calmer.

- I can't talk to you when you are yelling.

- I appreciate that you feel strongly about this, but I need to delay this discussion until tomorrow.

If your partner is emotional and wants to "talk things over," try to delay the discussion so they have some time to cool down. You might say something like, "What you have to say is really important to me, but I'm trying to figure out a work problem right now, and I want to give you my full attention. How about tomorrow afternoon?" When tomorrow afternoon arrives, wait until they bring it up, because whatever was critically important yesterday may not matter that much today. Let them get used to the idea that you are no longer responding to their drama, chaos, and uproar.

Much of the time, anything that you want to change will have a better chance of success if you take action rather than talk about it. "Action" usually means either starting a new behavior or quitting doing something that you usually do. *Remember: You do not need your partner's permission.* Logic will not work. Actions are more believable and have more impact than words. By deciding what you want to do and then doing it, you stop caretaking and make advances toward having your own life. It's vital that by the time you do this, you have solidly established your confidence and self-esteem and understand completely that your partner's angry words have little to do with you—it's the mental illness talking. State what you have chosen to do and then reflect how they feel, for example:

- "I'm sorry that you don't like it when I go to my parents' house. It's important for me to see them, and I'm going to go."

- "I am not having an affair. I love you, and I'm going to continue having lunches with my coworkers."

- "I understand your feelings about me taking trips. I wish you didn't get so lonely. I'll be gone from Monday morning to Wednesday night."

Notice I did not use the word "but." It negates everything that went before it.

Stop Talking, Take Action

Sometimes your best option is to say nothing. You may have realized by now that your partner doesn't know how to resolve differences by having a conversation. Conversations simply bring out their HCP behaviors. They are not logical, they talk in circles, and they reside in an HCP universe in which they are always right and everything is your fault. They are masters of denial and delusion. To make changes in the relationship, take action rather than talking about what you want to do. Words don't work. Making changes on your own is the way to reclaim your power and control. For example:

- Don't count on your partner to do something important. Do it yourself.

- If your partner repeatedly breaks promises, don't ask for them. You will only be disappointed.

- If your partner objects to your friends and family and refuses to have a social life, create your own social life. Extroverts who are married to introverts do this all the time. If your partner objects, you can reflect their feelings, but go anyway.

- If you don't like living with your partner, find another place to live.

- If a conversation devolves into meaningless complaints and insults, stop the conversation and go to another room or leave the house after saying, "Let's talk about this when we're both calmer. I'll be back in two hours." Then leave.

Work on Your Sense of Self

Before you met your partner, you probably had a pretty good sense of yourself. But years of hearing your partner's distorted claims about you can shake the foundation of your identity. Before, you were sure of your values, needs, and wants, and you saw yourself as a caring, compassionate person, always concerned with the needs of others. But when your partner—someone who's supposed to know you best—repeatedly calls you selfish, thoughtless, mean, and wrong, you can have an identity crisis. When you lose track of who you are, you no longer know what you want. You lose confidence in your decision-making capabilities.

Chances are good that you have bent over backward to show your spouse what a good person you are. You've done what they've wanted and tried to correct your "faults." Yet you can't prove to them that you're a "good person," and that makes you doubt yourself. But you did not become a new, selfish person when you met your partner. You may become frustrated and angry at your partner's insistence that you are uncaring and selfish, yet at the same time, you doubt your own perceptions more and more.

You can't make yourself over to become a perfect partner because the claims of your "wrongness" are gaslighting and brainwashing. When you don't meet your partner's insatiable needs, they will fault you. If you don't give them exactly what they want in a robust way, they will claim that the real conflict is you.

Do not believe your partner has special knowledge of how you should change to correct your many "defects." The problem is that your partner is seeing you through the lens of their mental illness. They want you to change in ways that benefit them in one way or another, whether it means giving them more narcissistic supply (an NPD partner) or giving up things and people who interest you so you can comfort them (your BPD partner). Instead of doing this, you can create your own identity (or build off who you already are) and be very skeptical of ideas, beliefs, opinions, and feelings that attempt to influence who you are or will become.

Your HCP partner might take any differences between you as an insult. If you want to go out and they want to stay home, that means you have implied there is something "wrong" about wanting to stay home. Remember, they think in black and white, wrong or right. They must be right, which makes you wrong, and your insistence on your own point of view is seen as invalidating or shame-inducing. You may be vulnerable to this kind of treatment because it occurred in your family of origin.

But you don't like conflict, and after a while, you get tired of fighting and just agree with what they say to avoid an argument. Your HCP then uses your capitulation as proof of your unworthiness and reflects that back onto you. You may try to hold onto your sense of self, but it inevitably becomes twisted up with your partner's opinion. Enmeshment follows, and as that happens, your sense of self shrinks until you can't recognize yourself. Your partner pushes you into becoming more and more of a caretaker than an equal partner. You need to be alert to stop this from happening. Set a goal to become an authentic person.

How to Develop Authenticity

Here are some tips to help you find and express your authentic self. Authentic people behave in ways that dovetail with their core values, wants, and needs; your authentic self is your true self. When you act in inauthentic ways, you may experience negative feelings, ranging from mild discomfort to heavy guilt. More specifically, authentic people (Wright 2008):

- know and trust in their own motives, feelings, and opinions

- can identify their strengths and weakness without denial or blame

- behave in ways congruent with their values, wants, and needs—even at the risk of criticism, blame, or rejection

- have open and honest close relationships

The following are ways to develop your authentic self (Davis 2019, Paul 2019):

Be objective and watch yourself as you go through the day. What are your thoughts, emotions, and actions? Are these truly yours, or have you been pressured to act in a certain way by society, your family of origin, or your partner? Which thoughts, emotions, or actions feel authentic to you? Which feel inauthentic? Notice which responses feel authentic and which ones feel inauthentic.

Have the courage to explore what makes you who you truly are. Imagine a conversation between your "adaptive self," which may include societal messages that don't serve you and your authentic self. The "adaptive self" takes over when the choices we make by our authentic self cause hurt or pain. It's a form of self-protection. Be grateful to your adaptive self! That part of you is helping you get through challenging times. Treat it with gentleness and compassion. However, the pain you've suffered is part of your authentic self.

Identify conflicting beliefs to become more authentic. First, ask yourself what you truly believe. Try to become aware of discrepancies between your actions and your beliefs. It's probable that the longer you've been with your high-conflict partner, the more you will notice that you have not acted like your authentic self. You may have learned to behave this way early in life to protect you from a childhood that left a lot to be desired. However, it's not working anymore, and you're an adult now, not a child. Take what is healthy and leave the rest.

Overcome fear, obligation, and guilt (FOG). Change is hard, and the familiar—even if it's got its problems—can be inviting. We tend to go to those places automatically, so stop and think of what your authentic self would do. Examining your core values, needs, and wants can be like wandering around the home of a stranger in the dark. You might feel scared of looking too deeply into your own mind.

When you discover a disconnect between your adaptive and authentic selves, you may start to experience cognitive dissonance. As I mentioned previously, cognitive dissonance happens when you act in ways counter to your core values, want, and needs. You may attempt to relieve this tension—believing one way and acting another—in different ways, but the longer you act contrary to your values, the worse the cognitive dissonance will get. When you come across a thought, emotion, or action that doesn't represent your authentic self, work on letting it go.

Recognize that developing authenticity takes time. Examining our true self is a lifelong process because we change as we grow older. It takes time to find areas of cognitive dissonance. Stop behaviors that no longer serve you and replace them with more authentic actions.

Part of getting to know yourself has to do with your goals in this life. When you look at the future, what do you see? Maybe you want to go to school, start a hobby, travel, save for retirement, or buy a summer house. Start making life-affirming choices for yourself that take you away from the toxic interactions that have been destroying your peace of mind. Planning for your future is vital. Otherwise, decades can go by with your HCP's drama and chaos while you are living in a state of hope that things will get better.

Some caretakers spend decades in catfish hope (see chapter 5). Don't just wait; *build a life worth living*, no matter what problems your partner has, and no matter how they try to heap abuse on you. Allow yourself to envision more for yourself. Start out by figuring out what it is that you want, now and in the future. Essentially, make goals that don't involve your partner waking up one day to apologize to you, accepting they are an HCP, and going to therapy to become a new person.

Ask for What You Want

One of the unwritten rules of your relationship may have been, "Don't ask for what you want." You may have grown up with that message as well. But don't give up before you've tried. When making decisions about the relationship, you need to know what happens when you try to get your wants and needs met. You are not imposing on your partner; relationships are supposed to be give and take. Start asking for something small, such as to go to your choice of restaurants, and as you gain success, you can make your requests larger.

Stop Living by Their Rules and Create Your Own

In every relationship, there is a list of unwritten rules to follow. In an HCP relationship, the HCP has rules like "My needs come first," "We live in my reality," "You need to ask me permission," and "You are responsible for the kids' emotional needs." Your first step is to uncover the rules and determine who benefits from these rules. Write them down in a notebook. Ask yourself questions like these:

- Who is allowed which feelings?

- What is it okay to disagree about?

- If there is a disagreement, how is a decision made?

- Who makes decisions about social activities?

- Who makes rules for the kids?

- How are finances handled?

- What emotions are you both allowed to express?

- Do I agree with these rules?

- Do the rules seem fair or compassionate?

- Do the rules go along with my values, wants, and needs?

Begin a plan and work with a therapist, if possible, to create your own rules. For example:

- I will no longer be a caretaker.

- My reality counts just as much as my partner's.

- I don't need permission to live my life.

- I won't apologize for things that aren't my fault.

- My partner is responsible for the consequences of their actions.

And no, you don't need their permission to formulate your rules. You're the one who is going to put them into action by *your* actions (or inactions). For example, mentally, don't accept their reality. You don't need to convince your partner of your perspective. You just need to act as if your truth is the truth. You can ask for what you want—you may not get it, but if you learn your partner has no interest in meeting your needs, that will give you valuable information you need for making the best decisions.

Heal Your Trauma Bonds

As you learned in chapter 4, trauma bonds occur in relationships in which an abusive partner sometimes acts normal or even shows small kindnesses. That inconsistent positive reinforcement keeps you enmeshed in an overall toxic relationship. If you can't leave the relationship even when you believe you should, you may have trauma bonds.

Trauma bonds are deeply rooted in our universal need to attach to a loving person who we think can offer us safety and security. The power and control the abusers use to keep us in line works because we are often stuck in shame and embarrassment. Learn how to identify the signs of unhealthy or abusive relationships (chapter 4) so you can distinguish between the two.

Healing from trauma is not a simple task; it happens over time, with patience and great care. You have to unravel your past and determine where it all started, even if it starts with your own parents or caretakers. This type of healing requires a therapist who understands the complexities of trauma responses and helps you work through your experience without shame or judgment.

There is no single "therapy" for treating trauma bonds. Rather, there are a variety of trauma-focused therapies that effectively help survivors of trauma, and these therapies can be used to heal trauma bonds. Outside of getting professional support, here are some steps you can take on your own to break free from a trauma-bonded relationship.

Stay in your own reality. It's difficult to hold onto your own reality when your partner comes from an alternative reality caused by their mental illness. It takes confidence, which you may not feel right now. But take actions based on your reality even if you're a little shaky about your own truth.

Create some space. Here, "space" means both physical and emotional space. Have a part of the house that is reserved for you where your partner cannot go or talk to you. One husband had a hard time doing this, but his teenage son did not. He had a rule that his high-conflict mother could not come in his room. The father told me that he and his other children would seek refuge in the son's bedroom at night. Set limits. Creating space means mentally as well as physically. Sometimes you can be so close to a situation that you cannot see it clearly. Space gives you clarity. Take a step back and get some distance from your HCP partner so that you can see the relationship for what it is.

Give yourself permission to heal. You are deserving of health and happiness. To want these things is not selfish. Healing starts with giving yourself permission to do what you need to do to engage in the healing process. You are allowed to grow and move on from environments and relationships that do not serve you.

Stop self-blame. It's natural and common for victims of trauma bonds to blame themselves for being in such a situation, but that only makes it harder for you to heal. Besides, what difference does it make? What matters is where you go from here.

Continue Working on Compassionate Detachment

In the past, you focused most of your thoughts, emotions, and behaviors on your HCP partner. You've done it to protect yourself and your children if you have them, because you wanted the relationship to work, and because you've focused all your energy on making your partner happy and denying your own needs. Admit it: None of that has worked for any length of time. It's time to change what you're doing. As you start working on yourself and treating yourself with compassion, you will begin to feel less responsible for your HCP partner.

Detaching means becoming the person *you* want to be instead of the person your partner wants you to turn into. It means being more concerned about your own opinion than theirs. Let go of the need to please, appease, and control your partner. Set limits for yourself and make them strong enough that the quality of your life improves and you are no longer an emotionally bereft person trying to change someone else, which is like chasing your own tail. Detaching means living in reality instead of the way you wished things would be. Letting go can release your feelings of anxiety, depression, confusion, and hopelessness. It reduces your self-imposed pressure to fix your partner, be perfect, or get your partner's approval.

Solve Your Problems and Let Your Partner Solve Their Problems

Before you start trying to solve a problem, figure out whose problem it is. That person is responsible for solving the problem. Be responsible for your own problems and let your partner be responsible for theirs. One reason high-conflict relationships are so toxic is that neither person is taking responsibility for their own problems. Caretakers try to solve their partner's problems, which HCPs encourage. For example, you try to solve your partner's need for attention by giving them plenty of it. In reality, that's your HCP partner's problem to solve.

You try to solve your problems by waiting for your partner to change instead of taking care of your own needs. Remember, the person with the problem is responsible for solving it. The first table lists examples of problems that are not yours, the reason why it's not your problem, and the solution. The second table describes examples of caretaker problems in the same format.

When It's Your Partner's Problem

What Is the Problem?	Why It's Their Problem	One Solution
Your partner doesn't want you to leave on a business trip.	Your partner is responsible for managing their own emotions	Make do with an appropriate number of texts or calls or leave notes that they can open every day you're gone.
Your partner is suicidal and threatens to cut themselves.	Seek professional help right away. Support your partner but do not take responsibility for keeping them alive and safe.	Tell them that you love them, but you're not qualified to handle these issues. Tell your partner that you're scared for them and offer to find a therapist, hospital, or whatever else. If your partner threatens suicide, tell them that if this is true, they need to get to the hospital right away.
Your partner wants you to do something you're not comfortable with.	Your partner may want something, but when it goes against your values, needs, and wants, you are under no obligation to do it or provide it.	Simply tell them no.
Your partner insults you and points out all your shortcomings.	Your partner chose you. If they don't like who you are, they have the freedom to find someone who meets their needs better than you do.	Stop needing their approval and realize you cannot change what they think or how they feel about you. Compassionately detach.

When It's Your Problem

What Is the Problem?	Why It's Your Problem	One Solution
Your partner is not giving you something you need or want.	You are the one who feels that something that is missing.	Provide it for yourself, get it elsewhere, or accept that you're not going to get this thing from your partner.
You are not happy in the relationship.	We are all responsible for our own emotions.	Get your happiness elsewhere. Plan your life according to your values, wants, and needs.
Your partner says something about you that isn't true.	You feel uncomfortable, not your partner.	Realize you cannot control what they think about you. You can only say your truth.
You want your partner to change back to who they were during the love-bombing stage.	This is your desire, not your partner's.	Realize you didn't cause it, you can't cure it, and you can't control it.

Work on Your Schemas

In chapter 3, I talked about schemas and how they made you more likely to choose and stay with an HCP. When you recover from these schemas, you can make clear, conscious choices about your relationship and free yourself of feelings of fear, obligation, and guilt. You can give up limiting beliefs, such as the belief that you need someone else to make you feel worthwhile and no one else will love you except your HCP. Recovering from limiting schemas takes time and therapy, but you can start to see changes in the way you view yourself long before recovery. Let's talk a bit more about what schemas are and how you can recover from them.

As a reminder, schemas act as a sort of filter through which all your thoughts, feelings, behaviors, experiences, and situations are viewed. For example, someone with the "defectiveness schema" sees themselves as a worthless failure whom no one will love. Someone with the "unrelenting standards" schema sees themselves as someone who will only be cared for if everything they do meets their high standards.

In their book *Reinventing Your Life*, Jeffery Young and Janet Klosko (1994) call schemas "lifetraps." They say that lifetraps (or schemas) begin with our experiences in childhood with our caretakers. For example, we might have been (or felt we were) abandoned, criticized, overprotected, abused, excluded, or deprived. Those experiences "programmed" us, affecting the way we see ourselves and the world, creating our schemas. Then, long after childhood, we manufacture situations in which we are abandoned, criticized, overprotected, abused, excluded, or deprived—especially when choosing a life partner.

I can hear you thinking, *What kind of demented person would choose to recreate painful experiences from their childhood?* The answer is that we don't do it on a conscious level. We recreate these painful situations subconsciously. Our subconscious (also called the unconscious) directs us to what is old and familiar to us. It's like having a favorite pair of sneakers that are old and ratty, but we slip into them because they're so comfortable and we're used to them. Change is hard, and often we fear the unknown. Young and Klosko write (1994):

> Why do we do this? Why do we reenact our pain, prolonging our suffering? Why don't we build better lives and escape the pattern?... Schemas are deeply entrenched beliefs about ourselves and the world, learned early in life. These schemas are central to our sense of self. To give up our belief in a schema would be to surrender the security of knowing who we are and what the world is like; therefore, we cling to it, even when it hurts us. These early beliefs provide us with a sense of predictability and certainty; they are comfortable and familiar. In an odd sense, they make us feel at home. This is why cognitive psychologist believes schemas, or lifetraps, are so difficult to change (18).

For example, Shana had a mother with BPD and a father with NPD. Her mother was blaming and critical, although intelligent and intermittently caring. Shana married Sam, a man who had some of the same good and bad traits as her parents. She fell in love with Sam's wit and intelligence, but he was emotionally unavailable and, in a sense, abandoned her. Like her mother, sometimes Sam was loving and caring. But he criticized and blamed her for literally everything wrong in the marriage.

Shana let Sam take the lead in everything because his way was always the better way. After all, she was used to being blamed and being thought of as inferior. When they went to marriage counseling, her husband spent the majority of the session listing her faults over the past week, trying to get the therapist on "his side." When she refused to do any more counseling, he was so verbally and emotionally abusive that she finally got up the nerve to leave him after twenty-five years. His last words to her were, "Go and ruin some other man's life." Luckily, though, once we become conscious of our schemas, we can avoid them, change the ways we view ourselves, and make different choices.

Let's take another look at the schemas that people in high-conflict relationships relate to the most. Keep in mind that a person can have several schemas at the same time.

The unrelenting standards schema. This schema whispers in your head, "I need to give 100 percent when I try to accomplish something, but no matter what, nothing I do is ever good enough. No one will love me unless I am perfect. I am anxious about achieving more in life and guilty when I am doing nothing. If something is not done right, it really bothers me." The opposite of this schema is trying your best to do something without obsessing over whether it is "right" or "wrong." It's also accepting that no one is perfect and everyone makes mistakes, yet we are all worthy of love (Young and Klosko 1994).

The subjugation of needs or emotions schema. People with this schema usually subjugate themselves out of guilt or fear. They go to great lengths to avoid confrontation, and they often fear anger (from themselves or others) and derive their self-esteem by thinking of others more than themselves. If you have this schema, you are probably too eager to please, feel guilty for asking what you want, and repress your anger. You have trouble standing up for your rights, and you act submissive, letting other people make decisions for you.

If you have this schema, you probably believe that putting yourself last is one of your most positive qualities. Thinking of others is good, but it's also true that you can have too much of a good thing. Sometimes you need to put yourself first to get your needs met, and it's not selfish to have your own needs! The opposite of this schema is not feeling guilty for saying no and clarifying and prioritizing your needs and values. Recovered people know what they want in a relationship and choose mates who will meet their needs.

The defectiveness or shame schema. Feeling defective is a schema you may share with your partner. However, while they react to it by projecting their feelings of defectiveness onto you, you have to deal with these emotions. On top of their projections, you likely bully yourself with an inner critic that tells you you're worthless, you're flawed, and something is fundamentally wrong with you. Since your partner knows where your sensitive buttons are, they can push them again and again until you agree with them, do what they want, or otherwise meet their needs—whether doing so is good for you or not.

If you have this schema, you probably take the blame for things that aren't your fault and continually apologize even though you haven't done anything wrong. This schema gives rise to the unrelenting standards schema: because you feel so defective, everything you do needs to be perfect. The opposite of this schema is feeling free to assert yourself, set limits, and express your feelings—including anger. People healed from this schema lack shame, have a healthy self-esteem, and treat themselves with compassion.

The self-sacrifice schema. If you have this schema, you have a pattern of helping others and ignoring your own needs. You may be manipulated by someone who uses emotional blackmail—fear, obligation, and guilt—to get what they want. Self-sacrifice is a pathway to resentment and burnout. Religion can play a part in this, as can sexism. Our culture glorifies women who put themselves last. The fear of being called selfish dictates your actions. You may be afraid to ask your partner to fulfill your needs because you fear having them dismissed, your partner getting angry, or even losing the relationship. Your partner will have a hard time when you heal from this schema because they want you to always put their needs first. But your needs matter! Healing this schema will make you feel better and have more energy as you start setting limits and taking care of your own needs. The opposite of this schema is having an equal relationship in which both people give and take. You don't fear asking for what you want, and you set limits on what you are willing to do for someone else.

The enmeshment or underdeveloped-self schema. People with this schema truly believe that when they're married, two become one—but the other person defines reality and calls the shots. You may find it difficult to know what you want or who you are, and you may not feel like your life is your own. The problem here is that your emotional state and sense of well-being are dependent on how someone else feels, and this is bad because emotions are contagious, and your partner's negative emotions are overwhelming. Someone who has healed from this schema knows their wants, needs, and values and acts upon them. They feel free to have their own interests, friends, opinions, and values separate from their partner.

The approval and recognition schema. Everyone wants approval and recognition, just like most everyone likes dessert. But just like binging on sweets can make you sick, your need for approval can become toxic. When you get it, everything is fine. But when it doesn't come, things can come crashing down on you emotionally. In other words, like people with BPD/NPD, you are counting on someone else to make you feel good about yourself. The opposite of this schema is to feel confident in your core sense of self and worthy of love as you are—whether or not anyone else approves.

Schemas grow deep within us like a plant, and they have long, thick roots that are difficult to pull up. You need a tool to do it properly, and in this case, the tool is a therapist—not only to help you beat the schemas, but deal with the everyday stress, trauma, and grief of having an HCP partner. So, do this work with a therapist if you can. You can find a list of schema therapists on Wendy Behary's (author of *Disarming the Narcissist: Surviving and Thriving with the Self-Absorbed*) website, https://disarmingthenarcissist.com. There is also a schema therapy program at http://www.schematherapyonline.com.

But you don't have to see a schema therapy practitioner. I suggest looking for a mental health practitioner who specializes in trauma. These are much more common. You may also wish to read *Reinventing Your Life* by Jeffrey Young and Janet Klosko, but it is a fairly old book and not all of the schemas I mention here are covered.

Because schemas are long-term patterns produced by the core wounds of our childhood, changing them requires time and hard work, with the reward of not being controlled by them anymore. You will also find that your partner has no power to control you either.

Each schema has its own treatment plan. But for space reasons, I can't go through each one. Here are some ideas that apply to all schemas (Young and Klosko 1994).

Choose one schema. With your therapist, choose one schema to work on. Pick the one that's having the most unwanted effect right now or choose the one that's the least difficult to change. Think of some alternate responses and different ways of acting or reacting. Pick easy things so you can build some success at the beginning of your journey, a journey that may last many years. Keep trying. When you have made progress and feel ready, pick another one to work on.

Understand the origins. Understand the childhood origin of your schema. Feel the wounded child in you. It is challenging to heal deep pain without reliving it. Visualize your childhood in your mind and try to recall your feelings. This kind of imagery can be painful, so it's essential you discuss this with your therapist.

Examine your schema. Disprove your schema at a rational level. Be your own advocate. Your thoughts create your feelings, and changing your thoughts can change your emotions and actions. Where is the evidence that you are a defective person? Just where is it written down that you'll be selfish if you take time for yourself? Who made that rule? What if your partner has been lying to you for their own benefit or because they can't see you for who you really are? For example, someone with NPD feels better about themselves when they put someone down. Do you want to put your partner in charge of how you feel about yourself? And if you decide there is some truth to what your partner believes about you, how could you improve that part of yourself, if that's what you want to do?

Build your identity. Start forming your own preferences and opinions in various aspects of your life. These could be preferences about movies, food, leisure time, politics, controversial issues, and so forth. Instead of pouring your mental energy into figuring out your HCP, start paying attention to yourself. Why do *you* want? What are your goals and dreams? Think about the long term and the short term. In what ways is your life running the way you want, and what would you like to change? What makes you happy? Are you doing it enough? You have the power to define yourself. Use it.

Do not repress anger. Learn to express your anger appropriately and constructively. Whatever your HCP does, calmly restate your position without letting them trick you into justifying yourself, arguing, defending yourself, or overexplaining (JADEing).

Use opposite action. Using what you've learned, do the opposite of what comes naturally and see how it feels. If you're a self-sacrificer, practice self-care and putting yourself first. Say no instead of yes. If you have unrelenting standards, deliberately do something imperfectly. Surprise yourself. Take small steps at first with things that don't involve people. Then try it around people other than your partner. As you build strength, bring it back into your relationship. Do the healthy thing, which is not necessarily the easy thing. Feel the fear and do it anyway.

Reward yourself. Schemas have the strength of a lifetime of memories and a multitude of repetitions. Deep inside, they feel as right to you as your HCP's beliefs and feelings do to them. Your self-image and view of the world are experiencing growth. So reward yourself for any kind of progress. Keep looking back at how far you've come rather than thinking about how far you have to go. Do not berate yourself for your schemas. This only hinders your efforts to change. If putting yourself down resulted in any positive changes, change would have happened already.

Identify pros and cons. List the disadvantages and advantages of having your schema. On the upside, it is familiar and as comfortable as a feather bed. On the downside, it is trapping you in all kinds of situations you don't know how to exit. What could you do in life if you weren't burdened by this schema? Do this for each schema.

Identify triggers. Take notice of when your schemas are being triggered. Are you at home, work, school, or someplace else? Who or what triggered you? Spend less time around people and places that trigger your schemas. This may be difficult because it's your partner, but there are other people in your life who may also trigger you, like a parent.

Work on your inner critic. All of us have a critic within us, a voice that mimics the awful things people have said to us (or we just say to ourselves) that are hostile, critical, and unfair. For example, you may be telling yourself, *This is all I deserve, No one else will want me,* and *I'm bad at asserting myself, and I always will be.* These thoughts lead to self-defeating emotions and limit your ability to believe in yourself and make positive changes in your life. Check whether your feelings reflect reality. What proof do you have that your emotions are telling you the facts? For example, if you feel defective, list all your supposed faults. Ask yourself if these are objectively true and how you know they're true. Ask people who love you to help brainstorm your strengths.

Write letters. Write two letters that you will not send: one to the person or people who were responsible for installing your core wounds, and one (or more) for the people in your life who activate that schema. The act of writing a letter to an abuser can be incredibly healing, validating, and empowering. Tell them what they did and how it has affected you now and in the past. You can say anything you want without measuring your words because the letter is not for anyone else besides you and perhaps your therapist. But *do not* send this letter, because your partner will DARVO: deny, attack, and reverse victim and offender. It's the same reason you don't tell them you suspect they have BPD/NPD.

Journal. The main problem with schemas is that they're often invisible. You need to be mindful of your thoughts and actions and catch yourself before you respond in an unhealthy way. Keeping a journal is well-known as a valuable way of uncovering your true thoughts, beliefs, wants, and needs.

You may be wondering how to balance wanting to make changes in yourself while rejecting the necessity of perfection. You do this by embracing the "dialectic," a word that signifies the integration of opposites or merging of two simultaneous—yet opposing—truths. For example, *I'm doing the best I can, and I want to be even better,* and *I can accept myself and still want to make some changes.*

Advice for People with BPD Partners

Participants in the Moving Forward online family support group offered the following advice for people with BPD partners:

- "Take care of yourself and stop taking care of him. Caring for and taking care of are not the same thing. Ask yourself, 'What do I need?' Then listen to your instincts. I sometimes ask myself, 'What would I be doing right now if this was not going on in my life?' Then I try to go do it."

- "Find a good therapist for yourself to get support. Sometimes your partner's therapist is not the best therapist for you. Listen to your gut. You know what you need. The Moving Forward internet support group helped me see that." (You can join the Moving Forward group at http://stopwalkingoneggshells.com.)

- "Get therapy for yourself as early as possible. Anyone involved with someone with a personality disorder needs appropriate support and assistance in dealing with the emotions that arise as well as assistance in separating themselves from the projections, and so forth."

- "Write in a journal daily. My written notes on things from last year helped me stay out of my denial that this was not that bad...I tend to do that in relationships...but it was that bad. My notes also helped his therapist understand what the patterns were in his splitting and his abusive outbursts."

- "Read *The Essential Family Guide to Borderline Personality Disorder* by Randi Kreger." (You can purchase a copy at my website, http://bpd central.com.)

- "Build the biggest support network you can of people who understand and accept you."

- "Build and observe appropriate boundaries without fail."

- "Make your own decisions."

- "Only trust or expect help from people who truly believe everything you relate to them without judgment or prejudice."

- "If you're not consulting with someone who has *personally experienced* the suffering BPD behavior can cause, then you're consulting with an uneducated consultant, regardless of their worthy intent to aid you. They may not anticipate the BP's puzzling, dangerous, and deceptive behavior and may cause you more harm than good and prolong the worst of your suffering."

- "Stop feeling guilty for your 'failure' to make your mate as happy as you once were. It's not your fault any more than it is the moon's."

- "Don't place your mate on a pedestal. Don't let your mate put *you* on a pedestal. What goes up must come down."

- "BPD and NPD have their own reasons. Don't let yourself get sucked into the bad feelings and emotions or the blame and criticism. Know that it's not about you."

- "Create a timeline if you decide to leave."

- "Document, document, document! Do *not* let your high-conflict spouse take control of the children, property, finances, and your life!"

- "Be very consistent with your boundaries. If you let up, the BP will test them again and again."

PART III

Kids, Custody, and Making Decisions

CHAPTER 10

Raising Resilient Children with a High-Conflict Parent

If you are a parent raising children with someone who has borderline or narcissistic personality disorder and they are also an HCP, you are probably worried about the effects of your spouse's behavior on your children. There is good reason to be. Your children are struggling to cope, without the experience, maturity, and perspective that you have. In this chapter, I will outline the effects of high-conflict parenting and give you suggestions to help your children through it. Some suggestions in this chapter come from the book *Raising Resilient Children with a Borderline or Narcissistic Parent* by Margalis Fjelstad and Jean McBride, the only book I know of (as of this writing) on the subject.

First, a disclaimer: some mothers with BPD are good parents—mostly those who know they have BPD and are getting treatment. One example is Rachel Reiland, author of the memoir *Get Me Out of Here: My Recovery from Borderline Personality Disorder*. The effect her disorder was having on her children was one of her prime motivations for seeking therapy. But even in the best-case scenarios, borderline parents have difficulty parenting in ways that affect their children negatively (Macfie 2009).

Parental Deficits

HCPs have many deficits that "good enough" parents should not have. Here is a partial list.

- HCPs have a high need for attention, draining away attention that should go to the children.

- HCPs create chaos and are unpredictable, while children need consistency and stability.

- HCPs (BPD) are highly emotional with mood swings and direct some of the blame for that on their children.

- HCPs are fun some of the time, but don't hesitate to devalue their children when they disagree with them, criticize them, or cause a narcissistic injury. They (NPD) may also have no interest in the mundane aspects of raising children, such as supervising homework or getting them to bed or off to school.

- HCPs don't consider the needs and feelings of others, including their children, because they are too consumed with their own needs, have limited empathy (NPD) or struggle with accessing empathy when emotionally aroused (BPD).

- HCPs alternate between being overcontrolling and neglectful, creating confusion and a sense of unfairness for the children (for example, when a behavior that was fine on Tuesday is forbidden on Thursday) especially when they are punished for it.

HCP Parents Begin to Affect Their Babies

The effect of high-conflict parenting on children begins very early—when the children are infants. While caretakers usually believe that being with both parents is more important when the children are young, the truth is that the younger the child, the more HCP behavior damages them. To explain why, I'm going to give you a quick lesson about something called "attachment bonds." For space reasons, this section will be brief. I encourage you to do further research and learn more on your own.

Attachment bonds become a blueprint of your child's social, emotional, and cognitive development. The attachment style your child develops in early childhood can have a lifelong influence on their ability to communicate their emotions and needs, respond to conflict, and form expectations about their relationship bonds, for better and worse. These early bonds also foster and stimulate growth of the child's brain. Neuroscientists believe that attachment is such a primal need that there are networks of neurons in the brain dedicated to it (*Psychology Today* n.d.).

Secure Attachment

When a child is brought up in a warm and nurturing environment, wherein the caregivers are responsive to the child's emotional needs, they develop a secure attachment. A secure attachment is the basis for developing key dimensions of a healthy personality, including (Hall 2022):

- being able to regulate their emotions

- having high self-esteem

- having the ability to empathize with others

- having an understanding of their emotions and the ability to talk about themselves

- having the ability to set appropriate limits

- having the ability to be emotionally intimate with others

Other Attachment Styles

Children with parents who ignore them, yell at them, punish them, or otherwise make them feel unsafe usually end up with an insecure, disorganized, or anxious attachment style. The child blames themselves for the caregiver's behavior, feels shame, and may have low self-worth.

An insecure attachment style can develop when:

- parents are not sensitive to the child's needs or distress

- parents are loving and caring in one moment and then in the next are emotionally distant

- parents are strict and emotionally distant, do not tolerate the expression of feelings, and expect their child to be independent and tough

As adults, people who had an insecure attachment may:

- have problems trusting others

- worry that people will abandon them and need constant reassurance in relationships

- crave an intimate relationship but feel uncomfortable with closeness and find it hard to trust others

- be fearful in of getting hurt if they get close, so they may avoid relationships

- stay in rocky or dramatic relationships, with many highs and lows

- cling to their partner when they feel rejected and then feel trapped when they are close

- wind up in an abusive relationship

Parents with NPD/BPD

You might ask, "How do we know people with NPD/BPD foster insecure attachments?" A number of studies have answered that question.

Narcissistic Personality Disorder

In the *Psychology Today* article "Insecure Attachment in Children of Narcissists," author Julie L. Hall (2022) says that people with NPD: "lack the self-regulation, emotional maturity, and capacity for intimate connection needed to form trusting bonds with anyone. Even if there is a loving parent in the family system, as the narcissist's partner, that parent may be likely to have an insecure attachment pattern (trauma bond) that denies and enables narcissistic abuse and models a fear-based relationship to the narcissist."

Hall (2022) also says that parents with NPD often "create a survivalist home environment characterized by rage, neglect, inequity, boundary violations, and explicit or passive-aggressive abuse." She adds that dynamics like the following are often the norm in narcissistic families: bullying, blaming, competing, humiliating, hypercriticism, projection, denial, harsh comparison, scapegoating, smear campaigns, triangulation, parentification, and gaslighting—all of which harm children.

Borderline Parenting: Effects on the Children

Researcher Jenny Macfie (2012) has conducted her own studies on the topic of borderline mothers and the effect of their parenting on children and adolescents. In a presentation to the National Education Alliance for Borderline Personality Disorder (NEA-BPD), she discussed her own research and those of other researchers on the topic of the effects of having a BPD mother. She compared these offspring with those who have a normative (normal) mother. Following are some of the results.

Children. Children aged four to seven with mothers with BPD are more neglected, more fearful, and more frustrated than normative children. They are also more withdrawn, anxious, highly affected by their emotions, and more likely to develop ADHD (Macfie 2012). Children of BPD mothers are also at higher risk of developing BPD due to a genetic link.

Adolescents. Adolescents and preteens experience more stress and have more impulsive-control disorders, more emotional and behavioral problems, are more aggressive and are more likely to self-harm (Macfie 2012).

Children and adults who don't have a secure attachment with their mother are not doomed. Therapy and hard work can help them have a healthy outlook. Even though your child may have poor attachment with their high-conflict parent, you can empower your child by creating a secure bond using the suggestions in this chapter. This gives them a good chance to overcome the consequences of an attachment style that is not secure and develop healthy, meaningful, and loving relationships as adults. It takes the right tools, the right therapist, and a healthy dose of patience and love.

Mothers with BPD

One of the first and most complete books on parenting by mothers with BPD is *Understanding the Borderline Mother*. The author, Christina Lawson (2000), says that although borderline mothers may love their children just as much as other mothers, their thought, emotional, and behavior deficits may undo their love. For example, parents with BPD have difficulty loving their children patiently and consistently. Lawson (2000) says of borderline mothers: "They can be jealous, rude, irritable, resentful, arrogant, and unforgiving. Healthy love is based on trust and is the essence of emotional security. Their children, there-fore, grow up without knowing the meaning of healthy love" (29).

Although a mother with BPD can function quite well in other areas of her life, motherhood is one of their most daunting roles. Being a parent requires letting children be independent—especially around the age of two or three and in adolescence. But the borderline mother's fear of abandonment and her tendency to experience separation as rejection or betrayal "lock the borderline mother and her children in a struggle for survival," says Lawson (2000, 5). For example, one single mother would not let her daughter go on sleepovers with her friends because it "was not safe." In reality, being alone in the house terrified the mother.

Children need consistency and continuity to develop trust and security in their caregivers. But this is precisely what parents with BPD are unable to provide. After all, the hallmarks of borderline behavior include inconsistency, unpredictability, and inappropriate intensity. Rules and expectations are vague, nonexistent, unreasonable, rigid, or unpredictably enforced. This makes children feel uncertain because they never know what Mom will be like when they return home from school, just like you never know what to expect when you come home from work. Their parent's moods can suddenly change from affection to rage, creating an uncertain and insecure emotional environment. Lawson says (2000), "Without structure and predictability in their emotional world, children have no reality base upon which to build self-esteem and security" (7–8).

She writes, "When a child disagrees with the borderline mother or does not satisfy her needs or wishes, the borderline will attempt to shame, punish, degrade, or vilify the child... In their view, they are doing their job as a parent" (Lawson 2020, 15–16). Lawson also adds, "Children of borderlines become preoccupied with reading their mother's mood in order to ward off a possible crisis or to prevent being attacked" (16). She writes: "When parents use fear to control their children, they shatter the sacred bond of trust" (Lawson 2000, 17).

Researchers and other experts have found that:

- People with a parent or close family member with BPD are five times more likely to develop BPD (Canadian Mental Health Association 2014). It is unknown whether that is a result of nature, nurture, or both.

- Children of mothers with BPD are at a high-risk for mental health problems. This may be explained by these mothers' tendencies to go back and forth between "extreme forms of hostile control and passive aloofness" in their interactions with their children (Stepp et al. 2012).

- The damage of borderline personality disorder on children can begin in the earliest stages of infancy and disrupt the development of secure attachment and engagement (Petfield et al. 2015). Because attachment styles are created at a very young age, waiting until the children get older before leaving a relationship is the exact opposite of what you should do, if you choose to leave.

Mothers with BPD "often have difficulty identifying and appropriately responding to their children's emotional state. These unmet psychological and social needs at critical moments of development increase risk of disorganized attachment and rob children of security, comfort, and safety from the very beginning of their lives. As children grow older and become verbal, the impact of BPD on their understanding of themselves, their mothers, and the world around them becomes more pronounced" (Štajner 2018).

"The mother's unstable identity, mood volatility, fear of abandonment, and black-and-white thinking can coalesce to prevent nurturing parenting behaviors and deeply fracture the child's psychological, social, and behavioral development. Compassion, empathy, and validation are often withheld as your mother is unable to recognize your emotional needs or formulate appropriate responses. This, combined with the unpredictability, impulsivity, and extremity of those with BPD, is extraordinarily detrimental to the establishment of a secure emotional base from which to grow and flourish (Kvarnstrom 2015).

Narcissistic Parenting: Effects on the Children

So how does narcissistic parenting affect children? Karyl McBride is on the forefront of private research concerning children of narcissistic parents, with a primary focus on women raised by narcissistic mothers. She is also the author of *Will I Ever Be Good Enough? Healing the Daughters of Narcissistic Mothers*. The following list is adapted from her work. Children with a parent with NPD may (McBride 2018):

- not feel heard or seen

- not have their feelings or reality acknowledged

- be treated like an accessory to the parent, rather than a person

- feel valued for what they do (usually for the parent) rather than for who they are as a person

- not learn to identify or trust their own feelings and grow up with crippling self-doubt

- be taught that how they look is more important than how they feel
- be fearful of being real and instead be taught that image is more important than being authentic
- be taught to keep secrets to protect the parent and the family
- not be encouraged to develop their own sense of self
- feel emotionally empty and not nurtured
- learn to distrust others
- feel used and manipulated
- have stunted emotional development
- feel criticized and judged rather than accepted and loved
- grow frustrated trying to seek love, approval, and attention to no avail
- grow up feeling not good enough
- not have a role model for healthy emotional connections
- not learn appropriate boundaries for relationships
- not learn healthy self-care and instead be at risk of becoming code-pendent (taking care of others to the exclusion of taking care of self)
- have difficulty with the necessary individuation from the parent as they grow older
- be taught to seek external validation versus internal validation
- get a mixed and crazy-making message of "do well to make me proud as an extension of the parent, but don't do too well and out-shine me"
- experience jealousy from the parent
- not give themselves credit when it is deserved
- eventually suffer from some level of post-traumatic stress disorder, depression, or anxiety in adulthood
- grow up believing they are unworthy and unlovable: *If my parent can't love me, who will?*

- be shamed and humiliated by a narcissistic parent and grow up with poor self-esteem

- become either a high-achiever or a self-saboteur, or both

- need trauma recovery and will have to reparent themselves in adulthood

The good news is that having a close relationship with at least one parent is a huge protective factor no matter what (Macfie 2009). While ideally children should have two healthy parents, just one parent's love, support, strength, and modeling skills can help lessen the effects of HCP parenting.

How to Help Your Children Be Resilient

There are a number of other protective factors that help children overcome negative effects of high-conflict parenting. Some of these include the children having:

- a sense of being loved and a good bond with at least one parent

- positive self-esteem

- good coping skills (which you will model)

- positive peer relationships

- interest in and success at school

- healthy engagement with adults outside the home

- an ability to articulate their feelings

- parents who are functioning well at home, at work, and in their social relationships

- parents who are employed

- a warm and supportive relationship with one parent

- help and support from immediate and extended family members

That's why it's so important that your children have you and other close adults—a grandparent, aunt, uncle, or close family friend—to help. Use the ideas above with children of all ages, modifying them as necessary so they are appropriate to their age and maturity level. Yes, protecting children from HCP behavior while coping with it yourself is daunting, although they both reinforce each other. At times it may be tempting to stay at work a bit later, leave the house earlier in the morning, put on headphones, or watch a little extra TV to zone out; in other words, to disengage and remove yourself. You will need some breaks! But as much work as it may be to stay present, you will be able to tell your children you did everything you could.

You can't make everything perfect—no parent can. You'll make mistakes too. And even some children who grow up in terrible circumstances—war, poverty, unsafe neighborhood, unstable family unit—manage to come out all right. That's because they have something called resilience. In the rest of this chapter, we'll show you multiple ways to help your children develop this quality. To learn more, read one of the several books on raising resilient children including *Raising Resilient Children with a Borderline or Narcissistic Parent*.

Decide to Put Your Children First

It all starts here. You need to make a decision: Are you going to put most of your time and energy into your partner, who's emotionally stunted—or your children? Caretakers don't mean to put their spouse before their children, but they do, all the time. Some do it simply because the squeakiest wheel gets the grease, and an HCP can easily out-tantrum an actual child. Others do it because they mistakenly think they can control their partner's moods, and that that's the way to protect their children. This translates to mollifying their spouse when they have an episode and doing their bidding to prevent an argument.

But you cannot control your partner because their upsets are caused internally, not externally. Additionally, no adult should be in the business of trying to control another adult. It makes for a codependent relationship, and it discourages the disordered person from taking charge of themselves. It helps keep them in an everlasting childhood state, never having to be accountable for their choices.

In their book *Raising Resilient Children with a Borderline or Narcissistic Parent*, Fjelstad and McBride (2020) write:

> So many times over our years of being therapists, we've had clients with spouses who have BPD or NPD say, "I have no choice but to spend most of my energy pacifying my spouse." Our message throughout this book is that you have many choices. You constantly choose how you think, what you say to yourself and others, and what actions you take every minute of the day. Even the smallest change in any of these

actions can change the results of what happens to you and your children. Too often we go through days and weeks without even noticing what we're thinking or doing. However, we are still making choices.

Become more aware of what you're choosing to say and do each day. Are your actions congruent with your values? Are you basing your choices on facts in accurate information, or on what you believe you're supposed to think and do? Have you thought through how you want to respond or are you just emotionally reacting? Are your choices moving you towards your personal and parental goals?

Pick your battles and be aware of your choices, keep your children's best interests in mind, and take good care of yourself. Don't ignore the truth but try not to become overwhelmed. You are smart. You are loving. You are strong...You may not remember selecting your priorities, but you do so every moment of the day when you choose where to put your time, energy, and focus. Where have you been placing your energy? Has it paid off? Does it square with your values? What will be the long-term result? How do you get recharged? How are your children doing? These are questions only you can answer for yourself.

Don't Fight in Front of the Kids

In the book *What Children Learn from Their Parents' Marriage*, author Judith P. Siegel (2000) says that the health of their parents' marriage is critical to the well-being and emotional health of the children. She writes: "Even if they are barely remembered, these 'lessons' of love are very powerful. The marital relationship observed by the child acts like a blueprint upon which all future intimate relationships will be built. For this reason, it is important for parents to step back and examine the 'lesson plan' they have created for their own children. Parents should ask themselves what their children might be noticing and question whether they are helping them create the best possible future" (Siegel 2000). Children watching their parents fight may feel guilt and shame because they believe they caused the fighting. This can cause:

- low self-esteem and confusion
- stress about feeling the need to take sides
- poor academic performance

- mental and behavioral disorders because they don't have strong coping mechanisms in place

- behavioral issues, such as behaving recklessly or withdrawing and becoming introverted

- a lack of trust in others because they lost faith in the adults around them

Go to a Different Room in the House

When you see signs your partner is going to have a meltdown and rage, accuse, or criticize you or the children, remove them from the situation in the calmest way you can. Have entertainment devices you can pull out at critical moments when you need to remove and distract children from a parent who is out of control. Place these in different rooms of the house. What these are depends upon the age and interests of your kids. A puzzle on the dining room table might work, as might a new app or game to show them. Or you could just bounce on the beds. (Clearly, teens will need more thought-provoking activities.) Plan ahead so you can always bring out something new or something that everyone likes. Play music, bake something, dance, do arts and crafts, or ask the kids for their ideas.

Get Out of the House

When it's unsafe to stay at home, leave. You control the transportation. Compile a list of places to go and fun things to do beforehand and be prepared to leave the house at a moment's notice. Have gas in the car, coats at the ready, a destination in mind, and money in your wallet.

When you return, keep to your routines with the children. Observe your partner's emotional state. Don't engage them until they are ready. Don't mention the episode or try to talk things out. They are unlikely to remember things accurately, and there is no need to rekindle those emotions again. Have the courage to leave things unsettled.

Set Limits

Setting up clear boundaries that you're prepared to enforce (or "observe") will protect your children and yourself. These limits (such as not arguing in front of the children) need to apply to everyone, young and old. "Childhood exposure to parental psychological abuse—name-calling, intimidation, isolation, manipulation, and control—appears to be more damaging to children's future mental health than witnessing physical violence between parents, according to a new study conducted at the University of Limerick, Ireland... The findings, published in the *Journal of Interpersonal Violence*, show that young people who grew up in homes with psychological abuse only tended to have poorer long-term mental health than those exposed to both psychological and physical violence" (Pedersen 2017).

At a minimum, set limits on:

- name-calling and insults to either the child or the other parent

- harmful behaviors in front of the kids

- hostile threats in front of the kids

- shouting or screaming in front of the kids

- throwing or breaking things in front of the kids

- laying a hand on someone else or putting them in a harmful physical situation, such as yelling at them in a car when they can't get away

These limits should apply to every family member. For example, no one can throw or break things. Children learn most from what they see their parents do, not what they say. Once you have removed the children from the situation, talk with them about your attitude toward harmful words. Validate them (that comes next) and let them know your own thoughts. For example, you might say, "It was mean of Mom to say those words to you. You don't deserve to hear that, and it isn't true. I'm sorry I couldn't keep you from hearing that."

Behavior such as shouting, screaming, throwing or breaking things, and of course, pushing or hitting the children, are an absolute sign you need to do your best to remove the children from your spouse unless they have supervised visitation. If you excuse that behavior and wait for the other parent to calm down, your children will make three assumptions:

1. You agree with these behaviors.

2. You are powerless to change these behaviors.

3. They can't trust you to protect them.

Validate Them

Validation is one of the most important things you can do. Validation, as explained in chapter 7, involves listening to your child's emotions while being fully present, reflecting the emotions back in your own words, and asking questions to make sure you fully understand their internal experiences. When you validate your child's emotions (feelings, not thoughts or actions), you radically accept not only the emotions, but your child. You are saying, "I understand you have this very powerful feeling. This must be very difficult for you." And perhaps, "If I were in your position, I would feel that way too (if it's true)." Things you might say include:

- "I can see this is important to you."

- "I can see you were mad when your mom said that to you."

- "I can see right now you're not feeling so great about your mother (or father)."

- "Help me to understand what you're thinking."

- "I can hear (or see) you're feeling (mad, glad, sad, scared)."

- "So, what you're telling me is when this happened, you started feeling (mad, glad, sad, scared)?"

- "I can tell from your voice and tears you are feeling (mad, glad, sad, scared)."

- "If that happened to me, I would feel _____ too."

- "It must feel terrible for you to believe that. I am so sorry this feels bad for you."

- "Was that really (frustrating, disgusting, surprising) for you?"

- "Was that (difficult, upsetting, horrible, tough) for you?"

- "Did it make you feel (lonely, sad, worried, angry) when _____ happened?"

- "Wow, how hard that must be."

- "That really stinks!"

- "That's messed up!"

- "How frustrating!"

- "What a tough spot to be in."

- "We are going to get through this."

- "It makes sense that you feel _____."

- "Lots of people would feel that way."

Children naturally blame themselves when a parent is upset, angry, and negative. When their parent blames them for something that clearly wasn't their fault, they believe it. And unfortunately, one of the hallmarks of being a high-conflict person is blaming others and making them feel at fault. This is not a good combination.

Don't Underestimate the Effects

I hear lots of caretaker parents tell me they are concerned about their children, but they seem to put that concern on the back burner while they try to work on their relationship with their spouse. I can't say this more strongly: whatever you're feeling right now, whatever behavior you're trying to cope with, your children are going through the same thing. The difference is that their parents are God-like figures who control their world and are supposed to do everything they can to protect them. It's bad enough that someone is hurting them; the fact that this person is their parent makes it worse.

Model Tools and Techniques

Since your coparent can't be counted on to provide a consistent emotional role model for your kids, it's even more important for you to manage your own stress and keep calm in the face of high-conflict behavior. Show your child there's another way to manage strong emotions, to tolerate tension, and to solve problems without resorting to extreme, all-or-nothing thinking and behavior.

While you and the kids will experience some big upsets, be aware that emotional abuse and emotional neglect may be so subtle and ingrained that you don't recognize it. Once you become more sensitive to how it affects you—which can take a heavy dose of courage and facing reality—you will be able to better spot abuse directed to your children.

The 4 Big Skills for Life

Coauthor Bill Eddy has developed an easy approach to help children think in a positive way about their own behavior as well as their parents' behavior.

These are the 4 Big Skills for Life: managed emotions, flexible thinking, moderate behavior, and checking yourself. In daily life, you can teach these in almost any setting to help them think in terms of skills rather than good or bad people.

For example, if you see someone yelling on TV, you can ask your child: "Do you think that guy was managing his emotions right then? How could he have managed them better?" If your child has to make a decision about whether to talk to a friend who was rude to them, you can ask: "How can you use your flexible thinking to solve this? What are several possible things you could do or say?"

If the HCP parent was angry and threw a book at your child, and your child complains to you, you can ask your child: "Was that moderate behavior by your mother/father? At least we're trying to use moderate behavior ourselves, aren't we?" This way, you help your child process what has happened as a mistake by the HCP parent, without criticizing that parent or saying that they are an HCP. This keeps the focus on behavior and learning skills that your child can use throughout their life. Depending on your situation, you may also suggest to the HCP parent that you both try to teach these 4 Big Skills to the children.

Bill has an online course that teaches these 4 Big Skills at http://www.ConflictPlaybook.com. The following can also help you teach your child these skills for life.

Overcome Emotional Neglect

High-conflict parents don't do a good job tuning in to their children's emotions. But you can. Here are some tips:

- For young children, respond to their expressions and mimic them, which is a form of validation (you can read more about validation in chapter 7).

- Help your children identify their feelings. They may not have the words for what they are feeling. Help them identify their emotions by asking questions like, "How did you feel when that happened?" or "When that happened, did you feel scared?"

- Pay more attention when your children succeed or do something the right way and be less critical when they make mistakes. It's likely they already have self-esteem issues. Help them problem solve or remind them how they handled a similar situation.

- Establish routines. Rules and limits, while not always welcome, give them structure in what is probably a chaotic home environment. Try to be dependable, positive, and consistent, because their other parent probably won't be.

Let Your Children Make Small Decisions

Kids have no control over their parent's inconsistent and unreasonable rules, and they can't get away. So give them as many choices as you can. Even very young children have preferences. Let kids make as many decisions as is realistic for them. This shows you value and respect their opinion and choices. For younger kids, you can offer choices: "Would you like to wear these shoes or these shoes today?" "These socks or these socks?"

As kids get older, you can offer more choices (without going overboard and overwhelming them) as well as open-ended questions. "What would you like in your lunch for tomorrow?" "I'm going to the store. Is there something you feel like having for dinner?" Let kids have a say in what household chores they take on. Older kids can help set their own schedules, for example taking a break after school rather than starting homework right away.

Help Them Manage Their Emotions

Kids of high-conflict parents often struggle with understanding their own emotions. They may feel overwhelmed and express them in extreme ways, or at the other end of the spectrum, they may suppress them. Having a parent empathize, acknowledge, and label feelings helps kids gain coping skills.

As you're playing with your child of any age, observe and comment. "You like playing with Baby Bear, don't you?" "You do not like it when it's rainy out." "You seem to really like..." This shows your child you see them (and love them) as they are and recognize their separateness from you. Make your playtime about them; make them feel special.

After your child shares something difficult or that you don't agree with, stay calm. Don't get defensive. Tell your child you appreciate them talking to you and sharing their feelings honestly. You also can add something like, "I like talking to you. I always learn something new," or "You're a very good conversation partner." Tell your child you love them daily.

You can start with a simple observation. "Hey buddy, what's up? You look (sad, angry, disappointed)."

Your child will likely tell you why: "Yesterday Dad said he would play *Demon Team* with me, and now he says he never said that, and I should go play by myself. That's so stupid. You don't play *Demon Team* by yourself!"

Tuning in parent: "Yes, *Demon Team* is a game for two people. It sounds like you feel angry about what your dad said, and maybe a little disappointed."

Child: "I am! I hate it when Dad says he'll do something and then he changes!"

As you're listening to your child, show that you hear and "get" what they are saying. You can use your own body language—nodding, furrowing your brow, frowning. (By the way, you should also tune in to positive emotions.) Be sure not to "fake" your reaction or condescend; acknowledging feelings and empathizing are about putting yourself in your child's shoes.

Touch can help show your child you're tuning in too. "You look like you could use a hug before you tell me what's wrong." Or take your child's hand or rub their back while they are talking about a problem. When your child is excited and proud about an accomplishment, you can give a high five and a big smile.

Verbal responses that show your child you are tuning in to their feelings include:

- "I can see why you would feel that way. In that situation, I would probably feel that way too."

- "When I was your age. something like that happened to me too, and I felt kind of like you do now—I was disappointed that...and it made me feel angry too."

- "I understand."

- "I hear you."

- "Sometimes it's really hard, isn't it?"

- "Yeah, I know, it's not so easy when..."

You can help your child learn about the wide range of emotions by guiding them to label them. "From the way your hands are making fists, it looks like you're feeling angry right now. Is that right?" "From all the laughing I heard earlier, it sounded like you were pretty happy about..."

For younger kids, consider buying a set of emotion flash cards. Websites such as http://www.sesamestreet.org offer videos for kids and ideas for how parents can teach about emotions.

For slightly older kids, products such as Feelings in a Jar or Temper Tamers in a Jar (Free Spirit Publishing) can be helpful. Many products are available, so talk to a therapist, your child's teacher, or a school counselor for recommendations appropriate for your child's age and maturity level.

Help kids find ways to cope with the discomfort of negative emotions. Younger kids can "tell" their feelings to a favorite stuffed animal or snuggle with a blankie. Older kids might feel better playing with the family dog or calling a friend.

Some deal-breakers when tuning into your child's emotions include:

- Minimizing, dismissing, judging, or punishing what your child is expressing. "That's not something you should be angry about…" "It's not that bad." "That's no reason to cry."

- Denying or lying. "Oh, Dad's not really in a bad mood." "Mom wasn't angry (even though she was yelling)."

- Trying to use logic to show your child why a feeling is unjustified or wrong.

- Letting a child's extreme feelings justify unacceptable behavior.

Make a Feel-Better Basket

Encourage a child of any age to create their own "feel better basket." Adults can do this too!

Give your child a woven basket, plastic bin, or shoebox. Have the child fill the box with a few meaningful items that will make them feel better, such as:

- favorite or funny photos

- stress ball, crystal, rock, or special seashell found on a vacation

- small notebook for writing and a pen or pencil

- book or coloring book

- toy, game, or deck of cards

- stuffed animal, doll, or action figure

Contents will vary based on the child's age, personality, and interests, of course. Just letting your child put his or her own basket together and putting their name on it or decorating the outside of the basket (or box or bin) itself will show how much you value their individuality.

Strengthen Bonds with Your Children

This is one of my most important suggestions. Attachment is a type of connection with your child that, ideally, balances security with encouragement to explore and gain independence. It's a connection that helps a child feel safe in relation to a parent, and others, as well as confident in themselves as a separate person. This is known as a secure attachment.

High-conflict parents tend to form insecure attachment bonds with their children because they lack the emotional tools to consistently recognize the child's emotions, soothe the child when the child experiences strong emotions, and encourage the child's need for separation.

In an ideal world, children would have secure attachment relationships with both parents. But we don't live in an ideal world, and a secure attachment relationship with one parent or another healthy adult can also provide the connection children need.

It's never too early, or late, to provide experiences that strengthen the bond between you and your child. These same experiences help your child's developing brain form the nerve pathways and connections that create a strong brain architecture. Not surprisingly, earlier is better; a child's first four years are the most critical to many important aspects of development.

Even simple games can help you bond with your child. Theraplay, one particular type of play therapy, helps parents connect in fun ways that encourage closeness. If you're interested in learning more, visit http://www.theraplay.org.

Make Memories

Making memories is also part of the attachment bonding process. Document the time spent with your children. If you end up in divorce court and you want custody, documentation will demonstrate how involved you are with them. You can take pictures, write down the dates and what you did, and have a friend there who can serve as a witness. Save Mother's or Father's Day cards and birthday cards.

Psychologist Susan Newman, author of *Little Things Long Remembered* and many other books about parenting and families, emphasizes the value of making memories with children. "Small parcels of time well used assure stellar memories," writes Newman (1993). Those memories and traditions act like glue that helps parents and children stay connected. Your child likely has their share of high-conflict memories, so why not help balance them out with happy ones? Here are three simple ideas:

Young kids. Create "a special place" by putting an extra chair or stool in the kitchen, your home office, or workshop so your child can be with you to watch, talk, or help.

All ages. Create a special gesture with your child that means "I love you." Newman suggests to use it regularly and when your child least expects it—such as at a school event or sports game, in the grocery store, or when out with friends or relatives.

Pictures. Use a photo your child has taken as your screensaver or home screen on your mobile devices, or ask your child for help choosing an image to display.

Play with Your Child in an Age-Appropriate Way

Playing with your child is also part of the attachment bonding process. Here are some play suggestions.

- Do jigsaw puzzles.

- Play with dolls, trucks, airplanes.

- Give your children horseback rides.

- Perform puppet shows.

- Write a haiku, poem, or song together.

- Play hide-and-seek.

- Read books together.

- Sing, do karaoke, choreograph a dance number, or come up with a new dance move together. Photograph or video your child's performance. Be sure to use your child's name, for example, "Kaitlyn's debut silly-gopher dance. Saturday October 10, 2015."

- Play Words with Friends, or any number of other mobile games, back-and-forth during the day. Of course, limit the back-and-forth so it doesn't distract your child from school and other important activities. One mobile game specifically targeted toward building resilience, in both kids and adults, is SuperBetter (http://www.superbetter.com).

- Nature provides one of the best playgrounds ever.

- Swing together at a local park.

- Play fetch with your family dog (help young children throw a ball or Frisbee and to give Fido a treat when he returns it).

- Play soccer, kickball, softball, or catch.

- Visit a farmers' market; go fruit-picking; visit a pumpkin farm before Halloween.

- Do a five-minute scavenger hunt on the walk to or from the bus stop. Look for natural objects—birds, stones, leaves of different sizes, shapes, or colors.

While you're playing: Talk. Listen. Encourage your kids to share their ideas, beliefs, feelings, questions, and worries with you. Kids of high-conflict parents learn it's not safe to share these things with others, since they are often dismissed, invalidated, attacked, or shamed in response. Be someone your child feels comfortable talking to. Watch for opportunities. Be an opportunist (in a good way). Be alert for conversation openers and good timing. Kids may bring something up during a car ride, while watching TV, at bath time, or during other activities. That's great—you don't need to have a formal, sit-down, face-to-face talk. In fact, kids may be more comfortable talking while doing something else.

You can also create opportunities by engaging with your child while getting dinner ready or baking cookies together. (No time? Slice prepackaged cookie dough and let your child help put it on the baking sheet.)

Talk during play with puppets, dolls, stuffed animals, or while drawing pictures, painting, or working with clay.

In *Little Things Long Remembered*, Newman (1993) suggests calling yourself the "complaint department" and being "open" before bedtime, so your child has a chance to tell you if something is bothering them.

As a parent, you'll likely want to jump in and fix things. Not so fast... Ask your child if they want your help solving the problem or figuring out what to do. Sometimes just talking (to a good listener) is enough.

Try to ask questions that can't be answered with a simple yes or no:

- "What was the best thing about...?"

- "What was the worst part about...?"

- "How did you do that?"

- Ask about their friends: "How's Janie doing?" "What did Brett say about that?"

- Follow up on things you know were scheduled for the day: "What were some of the words on your spelling test?" "What did you do in music (or gym or art) class?"

- "And what do you think about that?"

- "What happened next?"

- "How did you feel when that happened?"

- "What do you think might happen next?"

- "What are some other things you can do to...?"

- "What are some other ways you can...?"

- "It sounds like you felt... Are you saying you...?"

Defuse Parent's Attacks on Kids

It's key to understand that when your spouse attacks someone—even a child—they do so because they feel like a victim. Their survival strategies are not working, and they feel out of control, both of which are genuinely frightening. Your HCP probably feels out of control, and while they can only control you so much, parents have an unlimited amount of power over a child. Or they feel unloved or lacking in narcissistic supply.

When you see your spouse being abusive to your child, the natural tendency is to want to protect them from their abusive parent. But in the long run it makes matters worse. It may make your spouse feel invalidated, injured, disrespected, and ganged up on. Psychologist and bullying expert Izzy Kalman (2014) says that if you can call yourself the same insult their parent calling you, then your children learn it is nothing to get upset about. But only do this if you know your HCP will see it as a joke and not as an attempt to belittle the way they are feeling.

Kalman (2014) says that when we try to rescue the apparent victim from the apparent persecutor, the hostilities between them escalate, and your spouse may get angry with you as well. This is how it works: Let's say you want to protect your child from a high-conflict mother. Outright disagreeing with her and taking the child's side sends the message that you shouldn't respect Mom because even Dad thinks she is wrong. Without realizing it, you are escalating hostilities because now Mom is mad at both of you. So by trying to protect your child from Mom in this way, you are actually making everyone more angry with each other. For the child, it now becomes "divide and conquer." You can do whatever you want, no matter how bad it is, and Mom and Dad start fighting each other!

The best way for you to help your child get along with their disturbed mother is to model the behavior outlined in the rest of this book, especially chapter 7, "Communicating Without Apology." If you get angry with your wife, you are teaching your child to get angry with her too. But if you can deal with her calmly and rationally and show that you love her despite her flawed personality, your child will pick this up as well. If you get upset when your spouse insults you, your child will learn to get upset when she insults them. But if you treat her insults as constructive criticism or something to detach from and not take seriously, then they are more likely to treat her insults in a positive way as well.

This advice does not apply when the HCP parent has said or done something cruel or unacceptable in front of the children. Depending upon what they say, refute it and remove the child from the area. For example, if they call your child "stupid," say, "You are a very smart person. Hurry up and finish breakfast, and I'll drive you to school." This gives you a chance to talk with your child.

Let Your Child Be a Child

Help children understand they're not responsible for others' emotions by reminding them that you and your coparent are the parents, and they are the child. It's not their job to worry about you or your coparent's extreme emotions. "You're the kid in this family. You get to think about (something your child loves to do or is looking forward to). Your dad and I will handle the adult issues (worry about the finances, figure out the schedule, and so on)." Don't shy away from tough topics. One of the toughest topics for coparents in a high-conflict family is the HCP's behavior.

Talk About the High-Conflict Parent's Behavior

We often hear parents ask how they should talk to their children about the confusing HCP behaviors and aggression. Rather than dread or discourage these kinds of conversations, I believe they can be excellent opportunities for you to help your children understand three critical things:

- HCP behaviors are not about the child.

- HCP behaviors are not the child's fault.

- HCP behaviors are not the child's responsibility to fix.

Susan Boyan (2017), cofounder and director of the Cooperative Parenting Institute in Atlanta, says there are gentle ways to plant the seed in children that the HCP's behavior is not about them. With younger children, that could mean a question such as, "Have you figured out that grownups are not perfect?" or a comment like, "Sometimes a problem is in the other person, and that person could be a grown-up," or "Both your mom and your dad—all parents—make mistakes; neither one is perfect." "Kids today understand that sooner [than they did in the past]," Boyan (2017) says.

Boyan (2017) goes on to describe how she might talk to a child-client with a high-conflict parent without naming the parent directly. "Let's say this problem is in your friend or mom or sister, someone you really care about. It can feel crazy, and you need to know that a situation is not always the way it seems, that the other person isn't always right."

If a child recounts a conflict with the HCP—for example, an accusation or distortion—Boyan (2017) might say, "Wow, that must feel kind of bad," and leave it open for the child to explore how they feel, which puts the focus on the child rather than the parent.

To older children, Boyan (2017) might say, "You know this isn't about you, right? It may feel like it, but it isn't." Or for an older teen, she might suggest that "something is wrong," and share some of the symptoms. She typically doesn't share the name of the disorder. What's more important for the teen is knowing there's a reason behind the confusing behaviors and that they can be explained.

Katrina Cochran (2017), a therapist in Oklahoma City, also shies away from clinical terms, such as "personality disorder," with her clients until children are in their later teens, opting instead to talk about problematic actions and behaviors. With younger kids, she sometimes talks about the high-conflict parent's brain using the analogy of a football stadium. In response to a child talking about a conflict when the HCP was screaming or raging, she might say, "It sounds like Mommy was overstimulated, and her brain was going bonkers. The fans were screaming so loud, Mommy couldn't concentrate. She's going to have to figure out how to get some of those fans to sit down and be quiet for a while."

After a child is involved in or observes an out-of-control episode with the high-conflict parent, Cochran (2017) encourages the other parent to help the child process their feelings. Some parents feel like this might be throwing the high-conflict parent under the bus, but children have feelings about what they experience, and it's important to help them cope effectively with them.

For example, with a child between five and ten years old, you might wait until you have some quiet time alone the next day and say, "I wanted to talk to you about what happened last night. What do you remember?"

Let the child talk about how they experienced the incident.

Child: "Mommy was really loud."

Parent: "That must have been scary for you."

Cochran counsels parents to stop talking at this point. Parents often over-talk out of their own anxiety, she says. Wait and see what the child says next.

Child: "It was very scary. Mommy was screaming. Loud."

Parent: "Sometimes Mommy gets very loud. I'm sorry you were scared."

An older child might ask, "Why was Dad so loud?" At this point, you can pose the question to your child to learn whether they feel responsible.

Parent: "Why do you think?"

Child: "Because I didn't do my homework."

Parent: "Well, let's talk about that a little. You're saying that if you had done your homework, Dad wouldn't have yelled?"

Child: "Mm-hmm."

Parent: "Remember a few days ago when Dad was yelling, and you had done your homework?"

Child: "Yes."

Parent: "One day you do your homework, and Dad yells; another day you don't do your homework, and Dad yells. How does that fit? You know what? I don't think it was about your homework. I think it was about Mommy. Let's make this about her and not you, okay?"

Cochran (2017) points out that other adults in the child's life can also have similar conversations with the child to help the child understand they're not responsible.

David's Story

With his three kids, ages twenty-one, nineteen, and thirteen, David makes sure not to directly say their mother, from whom he's now divorced, is wrong about things. Instead, he uses his conversations with the kids to teach them alternative ways of managing their emotions and behaving, including making the important distinction between feelings and actions. He says:

> I'll tell them that it's okay to feel very sad and depressed, as an example, but if they throw themselves on the ground and say they wish they were dead and threaten to kill themselves (like their mom has), I explain that's an action, and it has consequences. (David called 911.) We were in the car when a similar conversation took place, and I pointed to another car and said, "That car can cut me off, and I can get really angry. But if I ram the car because I'm so angry, I'd going to be taken to jail. Actions have consequences."

David has not used the term "personality disorder" with his kids, not even the oldest, who no longer lives at home. "I think she would confront her mother about it to try to help her, and that would create extreme volatility for the younger kids who still live in that environment." But this is his personal choice based on his child's personality.

Often, children are pulled into conflicts by the high-conflict parent. When David was throwing a birthday party for his daughter, he was concerned his ex-wife might show up uninvited, so he reminded her that neither parent is to interfere with the other's visitation.

> The morning of the party, my daughter seemed preoccupied with her phone, so I asked her what was up. My ex-wife had texted my daughter several times about how she was so sad I wouldn't let her come to our daughter's party and how my daughter is getting older and there won't be many more birthday parties. My kids get those kind of texts all the time—"Choose me," "Help me," "Manage my feelings for me."

Daughter: Mom's really sad she can't come to my party.

David: I understand. I can see how that would be something a person would be sad about. As you know, when your mom has parties, I don't go because we're separated. Over time, I can imagine there might be situations where, potentially, your mom and I could host a party for you together. But as things stand today, we're not able to do that. If you think back over all the things our family has been through, I think you'll understand the reasons why.

And I leave it at that. I don't bad-mouth her mom. The kids get it; they've lived it.

Sometimes, in response to those kinds of texts, I'll say: "Wow, that's a lot, isn't it?" The kids usually say, "Yeah, it is." I'll add something like, "I wonder what that's all about," to show them it's really not about them.

I talk with my kids about taking care of themselves and what it means to be healthy, how we try to eat well and get exercise, and what it means to be healthy in the mind. I talk a lot about the difference between feelings and actions and how we're responsible for ourselves and for our own feelings and behavior.

Instead of giving the disorder a label, I believe you can talk to kids about parents who are hurting inside, who parent inappropriately in some situations, and it might look like this type of behavior or that type of behavior, and this is an example of a better way (such as counting to ten, or twenty-five, before yelling at someone if you're angry).

I talk about negative and positive actions and reality—being honest with yourself no matter how painful it is—versus distortion. I give hypothetical scenarios and share stories of my own. I always relate things to myself. "When you mentioned…it reminded me of the time I…" I try never to mention their mom; I don't have to.

Lisa's Story

Lisa, mom of three kids, ages twelve, eight, and six, says she thought a lot about how much to share with her children. While she was married to her husband, she tried to shield them from their father's behavior.

Some of us are always playing a buffer role between the BPD and the kids. We are constantly monitoring what is said and mediating it both ways. We steer certain conversations to avoid blowups; we know which things should be hidden. We coach the kids what things to say and not say. We know which behaviors in the children we need to encourage and discourage in the presence of the HCP. If we weren't there to intervene and distract, the children will inevitably step on land mines, and the other parent would explode.

But as we've said already, you can't control someone else's behavior—not the HCP's and not your kids'. The constant high anxiety Lisa felt and saw in her kids drove her to the decision to separate.

Throughout the marriage, his blame, projection, and distortion were constant. Everyday conversations about mundane things turned aggressive, hostile, and irrational. When I made the decision to split up, I felt that at least my kids would have a calm, safe home to come back to after spending time with their dad. That way they could understand that what they experienced with him was not what all families are like.

Once the kids spent time alone with their father, they began asking Lisa point blank about his confusing traits.

The kids would come back to me and ask, "Why does Dad say something and then say he never said that?" "Why does dad lie?" At that point, I thought they deserved to know something. I explained that Dad has a condition (undiagnosed, although I didn't get into that) that causes his brain to think about things differently than other people.

I called it a "mental health issue" and explained that it's no different than when your body gets sick, but it's in your brain, and Dad can't help it. I told them when Dad thinks something happened differently than it really did, he believes that's how it actually happened, so it doesn't do any good to argue with him.

I talk to my twelve-year-old a lot about using "I" statements with his father. For example, "When Dad makes you leave football practice before it's over, try saying, 'It makes me feel like I'm not part of the team when I can't stay for practice,' instead of raising your voice and saying, 'You always make me leave practice early!' He gets it, but he's young, and it's hard for him to carry out.

I don't ask or expect the kids to keep secrets from their dad. I would never tell them something if I had to add, "…but don't tell Dad." In this case I really debated whether telling them was the right thing to do. I said that Dad does not think he has a disability and that is part of his disability. I told them if they mentioned it to their dad, it would probably make him angry. The kids had already learned to walk on eggshells with their father, so this was not new.

My kids seemed relieved to learn that Dad's confusing behavior wasn't in their heads, and that something wasn't wrong with them. I was particularly concerned about my middle child, who is less self-assured and more malleable than my oldest. I told them to trust their gut; they know the truth. I make sure they take things to do when they stay with Dad since Dad takes away electronics. We talk about how they can go in their rooms at Dad's and keep themselves occupied if the "weather is stormy."

Lisa's comment refers to a book called *The Weather House: Living with a Parent with Borderline Personality Disorder,* available through the Personality Disorder Awareness Network (http://pdan.org). She, and other parents, also have found the book *An Umbrella for Alex* helpful in explaining a parent's abrupt mood swings and helping young children understand they're not responsible. Books such as *The Invisible String* and *The Kissing Hand* can help kids of divorced parents as they learn to navigate transitions between parents.

Comments such as "Sometimes Dad has trouble managing his emotions (or his behavior)" can go a long way toward helping kids realize the outburst wasn't their fault. When you're driving, at the grocery store, or watching TV or a movie, you can point out examples of people who are doing a good job of managing their emotions, and those who are not doing such a good job of managing their emotions. Help kids identify what healthier responses to stress and strong emotions look like.

Margalis Fjelstad and Jean McBride (2020), the authors of *Raising Resilient Children with a Borderline or Narcissistic Parent,* have the following suggestions for talking to children of different ages:

Preschool Children

- "Daddy's voice was very loud, you were shaking all over, and that was scary. You just made a mistake. You're not a bad girl. I'll help you fix it."

- "That hurt your feelings when Mom took your toy away. I'll help you find something else to play with."

- "Daddy has mad days sometimes. Just because he said it was your fault doesn't make it your fault."

- "Mom doesn't feel good today. She is very tired and sad."

Middle School Children

- "Mom sure was angry. She's pretty mad at everything today. I'll help you pick up these toys, and then we will play a game."

- "Dad said he'll take you to a movie, but he changed his mind. I don't know why, but I know it's not because you did anything wrong. I know you're disappointed. What would you like to do instead?"

- "Dad gets confused and changes his mind a lot. I think Dad forgets and asks you to do two things at once. Which do you want to do first?"

- "Some days Dad needs to be quiet and alone."

Adolescents

- "Your Dad calls you names a lot. I don't like it. How do you feel about it?"

- "Do you believe that what Mom said to you was true? What do you think will help? What help do you need from me?"

- "When Mom is in an angry mood, she doesn't think before she speaks. How does that feel to you?"

- "Well, Dad is getting upset at everything today. A good day for us to stay out of the way."

- "You're right, your dad didn't keep his promise. I'm sorry he chose not to. I don't understand why. How can I help?"

You may feel that you should never say anything negative about the other parent to the children. It's supposed to be one of the most important parenting rules. But when your children come to you and say their other parent is being mean or scary, denying the facts (and their feelings) would gaslight them. Instead, be honest but brief.

For example, if they heard your spouse saying mean things to you, say, "Yes, that hurt my feelings. I am disappointed. No, I don't like being yelled at." This can be done without being dishonest or demeaning the other parent.

After your partner acts abusively toward your child, don't try to make it better by saying, "Your mother loves you." This may sound very counterintuitive. But it sets your child up to start associating love and abuse with each other, which could result in your child getting involved in abusive relationships (confusing it with love).

The exception to this honesty is that you should not burden your minor children with a diagnosis (unless you know your child can handle it). If your adult child has done their own research and comes to you saying they think the other parent has it, then you can be direct and honest with your own assessment. But until then, keep your language focused on ongoing patterns of behaviors, not labels, for example:

- "Mom's reasons don't always make sense to anyone else."

- "Dad's anger can be scary for all of us. He can't seem to control it. He doesn't have a shut-down switch."

- "Yes, Dad can't always act the way we like him too. His thinking gets very confused, and then what he says isn't true."

- "You didn't cause Mom to get upset. Sometimes her mind just makes her feel that way."

Don't forget to talk about the high-conflict parent's good qualities, talents, or strengths when appropriate (and not condescendingly). "You know, that's something I really appreciate about your dad… He has a real gift for…" It can be something simple too: "Your dad makes great Sunday breakfasts for us, doesn't he?" "Your mom has always enjoyed making unique crafts for our house." "Let's ask your mom if she can help with your math homework. She's really strong in math."

Don't Fret About Mistakes

If you make a mistake when it comes to a parenting decision or reaction, address it with your child. Say you thought more about it and share your change of heart. Accept responsibility and apologize, if warranted. Rectify the situation or ask the child how you can rectify it and work out a solution. Then move on. Don't go into martyr mode. Use humor (without belittling the child or minimizing the situation). Let your child see you doing things differently the next time.

If Needed, Seek Professional Help for Your Children

Marriage and family counselor Katrina Cochran (2017) recommends the healthier parent seek individual counseling with someone who understands family systems and toxic environments as soon as that person realizes there are issues. Often, the healthier partner spends a lot of energy trying to manage the HCP's behavior, which "will never work," she explains.

That said, not all therapists are skilled at recognizing personality disorders and dealing with related issues. It's important to find a therapist who truly understands HCP behavior and personality disorders.

Cochran (2017) also believes it is never too early to seek counseling and that children as young as two or three years old can benefit. In certain cases, both parents must agree for a therapist to see a child. If you are divorced and your partner won't agree to the child seeing a therapist, talk with your lawyer.

If you are still married, try to help your partner see the benefit of therapy for the child. I realize this may be easier said than done. Focus on the child's issues and behaviors that you both find concerning as coparents and how you think therapy will help. The less your partner feels threatened or blamed, the more likely they will be to consent. Do not take your child to a therapist in secret and expect that your partner won't find out.

Don't try to keep your child in counseling longer than the child reports feeling good about it. Children can start to feel that all the family problems are their fault if they are the only one in therapy. Teenagers especially have a wide range of feelings about being in therapy. Some really appreciate it, while others tire of it quickly and fear being identified as a child with problems. Sometimes brief or occasional therapy is best for adolescents so they can get help without feeling trapped by it.

Provide Consistency

Consistency, predictability, routine. Repeat. Since chaos and extreme emotions and behavior tend to run high in high-conflict families, the more calm, moderate consistency you can provide for your child, the better. This helps children feel secure, which in turn helps lower their stress level.

Lisa, who is married to an HCP, says:

Structure and routine help create consistency. Establish routines for the things you and your children do every day, such as bedtime, mealtimes, homework, bath time, tooth brushing. That doesn't mean you are inflexible. You may need to make changes to account for special events, busy weeks, or a change of season, for example. Think of earthquake- or wind-resistant buildings, whose strong materials have enough sway to move when the wind blows or the earth moves. That said, don't let the high-conflict individual be the earthquake or windstorm. You can keep the established routines with your kids no matter the storm that's around you.

Other ideas for creating consistency include:

Create menus. Even young children can give input on the foods your family eats. Establish some cornerstone themes each week, such as meatless Mondays or taco Tuesdays. Have a wildcard night to use up left-overs or have pizza delivered. Older kids can help plan and prepare a meal. One night the family can cook together. (And if the high-conflict partner has a meltdown, you cook with the kids or take them out to dinner, away from the fray.)

Create fun rituals. Set a weekend movie night. Take a Saturday morning family hike. Make Sundays ice cream sundaes night. Your family rituals can reoccur weekly, monthly, or annually and can be built around just about anything: physical activity, music, art, volunteerism, vacations, spirituality, nature, friendship, or reading.

Keep commitments and promises. Given the issues the high-conflict parent has, they might not follow through; you, on the other hand, must. This is one way children learn they can depend on you and learn to trust others. Be on time. Keep your promises. If you need to change plans, address it head on with the children by apologizing, explaining (simply and briefly) why, and then coming up with a new, revised plan for honoring the original commitment. Don't gloss over a broken promise, hoping the kids didn't really notice or don't really care. They more than likely do.

Help kids develop their own routines and learn to manage their own time and other resources. Teach them how to tell time and gain an awareness of how long things take. Give them a calendar and help them mark special events and days to remember. Help them learn about money and budgeting in age-appropriate ways.

Counteract the Messages About Marriage

You and your coparent individually teach your children many lessons about life, and you also teach them a great deal as a couple, no matter how happy or unhappy you are. In high-conflict relationships, parental energy is sapped by marital problems, leaving less of that important energy for the kids. Children also miss out on learning critical life skills from your relationship.

From their parents' partnership, children learn about trust, problem-solving, interdependence, and mutual respect. As Judith Siegel (2000) says in *What Children Learn from Their Parents' Marriage*:

Parents who want the most for their children should look at the freedom their children truly have to focus on themselves, as children should. It is much easier to create an environment where this can happen when parents are fulfilled in their marriage... If parents want their children to find happiness in life from a wife or a husband, they must look at the message they are sending by the example of their own marriage. When children see how much their parents value each other and their relationship, they are learning about an important source of fulfillment and gratification.

Siegel (2000) goes on to say that a good marriage gives children "the expectation and hope that one day they, too, will have a loving partner."

That's why lessening the conflict between you and your coparent is so important. We often hear parents tell us something like this: "I did such-and-such to protect my child, and as a result, the kids had no idea what was going on between us." Or, "I stayed in the relationship to shield my children, so they wouldn't be affected by my husband's high-conflict behavior." We are going to burst your bubble. Children know what's going on. They may not know the details, and they may not understand all the dynamics, but they know. They innately sense conflict, tension, resentment, hostility, subtle facial expressions, and body language. When it comes to sensing others' emotions, particularly ones that are extreme, confusing, and threaten their security, kids are very perceptive. Giving in or backing down shakes children's confidence in your ability to protect them. Differences between people become "no-win situations, and emotions something to be suppressed" (Siegel 2000).

Talk to Your Spouse About the Kids

Every marriage has its points of disagreement, of course, especially when it comes to child-rearing. But as much as possible, try to establish rules for addressing parenting issues together—away from the children. Some high-conflict coparents will be more able to have constructive discussions and modify their behavior than others. Here are some suggestions for trying:

- Address issues with your coparent when things are going well, not in the heat of the moment or when there's a conflict escalating.

- Talk about how you both want your kids to feel safe and secure in your home. "What can we do together to really have this be a safe space?"

- No matter what your coparent does, remain calm. If your partner begins yelling or name-calling, end the conversation. Say that you both need to find a better time to talk so that you can find solutions calmly.

- Always be respectful. Never engage in name-calling or verbal aggression yourself, no matter what is thrown your way.

- Remember that few issues are one-sided and there is rarely one solution to any given problem. Brainstorm some options and discuss the pros and cons of each. Make a proposal: "We're both concerned about Billy going out on his own now that he's getting older. He asked us about the game Friday night... I propose we do a trial run. Let him go to the game with his friends, but we offer to drive them there, and we arrange with the Smith family to bring the kids home by eleven o'clock. What do you think about that?"

If your partner tears your proposal to shreds, ask them to make another proposal. Try to negotiate in this way. Continue to point out your shared goal: to keep your child safe while allowing them to be a child. (Your individual goal as the healthier coparent is also to encourage your child to explore the world, but that may threaten your spouse. Think about how you frame your shared goal.) And remember, it's not about who is right or wrong, who is the better parent, or who got their way last time.

Validate the other parent's concerns. "I hear you—I'm concerned about Melissa's grades also." "When you talk about how worried you are about Cassidy going on that scouting trip, I can hear how much you care about her. I do too, and this trip might be a good way for her to learn some skills for traveling safely. She won't be alone; she'll have a lot of adults around to keep an eye out."

After your discussion, don't talk to kids about your disagreement or your anger at the other parent. With older kids, it's fine to say, "Your dad and I have different opinions on this issue, but we've come to a compromise and made a decision."

Appeal to Your Partner's Self Interests

No one likes getting mad or upset. If one of your children is bothering Dad when he wants to watch the news, ask your child to play in a different room or suggest that Dad go to a friend's home or a bar. The point is that you are separating them. If your spouse thinks you are doing it for their benefit, great.

Have a Plan B

High-conflict people are known for exploding, becoming intolerable, or having a meltdown over very little. Have a plan B in case this happens, especially when you are out and about with your family. Be very cautious of instances when your spouse is providing the transportation, because cars can be traps. Install the Lyft or Uber app on your phone or carry around the phone number of a cab company or a friend who can pick you up. Know your spouse and be careful.

Thinking about how your HCP may react can create a fountain of guilt. But your guilt won't help them. Instead, take the suggestions in this chapter, particularly the section on creating a bond between you and your children. Remember that children are naturally resilient.

What About Therapy?

Psychotherapy for your child might be helpful if your child (Ceder 2022):

- has behavioral problems, such as excessive anger, acting out, or bedwetting

- has a substance abuse problem or eating disorder

- has had a significant drop in grades

- shows signs of social withdrawal or isolation

- has episodes of tearfulness, sadness, or depression

- exhibits overly aggressive behavior, such as kicking or biting

- has had changes in eating or sleeping habits

- exhibits negative behaviors, for example acting out, talking back to teachers, or fighting with friends

- shows signs of regression or behaviors of a younger child, such as bedwetting, tantrums, and clinginess

- has physical complaints

- talks of suicide or death

Additionally, if your child seems to be enmeshed with their HCP parent or is showing traits of BPD or NPD, therapy may be warranted. If it looks like your child shows the traits of BPD, I strongly recommend my book, with coauthors Christine Adamec and Daniel Lobel, *Stop Walking on Eggshells for Parents*.

CHAPTER 11

Making Tough Decisions

There is no greater enemy than one's own fears.

—General Martok, "By Inferno's Light"

When divorce is involved, we find it hard to say our marriage is over. Being in a difficult relationship may force us to admit and accept that we made poor decisions in the beginning and during the marriage. Some people tend to act like the ostrich who buries its head in the sand.

I've learned that I can't change the past, but I can let it go. Some of us turn to indifference, and some can truly forgive and move on. Some stay but depersonalize the abuse and learn how to manage life with an HCP. Moving on, either by divorcing or staying and fashioning a new life for yourself, is not done overnight, and it's not an easy road to travel. Are you ready to move on with your life and face a new world?

—Ellen

Hitting Bottom

Most caretakers start seriously considering leaving the relationship once they've hit bottom. It's similar to alcoholics hitting bottom. Sometimes an event happens that gives them sudden clarity, and they can no longer deny the reality of their situation. Other times, this clarity comes after years of hard work on the relationship. Either way, the caretaker finally accepts they have tried everything, and they've concluded that the situation is untenable the way it is.

Have you hit bottom? Some caretakers have had these symptoms, which usually appear when the relationship has lasted for many years. Other people leave before the symptoms get too serious.

Caretakers Talk About Hitting Bottom

I hit bottom when I knew I had tried everything I possibly could: I educated myself on BPD, I tried to communicate differently, I removed stress, and I got him doctors and therapists. I gradually came to the conclusion that there was absolutely nothing I could do to change the situation for the better. I surrendered. I chose to invest all my time and energy into the brand-new life I created.

—Karen

Over the years I've found myself saying, "The next big blowup, I'm out." He's never cheated, he's never physically abused me, and his blowups were usually over really stupid stuff. I thought this wasn't "divorce worthy." One day I read the quote "Death by a thousand paper cuts." That described our marriage perfectly. I had been waiting for the vein or artery to bleed out when I was actually dying from a thousand paper cuts.

—Sheena

I reached a moment of surreal clarity during a time when my ex split me all bad. I was three weeks postpartum with his child, and he was attacking me verbally and throwing things at me while I was dealing with the stress and sleep deprivation of a new baby. As he was tossing food at me, I felt this eerie calm, and I said to myself, "I cannot raise a daughter in this chaos, and I sure as hell can't show her this behavior is okay to accept."

—Samantha

I've been with my wife nearly twenty years. I'm still with her, but I know I've hit bottom. I just have no way to leave right now. My bottom was when my father died of cancer and she was so mean and awful to me during that. The absolute worst time in my life, and she didn't see my pain, she didn't empathize with me, and she didn't try to step up when I couldn't carry the load emotionally or physically. That was when I finally realized I had been the one doing all the work in the relationship to keep us together. I realized how much of myself and my own well-being I had sacrificed, and I knew then that if I stayed, the next twenty years would be the exact same. It's very sobering when the person you have never asked anything from can see you as a shell of a person and still not be there for you.

—Juan

> *I hit bottom in January of 2022. My HCP husband threatened to move out for the millionth time, and I finally said "okay"—after which he had a huge rage-filled tantrum. He kicked in my front door after I closed it behind him (per his request—remember, he was moving out!), threw a big metal fruit holder at me, and then kicked in my bedroom door. He had never directed his rage at me before, and frankly I had just had enough. He had worn me down to a place of feeling suicidal. I had literally lost touch with reality (I was very afraid of myself and my mental health), and I knew that if stayed married to him that I would take my life. So in that moment, I chose myself. And that's what I believe any experience with a personality disorder person teaches you: choose yourself.*
>
> —Mark

Right now you're probably thinking, *What now?* You've learned your partner is a high-conflict person with borderline and/or narcissistic personality disorder. Most likely, this is a shock that has turned your life upside down. On the one hand, it's good to know you aren't crazy. On the other, you've realized that your partner is not going to change unless they seek therapy, and your partner has made it clear they are not going to do that. Where do you go from here when you're feeling so overwhelmed?

The answer is to put yourself first for once, especially when the way things are is worse than the thought of the unknown. My goal with this book is to raise the bottom and give you information that motivates you to make decisions on your own, including the decision to leave, stay with sufficient changes, or stay with things as they are, before the emotional effects of hitting bottom make it hard to think. If you wait until you are broken down, leaving will be harder. Once you've hit bottom, becoming your own person within the relationship will also be more difficult.

Putting yourself first may go against everything you believe. But putting yourself first is like a flight attendant's warning to put the oxygen mask on yourself before helping your children. While you're overwhelmed, lost, and in a highly emotional state, you're no good to anyone, including yourself. Here's how to put yourself first.

1. Determine if you have been traumatized. If your partner is an abuser, you may have physical complaints and mental challenges as the result of trauma. Ask yourself if you have signs of complex post-traumatic stress disorder.

As mentioned in chapter 4, complex PTSD is a form of PTSD in which the person undergoes repeated trauma for years, versus regular PTSD, which can happen if a person is exposed to one big trauma, like war or a serious car accident. Signs of C-PTSD include having flashbacks or bad dreams; feeling anxious and scared at the thought of going home after being gone; and avoiding situations, places and other things related to the traumatic person or event.

2. Find a therapist. A therapist is especially essential if you have trauma bonds (see chapter 4) or C-PTSD because these things are known for making people confused, stuck, and less likely to act in their best interest. As a reminder, people who have trauma bonds feel addicted to the relationship. If a trauma-bonded partner decides to leave and move out, a person with trauma bonds is likely to be persuaded to change their mind and move in again. These cycles—back and forth, back and forth—are destructive to your health. If this describes you, you may also be addicted to the drama of the relationship. This is unhealthy.

Signs of trauma bonds are nearly universal among the caretakers I talk to in my coaching practice. Signs include:

- The thought of cutting them out of your life fills you with dread.

- You keep the abuse a secret or defend their negative behaviors to others.

- You know they are abusive and manipulative, but you can't let them go.

- Little crumbs of affection make your day.

- You crave the drama: the high highs and low lows of the relationship.

3. Refuse to participate in gaslighting. Next, do everything you can to stop believing the criticism and blame your partner has been dishing out for years. Your partner's moods, problems, and anger have almost nothing to do with you. You've just been a trigger and a convenient scapegoat who has been manipulated and tricked into believing that you're selfish, bad, and not a good person. That is a lie. If you are a caretaker, you are most likely concerned about others with no thought of yourself. Compassion and empathy are wonderful qualities to have, but not at the expense of self-preservation.

4. Write down your experiences. You're so close to the situation that you can't think straight. Buy a journal or create a computer file and write down everything you're experiencing and how it is affecting you and your children. You can make it as long or short as you want to. You can do it in one sitting or over a few months. You may wish to do this as a letter to your partner. Then put your letter or journal away for a few days, weeks, or months. Then read your journal as if it were something happening to a friend. Or picture someone who loves you reading it. What would they think and what advice would they give you?

5. Tell your story to other people who have a high-conflict partner. It's hard to overestimate the importance of this step. People with an HCP in the family are often desperate to tell their story because they need to be validated. They can't believe their HCP's senseless actions, and they need to know it's not their fault and they're not crazy. While you can tell your story to anyone, the best people to talk to are those who are going through the same thing. I don't know of any in-person support groups, which is why I started my online group Moving Forward. You'll find plenty of people there with HCP partners. You can join at my web site, http://stopwalkingoneggshells.com.

6. Don't give your HCP any ammunition. If conversations trigger useless arguments and conflict (which of course they do), I suggest that you keep conversations to a minimum and use the Gray Rock method (described in chapter 7) without letting your partner know that's what you're doing—otherwise they may think you're going to leave them. Even if it's true, now is not the time to tell them. So use Gray Rock with a smile and nonthreatening body language. Make sure you do not JADE (justify, argue, defend, explain), which begs for a fight.

7. Set a time limit on the waiting game. Make a list of everything you've tried, how long you've tried it, and the results. Then ask yourself this question: Am I willing to stay in this relationship if nothing changes? Then select a deadline for noticing change in your partner, circle that date in your calendar, and stick to it. If your partner hasn't changed by then, acknowledge that you have tried everything you can think of and nothing has worked. At that point, you can leave or build a separate life for yourself while staying in the relationship.

8. If multiple sources tell you to leave, that may be what you should do. In my coaching practice, I get calls from people who tell me their family, best friend, and their therapist advise that they leave a marriage. They want to consult with me to make sure they have tried everything. If multiple sources—especially a therapist—suggest that leaving the relationship is the healthy thing to do, that may be what you should do. Yes, you have tried everything. It may have become evident that your partner is not going to change no matter what you do.

9. If you are considering leaving, know when to leave. In some instances, it may be best for you to leave the relationship immediately. Following are some situations that indicate you should get out of the relationship sooner rather than later:

- **If you feel suicidal or homicidal.** It is not unusual for caretakers to feel suicidal; most likely they have been traumatized and have trauma bonds. Other caretakers behave in risky ways, such as driving recklessly. If you feel this way or find yourself in dangerous situations, know that you do have options, you are strong enough to leave this relationship, and you are a lovable person who can attract a much better partner—even if you don't feel that way right now. Your feelings are side effects of trauma and trauma bonds. Get professional help right away!

- **If your partner has threatened to falsely accuse you of domestic violence or of sexually abusing your children.** False accusations can be tough to fight because often HCPs start to believe their lies, especially BPD HCPs. Don't dismiss this and think it couldn't happen to you. You could potentially be arrested or lose custody because of these false accusations.

- **If you are experiencing severe abuse.** How do you know when the abuse is severe? When you feel severely abused. Look to your feelings to guide you, not a laundry list of things your partner is doing or not doing. You are an expert on yourself. You don't need to explain this to your partner; they will simply DARVO (deny, attack, and reverse victim and offender). Learn to trust yourself without second-guessing yourself.

The Four Horsemen

Famed relationship researcher and psychologist John Gottman is known for his work on marital stability and the factors that cause marriages to disintegrate. When looking at factors that predict divorce, he developed the theory of the Four Horsemen: criticism, contempt, defensiveness, and stonewalling. In religion, the Four Horsemen of the Apocalypse are dramatic and symbolic warnings of the death and destruction that is supposed to occur at the end of days. In a marriage, the presence of the horsemen—which you can find aplenty in typical HCP relationships—predict that divorce is more likely than not. Let's take a closer look at the horsemen.

Criticism. Criticism is feeling that nothing you ever do is right. Gottman writes, "A complaint focuses on a specific behavior, but a criticism ups the ante by throwing in blame and general character assassination. Here's a recipe: To turn any complaint into a criticism, just add my favorite line: 'What is wrong with you?'" (Gottman and Silver 1999).

Contempt. Contempt goes far beyond criticism. The target of contempt is made to feel shamed, despised, and worthless. It looks like disrespect and mockery. Gottman says, "sarcasm and cynicism are types of contempt. So are name-calling, eye-rolling, sneering, mockery, and hostile humor. In whatever form, contempt—the worst of the four horsemen—is poisonous to a relationship because it conveys disgust… Inevitably, contempt leads to more conflict rather than to reconciliation" (Gottman and Silver 1999).

Defensiveness. If your partner is instantly defensive when you bring up a concern, no matter how you couch it, this intense defensiveness makes problem-solving near impossible. They are not just defensive: as I mentioned before, HCPs tend to DARVO (deny, attack, and reverse victim and offender). It's unfair; you can't share your concerns with your partner while they get to complain about you twenty-four hours a day—especially when you want to sleep.

Stonewalling. Stonewalling is the silent treatment, which means that the stonewalling partner refuses to engage with you on any level. It is an extremely passive-aggressive maneuver. Stonewalling also refers to tuning out, turning away, acting busy, or engaging in obsessive or distracting behaviors.

Considering Divorce

If you are considering divorce or your partner has made threats to leave, your first step should be reading the book *Splitting: Protecting Yourself When Divorcing a Borderline or Narcissist*, written by the authors of this book (Bill Eddy as lead author). It can take between six months and a year of planning to achieve the best outcome for you and your children. An HCP can seem very credible in court and can try to tear you down. I also offer two guides written by Bill, who is an attorney as well as a therapist, on my website http://stopwalkingoneggshells. com. One download is for people seeking custody, and the second one is for those without children. The closer you follow the guidelines in the book and downloads, the happier you and your children will be.

Divorce is a reasonable solution to an unhappy, acrimonious, destructive marital relationship. Studies that showed that divorce is bad for the family compared people who divorced to those in a happy, two-parent household. But you're in an entirely different situation. You are comparing the effects of divorce versus a chaotic home ruled and controlled by your HCP, who demands that their needs be met before anyone else's. Even the children are a lesser priority. From our experience, people who go through the worst divorces still end up better than people who stay married to an HCP.

Richard Skerritt (2005), who left his abusive relationship and wrote a book about it (*Tears and Healing*) says, "Often our concepts of obligation run completely contrary to our needs. We know we want something else; we know we need something else; but we persist in what we're doing because we believe that we **must**. Thus, obligation, together with fear, is what hooks us and locks us down in hurtful relationships." Caretakers often help keep their spouse by enabling them and acting codependent. What might make them confront their behavior is losing a loved one because they failed to make needed changes.

But it can be a long and difficult road, especially if the HCP is a persuasive blamer, meaning your HCP is bombastic, seeks revenge, or draws out the divorce process. Once they sense you may be leaving, your partner may panic because they are terrified of abandonment and losing narcissistic supply. When a marriage fails, it's always a hit on the self-esteem of both parties. This is intensified when one of the partners is an HCP. They may make all kinds of promises to get you to change your mind. If this doesn't work—and they can never keep it up for any length of time—they split you all bad.

The first rule of divorce is do not let your HCP know you are leaving until you are completely prepared. Don't act any differently or give hints you may be leaving. Keep important files in a safe place, whether on computer or on paper. Assume your HCP will snoop and try to read your phone or get into accounts. Don't have shared passwords. (I'll give you more tips for leaving the right way in the next chapter.)

You may have to keep your plan to leave secret for a long time because you need to prepare a few months in advance, or even longer if you have children and want to get custody or primary parenting time.

Get support only from people you are 100 percent sure will not tell your partner. This may go against your natural inclination. But know that the minute that the HCP finds out (and they can sense it because they depend so much on you), they will split you as "all bad," and you will be less likely to get through the divorce process with your health and sanity intact. With your health and sanity intact, you will also be more likely to get custody or primary parenting time, if that is what you want.

There are two terms to get familiar with: parental decision-making (often called "legal custody") and parenting time (often called "access" or "visitation"). Parental decision-making is for decisions about healthcare, education, counseling, extracurricular activities, religious upbringing, and other big aspects of your child's life. In most cases, parents have joint decision-making or joint legal custody. Exceptions include when a parent sees the child less than once a month, is in prison, or has a history of serious behavior problems.

Parenting time is about the schedule of when each parent has primary responsibility for your child, including weekdays, weekends, holidays, and vacations. Today's courts are moving toward equal shared parenting time (such as 50-50) in some states, but not others because they don't think it is stable enough. Therefore, it is important to find out the standards in your state and the county of your court. The laws are set at the state level, but each county (and to some extent each judge) may interpret these laws slightly differently.

Men often fear that the court will favor the mother and award her primary parenting time of the children. However, many mothers today also fear that some courts favor fathers and may give the father primary parenting time. Unless there is physical abuse reported and documented by a mandated reporter or authority, courts will generally default to a standard parenting schedule of significant time with each parent when both are considered fit and "adequate" parents. Find out what is the standard for your state and county court to prepare yourself.

Unconventional HCPs who won't admit they have a problem and blame the caretaker for all of the marriage's ills can be quite convincing to the courts, which generally don't take a deep enough look to separate fact from fiction. They can be chameleons who adapt themselves to each situation to appear in the best light possible. They can be "persuasive blamers," as described in the book *Splitting: Protecting Yourself While Divorcing Someone with Borderline or Narcissistic Personality Disorder.*

Staying for the Kids, Leaving for the Kids

Erica decided to leave for her kids, and affirmation that leaving was the right decision came from her twelve-year-old son after Erica began a new relationship. The new relationship was not without its difficulties. Erica and her new girlfriend disagreed about things and argued like most people do in "normal" relationships. But there was no yelling, no insults, no blame, no threats, no nastiness. Disputes were settled quietly and not in front of the children, and the household was harmonious. When Erica talked to her son about how peaceful their household was, he said, "I didn't know it could be like this, Mom." His only experience of married life was yelling, shouting, and abuse. With her new partner, Erica can be a role model of a healthy spouse.

Andy felt he had no choice but to divorce his HCP wife, but the thought of his daughters being with their HCP mom, without him as a buffer and to explain her irrational behavior, kept him from leaving. He especially feared for his oldest daughter, who often butted heads with her mom and caused his wife to blow up completely and then insist that the daughter needed professional help. Caretakers believe they can put into perspective for their children whatever crisis the HCP creates on any given day. They can try, but the kids can be hurt anyway—not just for what the HCP does, but what they don't do—things like being a comforting parent the child can count on to support them like a good parent does.

People say the number one reason they stay is for the kids. It's also the number one reason they leave. Often the same people who stay for kids later report they ultimately left for the kids or wish they had left for the kids. Others who stay for the kids do not regret their decision. You might want to reread chapter 10, which is about the effect of BPD/NPD parents on children.

Many caretakers try to balance whether it's better to leave the children alone with their HCP parent within the marital household under their current arrangement, or for the children to be alone with their HCP parent in a separate household. Is it better for the kids to be alone with their HCP father for 10 percent of their day at home or for 50 percent or more of their time, and up to two weeks at a time, in separate households?

Many people know that their HCP will fight hard over the kids, and out of protectiveness for the kids, they try to avoid ending the marriage or partnership. They might stay so they can protect their kids from the emotional, verbal, and sometimes physical abuse of the HCP: "If I'm always here, the kids won't have to endure this." They couldn't live with themselves if they weren't there to stick up for their children.

Some caretakers stay to be the "sacrificial lamb"—the punching bag, if you will—for the HCP. Often when the HCP no longer has access to the caretaker, who has been the target of abuse for years, the focus will shift to the child, especially older children, who are beginning to exercise free will and stand up for themselves. This can result in the children becoming the target of the HCP's blame, projection, and manipulation. Sarah had been with her HCP husband for fifteen years and was committed to staying until he started to treat her twelve-year-old son the same way he treated her.

Over the years, researchers have studied the impact of divorce on children. Some older studies indicated that divorce had a more negative impact on children than keeping a family together. However, more recent studies have challenged these findings and many of those studies compared happy, two-parent households to divorced households. They did not include high-conflict, two-parent households with an HCP parent and did *not* measure the ways children suffer in a chaotic home with an HCP parent who emotionally or physically abuses the other parent and children. This is a big difference, and it's essential that you replace the old message of "divorce is bad for children" with "I need to look at my specific situation."

With very young children and an abusive partner, divorce with fifty-fifty shared custody could be worse than staying together. According to a Norwegian study, children as young as four may be worse off with a personality-disordered parent without the reasonable parent in the home to manage their extreme behavior. The authors say, "When parents were not cohabiting, the variance of the children's emotional problems explained by parental Personality Disorder symptoms increased from 2.9% to 19.1% (Berg-Nielsen and Wichström 2012). There are many variables, most of which are hard to measure, so this has to be a personal judgment call.

The reality is that families with a high-conflict parent really vary in terms of if it's better or worse for the children. A lot depends on the proportion of exposure to a reasonable parent's flexibility and a high-conflict parent's toxic behavior. If a reasonable parent has equal or majority parenting time, then the extremes of an HCP parent may be sufficiently managed. However, if the HCP parent is likely to get the majority of the time, it may be preferable for the reasonable parent to stay in the same home as long as possible.

It depends very much on the specifics of your situation. Consult with a lawyer or therapist. It can also be helpful to go to your local courthouse and sit in a few courtrooms for a day to see how judges in your area are making their decisions about custody.

In the long run, after a divorce, most children become reasonably happy and competent adults. Children generally do better when their parents get divorced, in comparison to their parents living together in a continuous state of conflict, instability, argumentation, hatred and uncertainty. Two informal social media surveys of about 50 divorced people revealed that despite the hardships, they would choose to divorce again. Two subjects did not initiate the divorce; their partner did. But even they were happier after the divorce, even if it was a long, drawn-out process.

Many caretakers I have coached seem to need my permission to divorce because they seem to believe that the only justifiable reason for divorce is physical abuse or infidelity. This belief causes untold distress to people who are being emotionally and verbally abused who don't think they have the right to leave. People who are not caretakers divorce for all sorts of reasons; for example, they grow apart from their partner, the communication isn't good, or they're unhappy with their sex life. You are allowed to leave a high-conflict relationship for factors that are intolerable for *you*.

This may go against long-held values and beliefs. Perhaps you need to closely examine your values and beliefs in light of the fact that having an HCP partner can ruin your physical and mental health, destroy your hopes and dreams, and scar your children.

You Are Not Responsible for Your HCP's Choices

Edwin H. Friedman (1990) is the author of *Friedman's Fables*, a book of tales that offer fresh perspectives on familiar human foibles. One of his stories, "The Bridge," is a provoking emotional fable that explores who is responsible for their own life. It also illustrates how hard it is for some people to let other people take accountability for their own choices and decisions.

In the beginning of the story, an unnamed man sets out on a much-anticipated journey. He had been searching for the right opportunity for a long time, and now it had arrived. He sets out on his journey, getting more excited with each footfall. He is walking over a bridge in the middle of town when he sees a person (their gender is never mentioned) with a thirty-foot rope around their waist. Unexpectedly, the stranger politely asks the man to tightly hold on to the end of the rope with both hands. Confused but willing, the man takes hold of the rope.

The stranger then jumps off the bridge.

The man is almost dragged off the side. Quickly, he ties the rope to his waist and asks the jumper, "Why did you do this?" But the jumper doesn't answer. "Just hold tight," they say.

Desperate to save the jumper, the man tries hauling them up. But he doesn't have the strength or the leverage. There is no place to tie the rope. Then a thought occurs to him: *If the jumper curls the rope around their waist several times, making the rope shorter, they might be able to get out of this mess.*

He explains his idea to the jumper. But they show no interest in any plan that requires them to make some effort. "You must try to haul me up," they say in tears. "I'm your responsibility. If you let me go, I am lost. My life is in your hands."

But the man doesn't want the jumper's life in his hands. What is he supposed to do? He can't haul the jumper up himself, and there is no one else in sight who can help. The man stands in thought, wondering what to do. Then a solution comes to him. He decides to give the jumper's life back to them.

"I want you to listen carefully," he said, "because I mean what I am about to say. I will not accept the position of choice for your life, only for my own; the position of choice for your own life I hereby give back to you... I mean, simply, it's up to you. You decide which way this ends. I will become the counterweight. You do the pulling and bring yourself up. I will even tug a little from here." The jumper says, "You can't be serious." Then comes a torrent of criticism and blame. "How selfish you are," they rage. The man waits to feel a tug that would indicate the jumper is trying to save themselves. It never comes. Finally accepting that the jumper won't help themselves, he gives the responsibly for the jumper's life back to themselves.

He lets go of the rope.

For many caretakers, the need to avoid hurting another person for any reason—even if it means sacrificing their own happiness—is like a computer program running constantly in the background of their subconscious, invisibly affecting their life choices. You may feel it's your moral or spiritual duty to stay with the HCP, even if it means sacrificing your life. Leaving feels like you're being disloyal.

Some people who have an HCP partner feel so trapped that they start behaving recklessly in ways that could get them hurt. Some people feel suicidal. *Remember, you always have a choice.* It may not be a desirable choice, but you own it. Being in a high-conflict relationship is painful, and HCPs don't make divorce easy. But if you leave, you will eventually feel you will have the opportunity to find peace, freedom, joy, love, happiness, fun, clarity, high self-esteem, and self-confidence. These feelings are rare in high-conflict marriages.

Considering Staying

I put stayers into two categories. The first category includes caretakers who want to end the marriage but are waiting for something (like the kids getting older or finishing high school) and are biding their time. The second group is composed of people who see staying as their best option. The people who are successful at this are skilled at defusing conflict, not engaging in crazy-making behavior, and sticking to their limits. If you are in this group, make sure you are aware of the mental and emotional toll the marriage is taking. The best decision for now may not be the best decision in the long run. If the positives about your HCP outweigh the negatives, staying may be an option for you.

Heather, a caretaker, stayed in an HCP relationship primarily because of her strong beliefs in marriage (for better or for worse, right?) and the length of the relationship, believing that the problem was hers to solve. Further, she and her HCP partner, Frank, owned a business together, she had no financial base of her own, and the notion of picking up and moving terrified her. Where would she go? What would she do?

Heather is an example of how FOG (fear, obligation, and guilt) largely kept her in the relationship. I certainly don't want to minimize the ways in which financial matters might keep you from divorcing. But I will challenge you with this question: What is a real challenge, like a job or money and what is a barrier you are putting in your own way? Self-induced barriers are things such as years invested in this relationship, not believing in divorce, not wanting to be alone, hanging onto catfish hope, or playing the "wait to see if they change" game.

If you believe that divorce is impossible, ask yourself what would make you stay with a partner who was physically or sexually abusing you. Would the length of the relationship be a significant factor in your decision, like it was for Heather? What about your marriage vows? Would you be able to scrape up enough money to leave or stay with a relative for the short term?

As I have stated elsewhere in this book, verbal and emotional abuse are just as serious as physical abuse. Instead of looking at all the doors closed to you, look for open windows and climb through. Don't focus on what you can't do but on what you *can* do. For example, you can open a secret bank account and save a certain amount of money each month, if money is the issue. If not being able to find a job is a problem, look into community college classes to gain a new skill, or do gig work or other temporary or part-time paid work. If you need to work at Walmart, work at Walmart until you find something better. What is your mental health and the mental health of your children worth to you?

Why I Stay: Comments from "Stayers"

"I can't imagine leaving my kids alone with my husband. He is incapable (or unwilling) of even basic parenting, such as preparing meals or having a normal conversation with the kids. Getting them dressed every morning and to school on time? Overseeing homework? Helping them see friends? Supervising them on the weekends? I shudder to think. No one exists in his narcissistic world but him. I couldn't subject my kids to that without another adult in the house."

"I made a commitment when I married him, and I'm not leaving."

"I stay because I love my HCP, and I want to treat him with compassion and empathy. We've been together for almost thirty-five years now, and it's only within the past five years or so that I've noticed this change in him. I see all the signs of unconventional BPD, I realize that I can't fix him, and he needs to come to the realization himself in order to change things.

"I'm approaching BPD for what it is, a mental illness, and I'm trying not to punish him or blame him for having this disorder. If he were sick with any other illness or disease, I would do my best to stay by his side, take care of him, and stay true to my vows (for better or worse, in sickness and health), so I'm trying to think of BPD in the same way.

"At the same time, I'm learning to not to walk on eggshells anymore around him. I'm constantly learning new skills, mostly through Dialectical Behavior Therapy (DBT), to be able to communicate effectively and understand his way of thinking. I'm learning to set stronger boundaries for myself, take care of myself and my children, and remember that I can only do my best. He can interpret (and distort) my actions all he wants—but that won't change the way I think about myself: I am a good person with good intentions, and I want nothing but to do good by myself and all those around me.

"I'm also staying because I want to teach my children (two teenage girls) that you stick by family and the ones you love, even if they have something like BPD/NPD. I want to show them what unconditional love looks like and that they can count on receiving unconditional love too. I want to teach them how to empathize with others, even if they're being really difficult, and give them skills that will help them navigate through all the difficult people they will encounter in their life. I explain that their dad is sick and having a hard time trying to cope with his emotions.

"I also want to teach them how important it is to deal with your emotions before they get the better of you and start to control you and hurt those around you. I want to teach them that there's ways of getting help so that you can still lead a meaningful, beautiful life even if you or your BPD/HCP gets emotionally dysregulated from time to time. I want to teach them that relationships are hard sometimes, but you do your best to work things out.

"However, I also teach them that you stay true to yourself, stay strong and independent so that you can still carry on by yourself if you have to, and if you've given it your all and you can't deal with it anymore, it's okay to say you're done. But I'm not there yet, so I stay. I still have hope that we'll get through this illness and find a way to be healthy once again, together."

Note: Most DBT books and information you find online are geared to people with BPD. I also offer a Stop Walking On Eggshells six-week class on DBT for family members. See http://stopwalkingoneggshells.com for the latest classes.

How to Survive Emotionally If You Stay with an HCP

While it is not possible to completely protect yourself from being hurt by an HCP partner, there is a way to prevent some of the pain. You need to have a secret, inner life and guard it ferociously. Whether or not it is instinctive or deliberate, sooner or later, HCPs—especially those with narcissistic personality disorder—may use things you told them in unguarded moments to manipulate or hurt you. If you think that some thing, idea, or person is good, the HCP will try to make that seem ridiculous or bad. If something makes you happy, your partner may use it to manipulate you, hurt you by taking it away from you, or somehow destroy your joy in it. If you are a creative person in any way—not just in terms of crafts, art, or writing, but also things like gardening and cooking—they will openly or passive-aggressively make you feel that you have no talent and everything you create is mediocre or laughably bad.

Things you should never discuss with or reveal to an HCP with narcissistic personality disorder:

- your hopes and dreams

- your emotions

- your problems, worries, or fears

- your achievements at work or anywhere

- career or personal goals

- compliments from other people

- anything you create, or even the fact that you want to create something

- any experience, activity, hobby, course, place, outfit, possession, television series, book, painting, flower…anything that makes you happy

- subjects you're learning in school

- any thing or person you admire, care about, or feel good about

- anything meaningful or important in the world

What can you talk about with a narcissistic person? Use Gray Rock (described in chapter 7). Talk to them the way you would talk to a stranger sitting beside you on an airplane. Make polite conversation about neutral subjects you don't really care about: the weather, your partner's favorite movies or television shows, sports, and so on.

If you decide to stay with a spouse who has borderline personality disorder, I suggest you get the book *Loving Someone with Borderline Personality Disorder* by Shari Manning. The book is for family members of the "conventional" type (as described in chapter 1) who self-identify as BPD, want treatment, and practice self-harm or are suicidal. It will teach you about the inner life of that type of borderline individual and may be useful to you.

Comments from "Leavers"

"We try not to fight in front of our children, but that's nearly impossible when your spouse is an HCP. Still, the kids feel the tension in the house from years of built-up hostility. They're walking on eggshells too—that's all they've ever known. I'm afraid the kids will consider this normal and get involved with an HCP when they grow up."

"My borderline wife is deliberately trying to undermine my relationship with our toddler. She comes up with all kinds of excuses why I can't be alone with him. For example, my son and I were going to spend some quality time at a playground. But when we were ready to leave, she asked our him, 'Don't you want Mommy to come to the park too?' When I said it was just us, my toddler started having a fit, crying. So I felt I had to miss out on time with my son alone. He is all my wife has. I am already preparing for a custody fight."

"Your marriage is a model for your children. You can't shield a child from within because you're sanctioning your spouse's [high-conflict] behavior. I needed to show my kids an alternative. As much as I didn't want to leave— I'm not an advocate for divorce—I was not able to show them that alternative while I was living with and married to their mother. I'm for a healthy family unit, and the only way I could give that to my kids was to leave."

"I decided to leave because my kids need at least one parent who is happy and whom they can depend on."

"I am going through a divorce after twenty-three years of marriage. I stayed because I thought I was being a noble husband and father. I stayed because I was married before God and took my vows seriously. No one said I had to be happy. I also stayed because I love her. This whole thing would be so much easier if I didn't."

"My counselor told me that although I thought I was doing the noble husband and father thing by taking my wife's stuff on the chin to provide a 'stable' environment for my kids, I actually was doing my kids a great disservice. She enlightened me that I was teaching my children that it's okay to suck up someone else's stuff all the time, which is not acceptable. And conversely it was teaching my kids that the way she treats me (and sometimes them) is acceptable as well. It was a paradigm shift for me to be sure. I now know that I have to do this for my children going forward. That I have to show them that I am worth getting myself out of a bad relationship. That they are worth me providing a more stable environment with less stress and tiptoeing around, waiting for the next shoe to drop. That I will no longer own other people's dysfunction. That my wife will never get better if she always has me to blame for everything."

Reasons Caretakers Stay Stuck

You want to make the right decision based on the facts. But all kinds of beliefs complicate that, and the decision to divorce depends upon your emotions, schemas, and assumptions. Following are some common beliefs that keep people stuck, which greatly affect their decision-making process. If any of the following beliefs resonate with you, you may need to reexamine whether that belief fits the circumstances you are actually in.

Things will get better if I wait long enough. Is this hope justified or is it catfish hope (described in chapter 5)? Ask yourself this question: Assuming that nothing is going to change, how many weeks, months, or years will you let pass before your sense of self-preservation kicks in? Write down the date and note it in your calendar. Then stick to it.

It's not that bad yet. The belief is a companion to the previous one, *Things will get better*. It's time to get a reality check. In her article "It Hasn't Gotten Bad Enough For Me to Leave—A Reality Check," author Kim Saeed (2017) asks readers what it would take for them to finally reach the conclusion that their relationship is "bad enough." The socially acceptable answer seems to be physical abuse and infidelity. But that doesn't take *you* and what matters to you into account. Would any of the following be "bad enough" for you?

- Being so isolated that a good friend or family member dies before you can see them again

- Losing your job because your partner called you incessantly, making you unable to get anything done

- Your partner threatening to kill the family pet

- Your child developing NPD/BPD because of trauma

- The loss of love, affection, happiness, trust, and all the other things that make relationships worthwhile

Both Saeed and I have seen all these things happen and much worse. She writes: "It's funny how being in a constant stress of fight or fight mode clouds our perception so completely that we cannot see the forest for the trees… To drive my point, what if you found out you only had three months left to live? How would that knowledge influence your daily choices? Would you still care about getting the approval of a person who has treated you with contempt and indignity? Or would you focus on other areas of your life and try to make up for lost time?" (Saeed 2017).

My partner holds the key to my happiness. You may still be clinging to promises said in the love-bombing stage of the relationship. The love-bombing stage was just that—a stage—and it's over. People with NPD do something called "future faking," which is vividly describing a beautiful life together ("Let's go to Paris!") that they never expect will actually happen.

I caused all the problems in the relationship, so I can fix them, and things will return to normal. What exactly is "normal"? If you believe normal is going to be similar to the love-bombing stage, I am sorry to tell you normal will not return. What is "normal" is the way they are behaving right now. Remember, you can't fix things. HCP upsets are not about you but their disorder and their schemas. Review chapters 1 and 2, which go over this.

Love will prevail over everything. This belief is especially strong in those who are "romance or relationship addicts" (described in chapter 3). You can't be blamed for feeling this way, since nearly every song, movie, and TV show perpetuates this belief. But life is not that simple. Love is one factor, but there are many others that are just as compelling: your hopes, fears, and schemas, and those of your partner. If you anticipate getting that romantic buzz on a reliable basis and you haven't experienced that for months or years, accept reality. Review the "Bargaining" section in chapter 5.

I am worthless, and no one else will have me. This is a normal response to HCP brainwashing and gaslighting. The truth is that the people who love you and know you best believe you are a worthwhile, lovely person. It's hard to believe that your partner was lying about all your faults because you were a convenient scapegoat, but they believe feelings equal facts.

Roxanne said, "I could not change my narcissist, and he didn't care for my love. The only approval he needed was his own. Today I realize that the only way out is to claim that I am worthy, valuable, and lovable. I need to be stronger than the doubt I had allowed him to create in my own mind. I stopped trying to fit into a box that was not mine and smashed the box because it's time for me to be free. This is my life, and I have the right to love and value myself. Just knowing I am enough, and that in order to love others, I have to love myself first. It is not easy. I still have moments when I'm one digit away from calling him. But I know I'm worthy of an amazing relationship with myself, and I will banish from my life anyone who tries to make me believe otherwise."

Sex and affection are not important to me. During the love-bombing stage, sex and affection were plentiful. Now, the sex is nonexistent, devoid of love, or problematic in some other way. Sex and affection are as important as anything else. If you long for sex and touch, that's a valid reason for wanting to leave. Some caretakers get their needs met by having an affair. This is really about buying time so you don't have to make a decision about the marriage. Oftentimes, people choose another HCP, and their problems are doubled. I am not judgmental about this. It may be a valid choice for some people. But make sure you're not doing this to prolong the inevitable.

I made a vow: "until death do us part." Caretakers often believe that husbands and wives are supposed to take the good with the bad, no matter how bad it is—for better or for worse, right? But things don't get better or worse—they are worse all the time. HCPs break these vows by failing to love, honor, and cherish their spouse. BPD/NPD renders them incapable of those things. Therefore, the "contract" is null and void because it was entered by someone who didn't have the capacity to fulfill it. Some stay because of religious beliefs, and the HCP might have known that and capitalized on it. One HCP told his wife after she divorced him that one of the reasons he married her was because he thought she would never leave him because of her religious beliefs.

I have to stay because of the kids. We've discussed the effects of BPD parenting previously. But I'm adding it here because many parents, consciously or subconsciously, use their children as an excuse for not having to face the personal failure that a divorce would mean for them. They may not want to be alone, give up that catfish hope, or finally take steps to part ways when the relationship is no longer endurable. Feel the guilt and still do what is best for you and your children. Your children are more important than your partner. The children are innocents. Your first duty is to protect them—at least, that's my opinion as the child of one parent who had BPD and another who had NPD.

I am a strong person. You feel you can put up with abuse. If you couldn't, you would feel weak. You tell yourself, "I can handle it." Frank saw plenty of red flags in his relationship before he married Erin. She would swing from depressed and lethargic to elated and almost childlike and hyperactive. He thought he could handle it: be supportive or give her space when she's down and roll with the ride when she's up. But even the most emotionally stalwart among us will get worn down over time. No one can be an emotional punching bag day after day, year after year, and bear no scars from it. That doesn't mean you're weak. It means you're human.

My spouse is sick—I feel obligated and guilty. Many people find it difficult to let their HCP partner take responsibility for their own life. Often these are people who had parents that made them highly responsible in childhood: for example, children who felt responsible for making their parents happy, taking care of a substance-abusing parent, or parenting their younger siblings.

The compassionate side of you is a good thing. Sticking with things is an important value to you. But your strong sense of empathy, when carried too far, will get you into trouble because you don't have an equal sense of self-preservation. When normative people would say, "This person is too sick for me, and I can't live this way," you double down and think, *I can save this person.*

If your partner is suicidal, insist they admit themselves into a hospital. If they really are suicidal, they are more likely to go. If they chronically think about suicide, set a limit that they call a therapist. Do this in a validating, compassionate way. In some cases, you can find ways to help your partner without having to live with them or take care of them. For example, one husband who left his wife because the relationship became intolerable, delayed getting a formal divorce when she had cancer so she could stay on his health insurance.

If you still feel the need to help, figure out something you can do at a distance that will not affect your emotions.

Today may be the first day that I'm accepting that I can't help my
husband. But right in the beginning, he told me I had a beautiful soul,
and I'm the only one who understands him. How do I not feel like
I'm throwing a human being out like a piece of garbage? Yes, he has
emotionally abused me for five years. And he almost broke me this time.
But the guilt I feel for being able to pick myself up and move on while
he struggles on his own with literally no one to turn to is unbearable.

—Elena

The Anti-FOG Retreat

Find a way to be alone for at least one week, ideally for three weeks (maybe at a friend's home while they go on vacation). During that time:

- Try to find some excuse to avoid texts or phone calls with the HCP.

- Walk in nature.

- Practice meditation or yoga.

- Each morning, think about ten things you are grateful for.

- Journal.

You don't have to make a decision right away. On the other hand, how many years are you going to beat a dead horse? The most important thing is to make the right choice for you and your children—especially your children.

CHAPTER 12

Leaving the Right Way

It seems to come down to this: stop trying to change the other person. You can only change yourself or your situation. So my choice is, do I go back and accept his behavior or do I leave? It's a hard decision to think about starting again at age fifty-three.

But I am planning—no rash decisions. But I have to be prepared since he will react to my leaving likely with rage, despondence, and revenge. I just keep telling myself that this will be short-term pain for long-term gain.

—Elle

This chapter is about leaving the right way, if you decide to leave. It is not a comprehensive guide, as Bill and I have already provided that with our book *Splitting: Protecting Yourself While Divorcing Someone with Borderline or Narcissistic Personality Disorder.* Here, we give you information about leaving the right way on an emotional level with a few crucial tips on a practical level. There are costs to leaving, but you can minimize them. This chapter offers an overview of the five phases you will go through in leaving your partner, what you can expect, what help is available to you, and the best way to handle each phase.

The phases of leaving an HCP are:

1. Secret preparations before you inform them you're leaving

2. Informing the HCP you're leaving

3. The HCP's behavior right after you inform them

4. The HCP's behavior during the breakup or divorce process

5. Healing after you leave

I recommend that you read *Splitting* as soon as possible, because knowing your options will greatly reduce your stress, and the book will help you avoid mistakes while proceeding in the best direction right from the start. Most libraries carry it. Other excellent resources include two audiobooks by Bill Eddy available at my website http://stopwalkingoneggshells.com: *Dealing with High Conflict People in Divorce (Without Children)* and *Dealing with High Conflict People in Divorce (with Children)*. Buy ebooks or audiobooks if there's a risk your partner will find hard copies. In his roles as both an attorney and a therapist, Bill has seen all the possible HCP strategies in the divorce process and understands how HCPs' mental illness drives their behavior. He knows what an HCP might attempt and your legal options for protecting yourself.

Divorcing an HCP is vastly different from a normal divorce between two sane adults. It's more like leaving a cult combined with escaping a prison. Fortunately, these days, more people understand the difference, and there are ways to make the process easier and less confusing for you. Some people who have gone through the process of leaving an HCP consider it to be the most valuable learning and growth experience in their life.

Phase 1: Secret Preparations Before You Tell the HCP

What you do during the preparation phase will dramatically affect what happens in all the other phases. Remember to keep everything a secret. Once an HSP knows you plan to leave them, they may become physically abusive, spread rumors about you, try to alienate the children against you, get a court order to remove you from the house, or other extreme possibilities may occur. You will want to be as prepared as possible.

Mindset: Your Foundation for Winning

Many people in a divorce have a mindset they are unaware of—beliefs, habitual thinking, emotions, and unconscious goals for their divorce—that can sabotage their divorce process and prevent them from "winning." For sane people, "winning" a divorce means ending up with safety, peace of mind, a life that is free, and a home that is financially secure. For parents, it additionally means being able to enhance your children's emotional well-being.

In order to "win" in a divorce from an HCP partner, you need a mindset that is radically different from a caretaker mindset. If you're a parent, you need to think like a general who is defending a village of defenseless children. For many caretakers, who feel more like a prisoner of war, this idea will seem daunting and unrealistic. But you can do it, with help from your therapist and lawyer, knowledge from this book and others we recommend, self-care, and preparation. Those who are prepared generally do well and often grow stronger. For many, the skills and strengths forged in the fires of divorce help them live a life that is better than ever before.

Countless experts advise people to remain calm in a divorce for good reason. If you're emotional and out of control, this can give the court a bad impression of you. The two main emotions you need to control are fear and anger.

Fear. Preparation, knowledge, and working with a lawyer and therapist can help you calm fears such as:

- My ex will charm and deceive everyone, and the court will think I'm crazy and not believe a word I say.

- I will end up homeless.

- My ex will hurt me.

- My ex will kidnap my children.

- The court will give full custody to my ex.

- My ex will hurt the children during visits or shared custody when I'm not there to protect them.

- My ex will commit suicide, and I'll be consumed by guilt for the rest of my life.

Anger. Work with a therapist to release anger. You surely have good reasons to feel anger, but seething anger can damage you in your breakup or divorce in various ways, including:

- making it easier for your partner to push your buttons and manipulate you

- driving unconscious, destructive goals in your divorce that make you look bad to the lawyers and judge

- preventing you from seeing your children's needs clearly at all times

- distracting you from focusing your time and energy in ways that will protect you and your children from the HCP and help you win

Now is the time to be strategic, not emotional. Remember this when the HCP makes you angry: winning the divorce is your best revenge.

Repeat this mantra in your thoughts: *keep calm and win.*

Three Ways to Protect Your Sanity During a Breakup or Divorce

1. Work with a therapist. As a caretaker used to ignoring your own needs, you may feel like getting a therapist for yourself is a luxury you can't afford. The fact is, you can't afford to *not* have a therapist right now. A therapist can make the difference between you winning or losing your divorce, as well as winning or losing custody of your children.

Working with a therapist who has extensive experience with BPD/NPD can help you:

- understand and predict your partner's behaviors, crises, and accusations

- learn ways to describe the HCP's behavior, without labeling it in court

- cope with guilt, fear, and anger

- vent to a safe person

- maintain your sanity despite smear campaigns and false allegations

- avoid being manipulated by the HCP

- develop techniques and the mindset to *keep calm and win*

2. Gather emotional support from loved ones and support groups. Tell your family and friends what to expect, how to respond, how they can help, and how to avoid splitting either of you into being viewed as all good or all bad. Tell them you need their unconditional support and make sure you trust them to not reveal information about yourself—especially the legal details. Consider joining an in-person or online support group for people dealing with an HCP.

Build Knowledge and Strategy

If you know the enemy and know yourself, you need
not fear the result of a hundred battles.

—Sun Tzu

Learn as much as you can about NPD/BPD and divorcing an HCP. One example of a useful strategy is to let the NPD feel like they have won. We know people with NPD are insanely competitive. So let the raging toddler "win" and go home happy. (Find ways they can win that are not important to you.) Ignore their gloating. What matters is winning in ways that are important to you and getting the divorce done.

I put something in the separation agreement I knew he'd want taken out.
So when he screamed about it, it came out and he thought he'd "won."

—Lynn

Another useful strategy is to pick the battles that are important to you and let the rest go. When you divorce a narcissist, you'll have to fight many battles! If you throw all of your time and energy into fighting every one of them, you'll end up broke and exhausted. You'll also stand a greater chance of losing the battles you care about most, simply because by the time the important battles come around, you'll be too drained to give them your all. Decide in the beginning which fights are worth your effort.

The Importance of Secrecy

It is absolutely essential that you keep your plan to leave a secret from the HCP as long as possible. Once they know, they will either guilt-trip and love-bomb you or sabotage you. Be aware of your behavior, because if you start distancing yourself or acting differently, you might trigger their alarm buttons.

You need to thoroughly complete all your preparations before your partner knows you're leaving.

Have a Safety Plan

Your partner could assault or evict you at any time. For your safety and your children's safety, it's crucial to create a safety plan ahead of time. If your partner has shown their violent side, keep in mind that leaving is the most dangerous time in the relationship. Figure out a safe place to go, get some ready cash, and think about who can help you on short notice. If you think that your partner may throw things or try to harm you, it's even more important that you don't signal your intention to exit. The "Leaving an Abusive Relationship" section on the US Department of Health and Human Services, Office on Women's Health, website contains information to help you make a complete plan.

Protect Documents and Valuables

One day I had to leave home after calling 911, and I haven't been able to go back to get a few personal items I really care about, like a painting my grandmother gave me. Don't make the same mistake I made. Get your important things to a safe place ASAP.

—Kelly

Once you take decisive action (or your partner does), they will likely believe you have "abandoned" them. When this happens, their splitting behavior will recast you as "all bad and always has been bad," and they may impulsively destroy any evidence or artifacts that contradict that narrative—even sweet, happy pictures of the kids.

Copy important records and keep them in a safe place. As soon as possible, secretly copy important documents, like joint bank account statements, your partner's pay stubs, tax records, lists of assets and debts, birth certificates, and so forth. When blamers are involved, valuable items may "disappear" or become damaged. Quietly move valuables to a safe location. Set aside money to live, but don't take more than your share (discuss this with your attorney). It may be a good idea to put all communications and documents on a thumb drive, so they're not on your computer hard drive and vulnerable to hacking.

Digital Protection

Protect yourself digitally. Block the HCP on all social media. Quit using any publicly accessible online social networking account that can be used against you someday. Ask your lawyer for advice on creating a secret account under a fake name, if you want to join online support groups, like Moving Forward. Make sure your passwords are secure. Change passwords for any personal accounts that they may be able to access (your own bank accounts, shopping accounts, and so on).

Collect Evidence

Begin collecting and preparing evidence immediately. HCPs are skilled liars in court, so it is vital that you prepare evidence to reveal their lies and their character. Keep it hidden in a safe place.

When author Tina Swithin was fighting for custody of her children, the court was completely charmed by her NPD husband's performance, until she showed them one piece of evidence that proved he'd lied to them: information from a tracking device she'd put in her daughter's backpack. That was the turning point when the court started taking her seriously.

Phase 2: Informing the HCP You're Leaving

To reiterate, don't tell your partner you want to separate or divorce until you have taken the first steps. The book *Splitting: Protecting Yourself While Divorcing Someone with Borderline or Narcissistic Personality Disorder* is an essential resource to prepare you. You need to be prepared and protected as much as possible before they start reacting and acting out.

Choose a place to tell them where they are more likely to behave safely—perhaps in a public place. Or, if you want to tell them at home, have another person (other than your children) somewhere in the house. High-conflict people are often very cautious about their public image, which you can use to your advantage.

Before telling them, make a list of things you will and will not do, discuss, or tolerate from your spouse. As a compassionate person, it will be difficult to stay on message when your spouse gets upset. Your message can get lost if you start caretaking them or get involved in their accusations. Stay on point by concentrating on your message—you will likely have to repeat it several times—and ignore their emotional upheavals and the garbage thrown your way. You might want to write a letter beforehand so you can plan your words (maybe with help from a therapist) and read it to them. Don't be so specific that they can seize one event and blame you for whatever happened. For example, you might say:

1. "We have been having problems in many areas for a long time."

2. "The healthiest thing for me to do is to end the marriage or relationship."

3. If they speak, validate, but come back to your point. "I can see you're upset. You have a right to all your feelings. But it's not okay to (insult me, threaten me)."

4. "Let's discuss the details at a later time. Right now, I just need to tell you my decision."

You want to give them time to absorb your plans before you discuss any details. If they make threats, ignore them. Say, "Let's not make any decisions until we both come to terms with the fact that we're breaking up." Then go back to your message. However, do take their threats seriously, such as, "I am going to tell the police that you abused me," or "I am going to take the children out of the country." If you have kids, they may say that they won't "let you" see the children. Remember that most courts want both parents to be involved.

Don't label your partner.

Do not tell your spouse or coparent (and anyone who talks to them) that you believe they have a personality disorder. We gave this advice to you in earlier chapters of this book, and it's even more important now. Labeling your partner to anyone but your most cherished helpmates will backfire on you personally and in court.

Phase 3. The HCP's Behavior Right After You Inform Them

The HCP's reaction to learning you're leaving them can seem like a mess of changing emotions and contradictions. One minute, they act like they'll die without you, and the next minute, they split you all bad. Once you understand their driving motivations, their behavior becomes clear. Lawyers and therapists experienced in dealing with NPDs and BPDs can predict many typical HCP things they'll do and help protect you.

When you leave an HCP, their prime source of narcissistic supply is threatened, their fear of abandonment operates on overdrive, and most of all, they are at a loss because they are losing control of you and the relationship. You have broken their unspoken rules. Is it any wonder they try anything to get you back or split you completely black and treat you like an enemy throughout the divorce process, or a changing mix of both?

In the preparation phase, I explained ways to protect yourself from the HCP's splitting behaviors that will likely occur after they know you're leaving and off and on throughout the breakup. Now I'll explain how to resist getting back together, breaking apart, and then getting back together over and over. This is confusing and exhausting—especially for children. This is one of the most important sections in this book. If you can resist going back over and over, you could avoid years of suffering.

Avoid Going Back

An informal survey of caretakers showed that they go through an average of seven breakup-makeup cycles. One respondent had left and gone back thirty times. This is why it is crucial that you keep a log (mental or physical) of the reasons you are leaving. When you are prone to reminiscing about the good times, substitute one of these reasons.

> *I've left and gone back more times than I can count. After the initial love-bombing, it became a monthly cycle that left me a shell of my former self. I think this is the final one because I let her know exactly how I felt and how she was treating me... That was five weeks ago, she's already moved on.*

> —Joe

> *I went back twelve times in ten years because of the love-bombing, but this time I got an order of protection, and I haven't spoken to him since he came to my workplace and told my bosses he was going to call the FBI on me.*

> —Tracey

> *I served him with papers last month. His gaslighting, hoovering, and blaming are limitless. I am so sad. I feel overrun. I don't stand up to him. I should be angry, but I am too sad.*

> —Rachel

To bring you back to the relationship, HCPs may threaten suicide, promise to attend therapy, pretend to be the romantic person you fell in love with, or show up at your home with donuts for breakfast (true story). They may call you for unimportant reasons to keep a connection going, even if it's a bad connection. People with BPD do this because they fear abandonment. This is often called "hoovering" because they are trying to suck you back into the relationship like a Hoover vacuum cleaner.

*She threatened to kill herself several times over the years including
making a video with a pile of tablets in front of her. She wanted pity
because her lies had been outed. She never went through with it. After
I started calling 911 each time she threatened suicide, she stopped.*

—Anthony

*He held a loaded gun to his head when I had just come home from the
hospital with our third child. My kids were four, two, and newborn.
When my youngest was six, I was feeling strong enough to leave.
Then I got pregnant again. Ten years later, I left with the kids. He
threatened suicide, and I went back. Thirty years later, my oldest
child has NPD, my second child had a suicide attempt, and my
youngest has agoraphobia. I hate myself for not saving my children.*

—Stacy

No Contact

The objectives of having no contact with your soon-to-be ex are to:

- avoid emotional abuse and manipulation by the HCP
- deny the HCP any chance or hope of violating your boundaries
- protect yourself legally
- protect yourself from smear campaigns
- deescalate negativity, for your adult children's sake (with minors and shared custody, you will need to use low contact methods, described later in this chapter)
- avoid even *thinking* about the HCP
- get over them

To this end, you need to avoid any discussions about the HCP or any interactions with the HCP, including the following ways:

- in private, in person
- through technology
- by snail mail

- in discussions with other people

- in public, such as at events you both attend

Privately (In Person and via Technology)

- Don't talk to them or let them talk to you, no matter what. This includes not sending or listening to voicemail messages (delete without listening if it's not about child logistics).

- Change your phone number and block it from showing up on caller ID. Don't share it with anyone you can't trust to not tell the HCP. Go through a third party if communication is necessary.

- Never answer phone calls that don't have a caller ID.

- Only communicate through your lawyers.

- Don't allow the HCP in your house and stay away from their home. If possible, move with no forwarding address.

- Ignore all sentimental or revenge impulses to inform them of big events, such as getting married, having a baby, getting a new job, or your children's happy milestones. Ignore such events in their life.

- Ignore them on holidays, birthdays, anniversaries.

- Prevent and avoid all visits, even hospital visits.Completely block them on all social media and other technology, including email. Remember, essential communication is possible through your lawyer.

Snail Mail

- Resist sentimental or revenge impulses to send any birthday, holiday, mother's or father's day cards, letters, or gifts.

- Return any mail or gifts, unopened, with "return to sender" and "addressee unknown" written in someone else's handwriting on the package.

Other People

- Ask everyone to never mention the HCP, no matter what. Period. If necessary, explain the objectives of "no contact" to them. If relatives or friends care about you, they will respect this boundary.

In Public

- Politely avoid them at family events, such as weddings. Be the classier person and quietly walk away. If necessary, ask a friend or relative to keep the HCP away from you.

- If you run into them on the street, turn and walk away. If they follow you, go to the nearest police station.

Beware of the trauma bond. Angie is a life skills coach who's read many books about HCPs and caretakers, so it was a shock to her when she broke up with her BPD boyfriend and proceeded to do all the wrong things. "I can't believe I've already broken 'no contact' after one week! This is way harder than I thought it would be. My mind knows what I need to do, but the rest of me is being stupid. It's like I'm under some kind of spell."

If, like Angie, you feel like you're under a spell, remember:

- You are not stupid. The "spell" is your caretaker programming from childhood combined with the trauma bond from your abusive relationship. These landmines hide deep in your subconscious, invisibly and powerfully controlling your emotions.

- Your knowledge is intellectual, but your programming is emotional. Even highly informed caretakers cannot use intellect to break an emotional "spell."

- The only way to undo the powerful emotional programming of your subconscious is to work with a therapist who understands HCPs and trauma bonding. A therapist can help you remember you deserve happiness and freedom from a relationship that drags you down.

- Therapy takes time, so in the meantime, your only hope of staying free is to remain "no contact." This is the only way to prevent your HCP from triggering your emotional programming and activating the "spell."

Therapist Genevieve McMath (2023) explains the technique she advises her clients use to cope with guilt and resist hoovering: "Guilt is not a good reason to stay in a relationship. It is important that the HCP be told, by the person leaving, that there will be no circumstance under which the relationship will be reconciled. When I am counseling individuals who are breaking-up with an HCP, I recommend they tell their HCP that, although they might be able to be friendly with them at some point in the future when the dust settles, for a minimum of three months post breakup, they will only communicate with them as necessary.

The HCP will likely try multiple strategies to get the person to drop this boundary. It is important to hold your boundary no matter what happens. In most cases the HCP's attempts to get the person to drop their boundaries will burnout within a couple of weeks."

> *He has never been so nice. I have a mental list of five specific things I have purposely chosen to think about every time I feel my heart slipping toward falling for it. These are five disgustingly horrific things he has done to me and our child. This tool has kept me strong for longer than I've ever been able to be while in this exact stage of our breakup.*
>
> —Maria

Avoid sex with your soon-to-be-ex. Having sex confuses things and could result in pregnancy. Having a child will tie you with the HCP for many years, if not a lifetime, and give that child a toxic parent.

No matter what they've promised you, the HCP hasn't magically cured their dysfunctional ways of thinking, feeling, and behaving. Their promised changes never last very long once you've agreed to give the relationship one more try.

Phase 4. The HCP's Behavior During the Breakup or Divorce

You can anticipate your HCP's behavior during the breakup or divorce by understanding what's driving their motivation. From Bill's experience, people with BPD and "vulnerable" narcissists (described in chapter 1) are driven more by their upset emotions, and their high-conflict behavior is volatile. Their "hot anger" often gets them into trouble, and what triggers their hot anger is often predictable. On the other hand, grandiose narcissists and HCPs with antisocial personalities can be mean and predatory, planning ways to get back at their partners for nonexistent bad behavior or exaggerations. They seem to have "cold anger," which can be worse than hot anger because they may really set up their partner for humiliation or violence if they feel offended, which they often feel when someone has the audacity to leave them.

Vulnerable narcissism is rooted more in poor self-esteem, although the person living with the condition often appears outwardly confident. Since vulnerable narcissists have low self-esteem, providing some reassurance may make them less prone to being complete devils.

Common HCP Behavior During a Breakup or Divorce

Smear campaigns. Because of splitting, high conflict people may imagine that you did bad things to them, or they may simply make things up. They then use these stories to try to turn mutual friends and family against you. In some cases, people who have heard these false allegations join the HCP in spreading lies. HCPs can be extremely persuasive because they come to believe their own lies.

Don't assume that the people your HCP talks to will realize that what is being said is absurd. Some will believe it and hold it against you. If the HCP communicates a smear message to people you know, immediately send those people a clarifying BIFF (brief, informative, friendly, firm) message like the following:

> You have received an email from my ex, which includes many inaccurate statements. Our separation (or divorce) is a private matter, and you don't need to get involved at all. If you have any concerns that their statements are true, or have any concerns at all, please feel free to contact me so I can clarify what is going on. I appreciate your friendship and support.

For more information about BIFF responses, see chapter 7 and the book *BIFF for CoParent Communication*, by Bill Eddy, Annette Burns, and Kevin Chafin, which contains twenty-eight sample BIFF responses for almost any common coparenting situation, including smear campaigns.

Once you've sent the clarifying BIFF message, let go of caring what people think about you. Remember how you were fooled by the HCP at first? They'll probably figure out the truth at some point. Meanwhile, focus on the loyal people who know you and love you.

Be mindful of venting about your feelings to mutual friends or family members who may still be in contact with your spouse. Your spouse might try to solicit others to "check on you," only to use that information against you later. In addition, negative gossip tends to perpetuate ongoing feelings of anger and helplessness. Remember: Keep calm and win.

Suicide threats. HCPs go right to the most extreme thoughts in difficult situations as part of their all-or-nothing thinking. Suicide threats must always be taken seriously. Express concern for them, but tell them you cannot be responsible for if they live or die. It's too much responsibility. It really isn't a relationship if one half of the couple is only staying in the relationship because of emotional blackmail.

Encourage the HCP to talk with a counselor to deal with the stress they are under. See a counselor yourself if you are not sure how to deal with your suicidal HCP.

Do not diagnose. Never label the HCP as a BPD or NPD in court. If you and your spouse are going through psychological evaluations, don't tell the interviewer you think your spouse has BPD/NPD. Court personnel expect each party to be critical of the other, so it will be labeled as "he said, she said" allegations. What you can do, however, is use buzzwords that they will recognize: for example, "fear of abandonment," "black-and-white thinking," a "sense of entitlement," and so forth. Let them connect the dots for themselves.

False allegations. Men are often at risk of false allegations at the time of separation, such as of domestic violence or child abuse. Women are often at risk of being accused of parental alienation (badmouthing the father) or making false allegations. Because courts want to err on the side of caution, they will often issue a restraining order (protective order) against the accused just to be safe, even though allegations may be based on lies or exaggerations. Careful planning and good recordkeeping can help regarding incidents that could be exaggerated or manufactured. *Splitting: Protecting Yourself While Divorcing Someone with Borderline or Narcissistic Personality Disorder* goes into more detail about times of high risk and what you can do to protect yourself.

Bias against fathers? Many fathers have experienced a negative outcome in a custody dispute because of gender bias in the court system. Until the twenty-first century, the belief in women's "natural superiority" with regard to child-care frequently served as a legal argument for the award of sole custody to mothers. The laws have changed in order to be gender neutral, but the belief often remains, depending primarily on the state and the professionals handling your case. Meanwhile, countless studies have shown the positive impact engaged fathers have on their children. Fathers have a positive influence on their children's social competence, performance in school, and emotion regulation. For children of HCP mothers, their father may be their only protection from a traumatically damaging childhood. Studies show that fathers are pillars in the development of a child's emotional well-being, for example (Landsford 2021):

- An involved father promotes inner growth and strength.

- Affectionate and supportive fathers greatly affect a child's cognitive and social development and instill an overall sense of well-being and self-confidence. Children with sensitive and supportive fathers have higher levels of social competence and better peer relationships.

- The way a father treats his child influences what the child looks for in adult relationships. The patterns a father sets in the relationships with his child will dictate how his child relates with other people.

Bias against mothers? In recent years, many courts have tried to compensate for their previous bias against fathers in parenting issues by becoming biased against mothers. If an HCP father raises concerns about the mother, some courts have a higher standard for how women should behave and a higher tolerance for the father's poor behavior. In Bill's experience, if a father makes a claim for primary parenting time, he is more likely to get it because the spotlight is drawn to the mother and the question of whether she is defective in her parenting by looking at every little flaw. However, if a father makes a claim for 50-50 parenting time, which means there is nothing wrong with either parent and the father is more likely to be the focus of attention especially if he started with less than 50% of the parenting time.

There are cases in which a father has argued parental alienation by the mother when in fact the mother was being protective and the father was a poor parent, abusive toward the child, or violent with the mother.

Cases of resistance or refusal. One of the biggest issues in family courts these days is that of a child resisting or refusing contact with one of their parents. Historically, such children have resisted contact with their father primarily, but in recent years they often are resisting contact with their mothers almost as often. The source of this resistance can be very controversial, because on the surface the child's resistant behavior looks the same whether: 1) the driving cause is one parent engaged in alienating behaviors with the child against the other parent (the "rejected" parent) through badmouthing and interference with their parenting time, or 2) the driving cause is the rejected parent's own dysfunctional or abusive behavior (child abuse or domestic violence) toward the child or other parent.

It is essential that you are careful not to engage in badmouthing the other parent around the child or abusive behavior toward the child (including emotionally abusive behavior). It is also essential that you are prepared for the HCP parent to engage in exactly these behaviors and try to blame you for them in court. Consult with or retain a local lawyer to find out how your court system and judges handle cases like this. For more on this topic, see the book, *Don't Alienate the Kids: Raising Resilient Children While Avoiding High-Conflict Divorce, 2nd Edition* by Bill Eddy (2020).

Ways You Can Protect Your Children

HCPs who've shown no interest in their children often try to get custody for two reasons: to hurt you and to avoid paying child support. When the HCP starts emotionally manipulating the children or trying to turn them against you, they will urgently need a neutral adult they can trust. For this reason, get your children a therapist who understands HCPs as soon as possible.

Children of a HCP are at high risk of being psychologically damaged, and the best way to protect them is to get them a good therapist, whether you leave or stay. Your own behavior during the breakup or divorce process can help your children or unintentionally make things harder for them, so it's important for you to get advice from the children's therapist.

Meanwhile here are some important dos and don'ts.

Don't:

- Say anything negative about your partner in front of the children, no matter how provoked you might be.

- Ask your children questions about the other parent.

- Discuss court with your children or within their hearing.

- Ask your children to compare you and your partner.

- Give your children choices between their two parents.

- Expose your children to your negative emotions.

Do:

- Give your children a safe space to process their thoughts and feelings.

- Provide a sense of consistency by maintaining their normal routines as much as possible.

- Read *Raising Resilient Children with a Borderline or Narcissistic Parent* by Margalis Fjelstad and Jean McBride.

- Give your children positive "you-talk" frequently. (Shad Helmstetter's book, *Predictive Parenting: What to Say When You Talk to Your Kids*, explains why and how to do this.)

Unfortunately, if you are coparenting with an HCP, you do not have the luxury of going "no contact" with them. However, there are ways to maintain "low contact" that can minimize your contact with them and prevent the HCP from creating drama and stress for your children.

One approach that Bill recommends is "parallel parenting," which usually has to be court ordered to be most effective, but some parents do this by agreement with the help of their lawyers. With parallel parenting, the parents have very little contact with each other throughout the year. When the children are with one parent, the other parent does not contact them, and the children don't contact that other parent. No phone calls, emails, texts, etc., unless there is an emergency. This way, the parents are not engaged in conflicts and the children are not exposed to the other parent's manipulations. The parents rarely contact each other except for necessary decisions regarding healthcare and school. The regular parenting schedule is followed rigidly, without flexibility for changing the schedule which would otherwise involve an HCP parent constantly trying to get the other parent to make changes as a form of harassment and contact.

Another form of low contact is to limit emails to one per day, one subject only. (HCP parents often like to raise endless topics all day long.) The BIFF method of emails is recommended, as mentioned earlier in this book, which means keeping them brief, informative, friendly, and firm.

Limiting exchanges of the children to the school or even a supervised exchange location can minimize contact. This way you rarely have to see the coparent, which avoids harassment and arguments.

Overall, consult with a local lawyer about how you can arrange a low contact relationship with the other parent and whether getting a court order for this will be necessary. Sometimes HCP parents are agreeable at first, but cannot follow their agreements, so that stronger court orders are necessary.

Phase 5. Healing After You Leave

Guidance about the process of healing from a relationship with an HCP requires an entire book to do it justice. For more resources, visit http://www .stopwalkingoneggshells.com/resources. The usual elements for healing from a traumatic experience are needed for caretakers (therapy, journaling, spending time nature, having a support network, self-care), but additionally, you need to understand some key factors that can confuse and hinder a caretaker's healing after leaving an HCP.

Landmines in Your Psyche

The HCP and, before them, someone in your childhood, have made you believe negative, distorted things about yourself and the world, and you are not consciously aware of these beliefs. Only time and working with a therapist who understands HCP abuse, C-PTSD, and trauma bonding can track down these landmines that dysfunctional people buried in your psyche and defuse them. Only a therapist can help you resist the compulsion to stay in contact with the HCP.

> Over the years since I started therapy, the landscape of people in my life has completely changed. I'm surrounded by caring, positive people. Therapy helped me see which friends, family members, and other people (even my boss!) were unhealthy for me and either remove them or set boundaries. My mother hated my boundaries, so she cut me off. It hurt, but looking back, it was like a dark cloud lifted. I now know how to protect my happiness no matter what, and this gives me beautiful peace of mind. I could not have reached this point without therapy. Now I really am free. I've healed my life.
>
> —Sierra

Many caretakers use relationships like bandages to distract themselves from other problems. The good feeling of giving and helping another person can help a caretaker ignore guilt or sadness over not improving their own life, education, career, finances, and so forth. Your therapist can help you with goals in these areas.

Now is your chance to jump off the hamster wheel of toxic relationships and heal your life. A one-year sabbatical from dating could be the most valuable gift you ever give yourself.

Don't Skip Telling Your Story

The things the HCP did are so bizarre, no one would believe it...except others who've lived with an HCP. You've probably wondered if you imagined things, if it was your fault, if it was really that bad, or if you are crazy. It is essential to talk about what you went through and get validation from other survivors of high-conflict relationships. Other survivors are the only ones who really understand how petty and insidiously hurtful HCPs' behavior can be. Non-survivors might think you're overreacting to a grain of sand, but survivors know that's a grain of sand in a vast beach of pain.

The magic of support groups is that, beyond receiving validation that you're not crazy or overreacting, you also will hear the stories of many other people. This gives you insights you can't get in individual therapy.

Everything I've seen in these online support groups has been truly eye-opening. I felt like I was in a twilight zone and going crazy. And finally calling out the characteristics and seeing the same answers everyone else experiences made me feel like I'm not crazy anymore.

—Janice

Don't Get Stuck Telling Your Story

There can be a dangerous paradox with telling your story. It feels good to receive validation and compassion, and it's an essential phase in your healing process. For some abuse survivors, their story becomes a self-limiting part of their identity. Without realizing it, they begin to feel an emotional reward when they tell their story, long after the healing benefits of the validation phase. Anyone who has survived abuse deserves to be admired, but that admiration can become addictive. Without realizing it, people become trapped in their memories and emotions of suffering, which are relived each time they tell their story.

Take as long as you need to tell your story and heal during this important phase, and know that you deserve all the admiration in the world—but also know that someday, you will want to stop telling your story so the negative memories no longer drag you down. At some point, let people admire you for reasons related to all the positive things about you.

The morning after Elizabeth Smart was rescued from her kidnappers (at age fifteen)—including from their leader, who had raped her repeatedly for nine months—her mother said to her: "Elizabeth, what this man has done is terrible... But the best punishment you could ever give him is to be happy. To move forward with your life. To do exactly what you want" (Smart 2014). She described what might happen in the trial, and how justice may or may not be served, and then said, "You be happy, Elizabeth. Just be happy. If you go and feel sorry for yourself, or if you dwell on what happened, if you hold on to your pain, that is allowing him to steal more of your life away. So don't you do that! Don't you let him! There is no way that he deserves that" (Smart 2014).

In your thoughts, tell yourself this: *After a lifetime of sacrifice, I have earned a year to be selfish. If being selfish is the only way to fix my life, so be it.*

When others call you selfish, reply in a relaxed and cheerful manner: "Yes. I'm a selfish person now." Expect some people to intensify their efforts to guilt-trip you and then have a tantrum when they realize they can no longer control you. Stay strong. You are the opposite of selfish. You are a beautiful soul, a giver who only *feels* selfish. Let this be your mantra for one year: "Feel the selfish and do it anyway."

You have a wonderful future ahead of you, Amazing Person. I wish you deep joy on your journey.

Acknowledgments

I am thankful to Bill Eddy, the co-author of this book, for all the help he has given me since I realized I needed to add content about narcissistic personality disorder (NPD) in my books, website, and so on. More importantly, he put together the whole concept of high conflict people. I use it a bit more broadly than he does, but I think it works well in the book.

Margalis Fjelstad is another person whom I couldn't do without. She doesn't use the term high conflict person, but she writes about the same people I do. I'm so grateful for her books and her advice.

Two other people deserve a special mention for their contributions to *Stop Walking on Eggshells for Partners*. First, a heartfelt thanks to Silvia Wilde, founder of Happyology Academy (happology.ca). As someone who divorced a spouse with Narcissistic Personality Disorder, Silvia provided unique additional insights. I also thank Genevieve McMath, MSW, a psychiatric nurse with a private practice specializing in helping spouses and family members of BPDs, for her important contributions.

References

Altınok, A., and N. Kılıç. 2020. "Exploring the Associations Between Narcissism, Intentions Towards Infidelity, and Relationship Satisfaction: Attachment Styles as a Moderator." *PLOS One* 15(11): e0242277.

American Psychological Association. 2019. "Mindfulness Meditation: A Research-Proven Way to Reduce Stress." APA, October 30. https://www.apa.org/topics/mindfulness/meditation.

Berg-Nielsen, T. S., and L. Wichström. 2012. "The Mental Health of Preschoolers in a Norwegian Population-Based Study When Their Parents Have Symptoms of Borderline, Antisocial, and Narcissistic Personality Disorders: At the Mercy of Unpredictability." *Child and Adolescent Psychiatry and Mental Health* 6(1): 19.

Boyan, S. 2017. Personal communication, telephone interview..

Canadian Mental Health Association. 2014. "Borderline Personality Disorder." https://bc.cmha.ca/documents/borderline-personality-disorder-2.

Carnes, P. 2019. *The Betrayal Bond: Breaking Free from Exploitive Relationships*, revised ed. Deerfield Beach, FL: Health Communications.

Ceder, J. 2022. "Why Your Child May Need to See a Therapist." Verywell Family. https://www.verywellfamily.com/signs-your-child-may-need-a-therapist-4130486.

Center for Substance Abuse Treatment. 2014. "Understanding the Impact of Trauma." In *Trauma-Informed Care in Behavioral Health Services*. Rockville, MD: Substance Abuse and Mental Health Services Administration.

Cherkasova, M. V., L. Clark, J. J. S. Barton, M. Schulzer, M. Shafiee, A. Kingstone, A. J. Stoessl, and C. A. Winstanley. 2018. "Win-Concurrent

Sensory Cues Can Promote Riskier Choice." *Journal of Neuroscience* 38(48): 10362–10370.

Cochran, K. 2017. Personal communication, telephone interview.

Davies, J. 2017. "Brainwashing: Signs That You Are Being Brainwashed (Without Even Realizing It)." *Learning Mind* (blog), April 8. https://www.learning-mind.com/brainwashing-signs.

Davis, D. M., and J. Hayes. 2012. "What Are the Benefits of Mindfulness." American Psychological Association, *Monitor on Psychology* 43(7): 64. https://www.apa.org/monitor/2012/07-08-ce-corner.

Davis, T. 2019. "Develop Authenticity: 20 Ways to Be a More Authentic Person." *Psychology Today*, April 15. https://www.psychologytoday .com/us/blog/click-here-happiness/201904/develop-authenticity -20-ways-be-more-authentic-person.

Dugan, M. K., and R. R. Hock. 2006. *It's My Life Now: Starting Over After an Abusive Relationship or Domestic Violence*, 2nd ed. New York: Routledge.

Eddy, B. 2018. *5 Types of People Who Can Ruin Your Life: Identifying and Dealing with Narcissists, Sociopaths, and Other High-Conflict Personalities.* New York: TarcherPerigee.

———. 2020. *Don't Alienate the Kids: Raising Resilient Children While Avoiding High-Conflict Divorce*, 2nd ed. Scottsdale, AZ: Unhooked Books.

———. 2021. *Calming Upset People with EAR: How Statements Showing Empathy, Attention and Respect Can Quickly Defuse a Conflict.* Scottsdale, AZ: Unhooked Books.

Eddy, B., A. T. Burns, and K. Chafin. 2020. *BIFF For Coparent Communication: Your Guide to Difficult Texts, Emails, and Social Media Posts.* Scottsdale, AZ: Unhooked Books.

Eddy, B., and R. Kreger. 2011. *Splitting: Protecting Yourself While Divorcing Someone with Borderline or Narcissistic Personality Disorder.* Oakland, CA: New Harbinger Publications.

Encyclopaedia Britannica. 2023. "Limbic System." *Britannica.* https://www.britannica.com/science/limbic-system.

Engel, B. 2002. *The Emotionally Abusive Relationship: How to Stop Being Abused and How to Stop Abusing.* Hoboken, NJ: John Wiley and Sons.

Fjelstad, M. 2013. *Stop Caretaking the Borderline or Narcissist.* Lanham, MD: Rowman & Littlefield.

Fjelstad, M., and J. McBride. 2020. *Raising Resilient Children with a Borderline or Narcissistic Parent.* Lanham, MD: Rowman & Littlefield.

Freyd, J. J. 1997. "Violations of Power, Adaptive Blindness, and Betrayal Trauma Theory." *Feminism & Psychology* 7(1): 22–32.

Friedel, R. O., L. F. Fox, and K. Friedel. 2018. *Borderline Personality Disorder Demystified: An Essential Guide for Understanding and Living with BPD,* rev. ed. New York: Da Capo Lifelong Books.

Friedman, E. H. 1990. "The Bridge." In *Friedman's Fables.* New York: Guilford Press.

Gilles, G. 2018. "Understanding Complex Post-Traumatic Stress Disorder." *Healthline,* September 29. https://www.healthline.com/health/cptsd.

Gottman, J. M., and N. Silver. 1999. *The Seven Principles for Making Marriage Work: A Practical Guide from the Country's Foremost Relationship Expert.* New York: Three Rivers Press.

Grant, B. F., S. P. Chou, R. B. Goldstein, B. Huang, F. S. Stinson, T. D. Saha, S. M. Smith, et al. 2008. "Prevalence, Correlates, Disability, and Comorbidity of DSM-IV Borderline Personality Disorder. Results from the Wave 2 Epidemiologic Survey on Alcohol and Related Conditions." *Journal of Clinical Psychiatry* 69(4): 533–545.

Greenberg, S. 2021. "The 10 Most Important Components of Self-Compassion." *Clearer Thinking,* October 20. https://www.clearerthinking.org/post/the-10-most-important-components-of-self-compassion.

Greenburg, E. 2021. Personal communication, email. December.

Hall, J. L. 2022. "Insecure Attachment in Children of Narcissists." *Psychology Today,* October 20. https://www.psychologytoday.com/us/blog/the-narcissist-in-your-life/202210/insecure-attachment-in-children-narcissists.

Hayes, S. C., and S. Smith. 2005. *Get Out of Your Mind and Into Your Life: The New Acceptance and Commitment Therapy.* Oakland, CA: New Harbinger Publications.

Hazelden Betty Ford Foundation. 2021. "The Five Most Common Trademarks of Codependent and Enabling Relationships." September 7. https://www.hazeldenbettyford.org/articles/enabling-fact-sheet.

Hendrix, H. 1988. *Getting the Love You Want: A Guide for Couples.* New York: Henry Holt.

Hobson, P. R., M. Patrick, L. Crandell, R. Garcia-Perez, and A. Lee. 2005. "Personal Relatedness and Attachment in Infants of Mothers with Borderline Personality Disorder." *Development and Psychopathology* 17: 329–347.

Kaimal, G., K. Ray, and J. Muniz. 2016. "Reduction of Cortisol Levels and Participants' Responses Following Art Making." *Art Therapy* 33(2): 74–80.

Kalman, I. 2014. Personal communication, email.

Kendler, K., S. Aggen, N. Czajkowski, E. Roysamb, K. Tambs, S. Torgersen, M. Neale, and T. Reichborn-Kjennerud. 2008. "The Structure of Genetic and Environmental Risk Factors for *DSM-IV* Personality Disorders: A Multivariate Twin Study." *Archives of General Psychiatry* 65(2): 1438–1446.

Kreger, R. 2008. *The Essential Family Guide to Borderline Personality Disorder: New Tools and Techniques to Stop Walking on Eggshells.* Center City, MN: Hazelden.

Kreger, R., C. Adamec, and D. S. Lobel. 2022. *Stop Walking on Eggshells for Parents: How to Help Your Child (of Any Age) with Borderline Personality Disorder without Losing Yourself.* Oakland, CA: New Harbinger Publications.

Kreisman, J. J. 2018. *Talking to a Loved One with Borderline Personality Disorder: Communication Skills to Manage Intense Emotions, Set Boundaries, and Reduce Conflict.* Oakland, CA: New Harbinger Publications.

Kvarnstrom, E. 2015. "Being Raise by a Mother with Borderline Personality Disorder." *Bridges to Recovery Beverly Hills* (blog), December 11.

https://www.bridgestorecovery.com/blog/being-raised-by-a-mother
-with-borderline-personality-disorder.

Lansford, J. E. 2021. "The Importance of Fathers for Child Development."
Psychology Today, June 15. https://www.psychologytoday.com/us/blog
/parenting-and-culture/202106/the-importance-fathers-child-development.

Lawson, C. A. 2000. *Understanding the Borderline Mother: Helping Her
Children Transcend the Intense, Unpredictable, and Volatile Relationship.*
Lanham, MD: Rowman & Littlefield.

Layton, J., and A. Hoyt. 2023. "How Brainwashing Works." *How Stuff Works*,
September 7. https://science.howstuffworks.com/life/inside-the-mind/
human-brain/brainwashing.htm.

Leonard, J. 2022. "Complex Post-Traumatic Stress Disorder (Complex
PTSD)." *Medical News Today*, December 23. https://www.medicalnews
today.com/articles/322886.

Leotti, L. A., S. S. Iyengar, and K. N. Ochsner. 2010. "Born to Choose:
The Origins and Value of the Need for Control." *Trends in Cognitive Sciences*
14(10): 457–463.

Lerner, H. G. 2014. *The Dance of Anger: A Woman's Guide to Changing the
Patterns of Intimate Relationships,* rev. ed. New York: William Morrow.

Linehan, M. M. 2014. *DBT Skills Training: Handouts and Worksheets.*
New York: Guilford Press.

Macfie, J. 2009. Call-in educational presentation at the National Education
Alliance for Borderline Personality Disorder.

———. 2012. "Mothers with BPD and Their Children's Development:
What Do We Know?" Call-in educational presentation at the National
Education Alliance for Borderline Personality Disorder.

Marks, H. 2023. "Stress Symptoms." *WebMD*, October 8. https://www
.webmd.com/balance/stress-management/stress-symptoms-effects
_of-stress-on-the-body.

Mason, P. T. T., and R. Kreger. 2020. *Stop Walking on Eggshells: Taking Your
Life Back When Someone You Care About Has Borderline Personality Disorder,*
3rd ed. Oakland, CA: New Harbinger Publications.

Mayo Clinic. 2022. "Friendships: Enrich Your Life and Improve Your Health."
January 12. https://www.mayoclinic.org/healthy-lifestyle/adult-health/in
-depth/friendships/art-20044860.

————. 2023a. "Stress Symptoms: Effects on Your Body and Behavior."
August 10. https://www.mayoclinic.org/healthy-lifestyle/stress
-management/in-depth/stress-symptoms/art-20050987.

————. 2023b. "Exercise: 7 Benefits of Regular Physical Activity." August 26.
https://www.mayoclinic.org/healthy-lifestyle/fitness/in-depth/exercise
/art-20048389.

McBride, K. 2018. "How Narcissistic Parenting Can Affect Children."
Psychology Today, February 19. https://www.psychologytoday.com
/us/blog/the-legacy-of-distorted-love/201802/how-narcissistic
-parenting-can-affect-children.

McLeod, S. 2023. "What Is Operant Conditioning and How Does It Work?
How Reinforcement and Punishment Modify Behavior." *Simply
Psychology*, October 18. https://www.simplypsychology.org/operant
-conditioning.html.

McMath, G. 2023. Personal communication, author interview. June 28.

Meyer, D. R., M. J. Carlson, M. M. Ul Alam. 2022. "Increases in Shared
Custody After Divorce in the United States." *Demographic Research*
46(38): 1137–1162.

Mental Health Systems (MHS). 2021. "Emotional Abuse vs. Physical Abuse."
The MHS Journals (blog), May 14. https://www.mhs-dbt.com/blog/
emotional-abuse-vs-physical-abuse.

Mirza, D. 2017. *The Covert Passive-Aggressive Narcissist: Recognizing the
Traits and Finding Healing After Hidden Emotional and Psychological Abuse.*
Monument, CO: Self Place Publishing.

National Child Traumatic Stress Network (NCTSN). n.d. "About Child
Trauma." *NCTSN.* https://www.nctsn.org/what-is-child-trauma/about
-child-trauma.

National Coalition Against Domestic Violence (NCADV). n.d. "Signs of
Abuse." *NCADV.* https://ncadv.org/signs-of-abuse. Accessed
January 2024.

National Domestic Violence Hotline. n.d. "Warning Signs of Abuse: Know What to Look For." https://www.thehotline.org/identify-abuse /domestic-abuse-warning-signs. Accessed January 2024.

———. n.d. "Identifying and Overcoming Trauma Bonds." https://www .thehotline.org/resources/trauma-bonds-what-are-they-and-how-can -we-overcome-them. Accessed January 2024.

National Health Service (UK). n.d. "Complex PTSD." https://www.nhs.uk /mental-health/conditions/post-traumatic-stress-disorder-ptsd/complex. Accessed December 2023.

Neff, K. 2011. *Self-Compassion: The Proven Power of Being Kind to Yourself.* New York: William Morrow.

Neuharth, D. 2017. "14 Ways Narcissists Can Be Like Cult Leaders." *PsychCentral*, March 20. https://psychcentral.com/blog/narcissism -decoded/2017/03/14-ways-narcissists-can-be-like-cult-leaders.

Newman, S. 1993. *Little Things Long Remembered.* New York: Crown Archetype.

Office on Women's Health. n.d. "Leaving an Abusive Relationship." US Department of Health and Human Services, Office of the Assistant Secretary for Health. https://www.womenshealth.gov/relationships -and-safety/domestic-violence/leaving-abusive-relationship.

Paul, M. 2019. *The Inner Bonding Workbook: Six Steps to Healing Yourself and Connecting with Your Divine Guidance.* Oakland, CA: New Harbinger Publications.

Pedersen, T. 2017. "Witnessing Parental Psychological Abuse May Do More Harm Than Physical Abuse." *PsychCentral*, May 16. https://psychcentral .com/news/2017/05/16/witnessing-parental-psychological-abuse-may-do -more-harm-than-physical-abuse.

Petfield, L., H. Startup, H. Droscher, and S. Cartwright-Hatton. 2015. "Parenting in Mothers with Borderline Personality Disorder and Impact on Child Outcomes." *Evidence-Based Mental Health* 18(3): 67–75.

Polcari, A., K. Rabiet, E. Bolger, and M. H. Teicher. 2014. "Parental Verbal Affection and Verbal Aggression in Childhood Differentially Influence

Psychiatric Symptoms and Wellbeing in Young Adulthood." *Child Abuse and Neglect* 38(1): 91–102.

Potter, D. n.d. "STOP: One-Minute Breathing Space." *Palouse Mindfulness.* https://palousemindfulness.com/docs/STOP.pdf.

Psychology Today. n.d. "Attachment." https://www.psychologytoday.com /us/basics/attachment.

Robinson, L., M. Smith, and J. Segal. 2023. "Emotional and Psychological Trauma." *HelpGuide*, June 6. https://www.helpguide.org/articles/ptsd -trauma/coping-with-emotional-and-psychological-trauma.htm.

Ross, J. A., and J. Corcoran. 2011. *Joint Custody with a Jerk: Raising a Child with an Uncooperative Ex.* New York: St. Martin's Griffin Press.

Saeed, K. 2017. "It Hasn't Gotten Bad Enough for Me to Leave— A Reality Check." Kim Saeed (blog). https://kimsaeed.com/2017/01 /03/hasnt-gotten-bad-enough-leave-reality-check.

Sander, L. 2019. "The Case for Finally Cleaning Your Desk." *Harvard Business Review*, March 25. https://hbr.org/2019/03/the-case-for -finally-cleaning-your-desk.

Sansone, R. A., and L. A. Sansone. 2011. "Gender Patterns in Borderline Personality Disorder." *Innovations in Clinical Neuroscience* 8(5): 16–20.

Scott, E. 2020. "The Benefits of Art Therapy for Mental Health." *Verywell Mind.* Updated January 12, 2024. https://www.verywellmind.com/art -therapy-relieve-stress-by-being-creative-3144581.

Selby, E. A., and T. E. Joiner. 2009. "Cascades of Emotion: The Emergence of Borderline Personality Disorder from Emotional and Behavioral Dysregulation." *Review of General Psychology* 13(3): 219.

Segerstrom, S. C., A. L. Stanton, L. E. Alden, and B. E. Shortridge. 2003. "A Multidimensional Structure for Repetitive Thought: What's on Your Mind, and How, and How Much?" *Journal of Personality and Social Psychology* 85(5): 909–921.

Seltzer, L. F. 2017. "What's 'Emotional Reasoning'—And Why Is It Such a Problem?" *Psychology Today*, June 21. https://www.psychologytoday.com

/us/blog/evolution-the-self/201706/what-s-emotional-reasoning-and
-why-is-it-such-problem.

Siegel, J. P. 2000. *What Children Learn from Their Parents' Marriage.*
New York: HarperCollins.

Skerritt, R. 2005. *Tears and Healing: The Journey to the Light After an Abusive
Relationship.* Kennett Square, PA: Dalkeith Press.

Smart, E., and C. Stewart. 2014. *My Story: Elizabeth Smart.* New York:
St. Martin's Press.

Štajner, E. 2018. "Part IV: Interaction Between BPD Mother and Child."
Eva Stanjer (blog), December 21. http://www.psychotherapeutic.help
/2018/12/21/part-iv-interaction-between-bpd-mother-and-child.

Stepp, S. D., D. J. Whalen, P. A. Pilkonis, A. E. Hipwell, and M. D. Levine.
2012. "Children of Mothers with Borderline Personality Disorder:
Identifying Parenting Behaviors as Potential Targets for Intervention."
Personality Disorders 3(1): 76–91.

Stern, R. 2018. *The Gaslight Effect: How to Spot and Survive the Hidden
Manipulation Others Use to Control Your Life.* New York: Harmony.

Taylor, K. 2004. *Brainwashing: The Science of Thought Control.* Oxford, UK:
Oxford University Press.

Tinman, O. 2005. *One Way Ticket to Kansas: Caring About Someone with
Borderline Personality Disorder and Finding a Healthy You.* Highland, CA:
Bebes and Gregory Publications.

Torgersen, S., S. Lygren, P. A. Oien, I. Skre, S. Onstad, J. Edvardsen,
K. Tambs, and E. Kringlen. 2000. "A Twin Study of Personality Disorders."
Comparative Psychiatry 41(6): 416–425.

United Nations. n.d. "What Is Domestic Abuse?" https://www.un.org/en
/coronavirus/what-is-domestic-abuse.

United States Conference of Catholic Bishops (USCCB). 2002. "When I
Call for Help: A Pastoral Response to Domestic Violence Against Women."
USCCB. https://www.usccb.org/topics/marriage-and-family-life-ministries
/when-i-call-help-pastoral-response-domestic-violence.

van der Kolk, B. 2015. *The Body Keeps the Score: Brain, Mind, and Body in the Healing of Trauma*. New York: Penguin.

Walker, M. 2017. *Why We Sleep: Unlocking the Power of Sleep and Dreams*. New York: Scribner.

Whitbourne, S. K. 2021. "How Emotions Go Downhill in People with Personality Disorders." *Psychology Today*, September 21. https://www.psychologytoday.com/us/blog/fulfillment-any-age/202109/how-emotions-go-downhill-in-people-personality-disorders.

White, M. P., I. Alcock, J. Grellier, B. W. Wheeler, T. Hartig, S. L. Warber, A. Bone, M. H. Depledge, and L. E. Fleming. 2019. "Spending at Least 120 Minutes a Week in Nature Is Associated with Good Health and Wellbeing." *Scientific Reports* 9: 7730.

Wright, K. 2008. "Dare to Be Yourself." *Psychology Today*, May 1. https://www.psychologytoday.com/us/articles/200805/dare-be-yourself.

Young, J., and J. S. Klosko. 1994. *Reinventing Your Life: The Breakthrough Program to End Negative Behavior and Feel Great Again*. New York: Plume.

Randi Kreger is coauthor of *Stop Walking on Eggshells*, and author or coauthor of three other books: *The Stop Walking on Eggshells Workbook*, *The Essential Family Guide to Borderline Personality Disorder*, and *Stop Walking on Eggshells for Parents*. Kreger is owner and moderator of the Moving Forward family support group, which can be accessed at her website: www.stopwalkingoneggshells.com. She has given presentations throughout the United States and in Japan. She also has a one-on-one coaching practice which can be accessed through her website.

Bill Eddy, LCSW, JD, is a family lawyer, therapist, and mediator in San Diego, CA. He is cofounder and chief innovation officer at High Conflict Institute, and trains lawyers, judges, mediators, and counselors worldwide in respectfully managing high-conflict disputes and personalities. He is author of more than twenty books and manuals, developer of the *New Ways for Families* method for separation and divorce, and blogger for *Psychology Today* with more than six million views. His website is www.highconflictinstitute.com.

Real change *is* possible

For more than forty-five years, New Harbinger has published proven-effective self-help books and pioneering workbooks to help readers of all ages and backgrounds improve mental health and well-being, and achieve lasting personal growth. In addition, our spirituality books offer profound guidance for deepening awareness and cultivating healing, self-discovery, and fulfillment.

Founded by psychologist Matthew McKay and Patrick Fanning, New Harbinger is proud to be an independent, employee-owned company. Our books reflect our core values of integrity, innovation, commitment, sustainability, compassion, and trust. Written by leaders in the field and recommended by therapists worldwide, New Harbinger books are practical, accessible, and provide real tools for real change.

 **newharbinger**publications

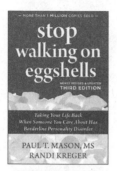